# Education in a Global City

# The Bedford Way Papers Series

19 *Teacher Pay and Performance*
Peter Dolton, Steve McIntosh and Arnaud Chevalier

20 *Childhood in Generational Perspective*
Edited by Berry Mayall and Hela Zeiher

21 *Homework: The evidence*
Susan Hallam

22 *Teaching in Further Education: New perspectives for a changing context*
Norman Lucas

23 *Legalised Leadership: Law-based educational reform in England and what it does to school leadership and headteachers*
Dan Gibton

24 *Theorising Quality in Higher Education*
Louise Morley

25 *Music Psychology in Education*
Susan Hallam

26 *Policy-making and Policy Learning in 14–19 Education*
Edited by David Raffe and Ken Spours

27 *New Designs for Teachers' Professional Learning*
Edited by Jon Pickering, Caroline Daly and Norbert Pachler

28 *The Dearing Report: Ten years on*
Edited by David Watson and Michael Amoah

29 *History, Politics and Policy-making: A festschrift presented to Richard Aldrich*
Edited by David Crook and Gary McCulloch

30 *Public Sector Reform: Principles for improving the education system*
Frank Coffield, Richard Steer, Rebecca Allen, Anna Vignoles, Gemma Moss and Carol Vincent

31 *Educational Resource Management: An international perspective*
Derek Glover and Rosalind Levačić

A full list of Bedford Way Papers, including earlier books in the series, may be found at www.ioe.ac.uk/publications

# Education in a Global City
## Essays from London

Editors: Tim Brighouse and Leisha Fullick

Bedford Way Papers

First published in 2007 by the Institute of Education, University of London,
20 Bedford Way, London WC1H 0AL
www.ioe.ac.uk/publications



**British Library Cataloguing in Publication Data:**
A catalogue record for this publication is available from the British Library

ISBN 978 0 85473 792 5

Extract from 'The London Breed' by Benjamin Zephaniah printed by kind permission of Bloodaxe Books. The full poem is published in *Too Black, Too Strong*, Bloodaxe Books, 2001.

Design by River Design, Edinburgh
Typeset by Chapman Design Limited
Printed by Elanders www.elanders.com

# Contents

# Acknowledgements

The editors wish to thank Anne Sofer, Ruth Lupton, Marianne Coleman and Alan Dyson for their advice and support; and to give special acknowledgement to Dina Mehmedbegović for her meticulous work in preparing this book for publication.

# Introduction

Tim Brighouse and Leisha Fullick

This book is about education in London in the first part of the twenty-first century. We thought such a book might be of interest at this time for two main reasons.

First, London has changed enormously, in ways that now make it different from many other UK, European, and world cities. Economically it has recovered from the long decline in its manufacturing base that continued from the 1960s through to the 1980s and has become one of the premier global cities for finance and the cultural industries. Its population is expanding and becoming more and more diverse. Divisions between rich and poor are greater. These changes have big implications for education, and education has become increasingly important to London as the future growth of the city will depend on a population with high levels of skills and knowledge.

Several of the essays in this book focus on the particular London context and the challenges and opportunities it presents for learners and for educators. The book begins within an overview of London's economic, demographic and social make-up, its rapid change, and the performance of its school system in providing access and achievement for London's diverse school population. London's state funded schools have always been the starting point of hope for disadvantaged children, particularly the many immigrants who for generations, on arriving in this country, have made London their first home. So Jan McKenley provides an authoritative essay on the history and present state of achievement of black and minority ethnic pupils and how they and their communities have interacted with the education system. Dina Mehmedbegovic brings penetrative new light to an issue of fundamental importance to London – its multilingualism. Her analysis should provoke fresh debate on an issue that is vital in a city where over 300 languages are spoken. Leisha Fullick focuses on adult education in a city whose economy is becoming increasingly dependent on high-level skills and knowledge but where low wages at the bottom end of the labour market, intense competition for work, high mobility, and high housing and living costs threaten economic and social polarisation.

Thus one of our interests is London's particularities, although, by taking this focus, we do not claim that London uniquely possesses these characteristics of diversity, mobility, inequality, or change. Other UK cities and parts of cities share the same characteristics of complexity and diversity, extremes in wealth and poverty, and high levels of immigration and mobility, albeit on a less extensive scale – London is far and away the biggest city in England and continues to expand at a rapid rate. Other world cities demonstrate these same characteristics on an even larger scale or, in some cases, in greater intensity. One of the interesting points for debate that we hope will emerge from this book is that of London's uniqueness, or otherwise. Which cities does London have most to learn from and which cities can learn from London? What are the points of similarity and difference? Anne Sofer's essay starts to do this by comparing London with some other world cities, and offers a basis for broader UK, European, and global comparisons.

The second reason why we thought the book would be of interest is that London has much to offer as a case study for urban education in England, and perhaps even for education in urban settings across the world, where there is common interest in the same set of issues: the quality of schools, staffing, funding, governance, the reproduction of a qualified and skilled labour force. There is a heightened level of interest in cities like London that are developing new strategies and approaches and where there appears to be growing knowledge and confidence of what works in urban education.

The 'city as case study' approach is particularly relevant in England, where education policy is highly centralised, and London's schools and colleges are operating under the same policy regimes, funding, and governance systems as those in the rest of the country. For readers unfamiliar with the English context, its background is a suite of major educational reforms beginning in the late 1980s, and continuing under governments of both political hues. The reform movement has had a number of distinctive features. The first is that of devolution, particularly the introduction of Local Management of Schools (LMS), which devolved resources and employment powers to schools and later to colleges. LMS, in combination with the adoption of the principle of parental choice as the basis for the allocation of school places, and the publication of comparative school performance information in 'league tables', created a quasi-market in education by which schools competed for pupils and resources, and the weakest schools could ultimately be forced into closure. Devolution of powers has been accompanied by a number of measures that have given schools further freedoms in admissions, governance, and curriculum and have given parents and pupils more choice in the kinds of schools and colleges available to them. These measures started with the introduction of grant maintained schools and city technology colleges in the early 1990s and have continued with the spread of specialist schools, foundation schools, and academies since New Labour came into power in 1997.

Diversity, choice, and devolution to the local level have been accompanied by a highly prescriptive and centralised accountability regime. Accountability has been ensured through target setting, testing, and inspection regimes at all levels of the system and has also been accompanied by high-profile interventions for underperforming schools and local authorities. Moreover, curriculum and pedagogies have become more standardised, beginning with the introduction of the National Curriculum in 1988, and become more systematised since the advent of New Labour governments in 1997, with national strategies and targets for the teaching of literacy and numeracy, and the introduction of an even stronger raft of standardised tests. Investment in education has also been increased under New Labour, with enhancements to teachers' pay, investment in professional development (along with standardised qualifications for headteachers, and the introduction of performance-related pay for teachers), smaller classes, improved technology, and a commitment to the modernisation or re-provision of every school building in the country. Curriculum, qualifications, and assessment have again come under scrutiny, with proposals to raise the compulsory school leaving age to 18 and to introduce a new set of diplomas, spanning the traditional academic/vocational divide and providing more personalised routes through the education system.

Most recently, education departments have been repositioned, being incorporated within 'children's services' departments in local authorities, under the Every Child Matters agenda, which sees education as part of a holistic approach to the welfare of children and young people and, perhaps some way behind other local authority services such as housing and environmental services, being repositioned as commissioners rather than providers of services, championing individual citizens in their legitimate pursuit of education.

Several of the essays in this book look at London as an example of the ways in which these reforms and changes are playing out at ground level. Geoff Whitty and Sandra Leaton Gray explore the impact of the current political imperatives of 'choice' and 'diversity' in the context of the drive to achieve greater equity in education in London. Janet Mokades examines the implementation of Every Child Matters, while Paul Grainger, Ann Hodgson and Ken Spours address qualifications and curriculum reform: the government's new-found interest and attention in creating a 14–19 phase, spanning secondary school and college participation. They highlight the particular challenges that this will bring to both London's secondary schools and colleges.

While these reforms affect education in general, there have also been specific policies aimed at improving urban education. Particularly since the advent of the New Labour governments, the urban context has been seen as a particularly challenging setting meriting additional interventions to support national policies. Education Action Zones (mostly but not exclusively in urban settings) were one of New Labour's first policy initiatives: partnerships of groups of schools along with local authorities and private sector partners trying innovative solutions to raise urban achievement. They were followed by Excellence in Cities, a larger scale programme, to raise standards in urban areas by providing extra resources for programmes such as mentoring, learning support, and out-of-school hours provision, as well as extra grants to support leadership development. In one sense, we can see these initiatives (and they are initiatives rather than reforms, in the sense that they sit alongside or on top of core national policies and structures) as a gradual scaling up of the problem and solution, from the level of the individual school, to groups of schools, then to whole local authority areas, but still with very much of an emphasis on school-based interventions.

In 2002, central government launched a new urban education initiative – the London Challenge – a central government-run programme taking an overview at the level of the urban education system, aiming to tackle school failure in London and to make London a world class leader in education. The London Challenge is, as far as we are aware, the only such nationally led big city education initiative in the world. The intended end of the London Challenge in 2007 was one of the original motivators for this book – a good time to take stock of London's continuing and emerging challenges and to see how its education system is responding and could respond. In fact, not only will the London Challenge continue, it will be extended to two other areas, Greater Manchester and the Black Country, in the form of City Challenge.

The London Challenge merits a dedicated essay in the book from one of its key agents, Tim Brighouse, the first Commissioner for London Schools. Brighouse describes the main features of the initiative and some of the lessons to be learned from it and attempts an inevitably subjective assessment of its effectiveness. Other authors address specific and perennial issues in urban education: Sara Bubb and Peter Earley focus on teacher development and the teaching workforce in London schools, while Hilary Emery and Kathryn Riley look at leadership in the inner-city and London schools in particular.

Again, when looking at London as a case study for the enactment of national policy, we come up against the question, to what extent is London different? A recurring theme in many of the essays is the history of educational provision in London, and the resulting governance structures. London has never had one single education authority: perhaps its scale prevents it. However, until 1990, there was a single authority for the 13 Inner London boroughs: the Inner London Education Authority (ILEA). For some commentators, the ILEA represented the worst of left-wing and progressive tendencies in education: inefficient and with low standards. Its abolition was a symbolic moment in the Conservative government's battle with Labour-led local government. For others, it represented a golden age in approaches to urban education, with a strong identity and commitment to education in the inner city, to social justice (for example, in its banding of admissions so that pupils were more equitably distributed among schools) and to collaboration in the development of urban curriculum and pedagogy. The legacy of the ILEA is still very much alive and kicking in the many ex-ILEA personnel who are still involved in education in London, and in the memory of a time when at least part of London was governed by a single authority, rather than as now, by 33 separate and small authorities, catering for students who cross boundaries on a daily basis.

Many of the essays in this book touch on the particular challenges for London that the post-ILEA fragmented governance structure presents, and we return in the conclusion to the question of the value and practicality of pan-London functions to overcome some of these difficulties. But these are not only questions for London. Many urban education authorities in England, such as Bristol and Nottingham, exist in urban education systems in which they are not the only authority, as neighbouring county or borough councils run schools outside the city boundary but within the conurbation. Political and organisational histories will be of greater or lesser importance in any urban setting. The essays here will be of particular interest to those who have lived through the evolution of London's education system, but also to those looking from elsewhere, who will recognise the importance of structural arrangements, institutional arrangements, political legacies, and embedded narratives in their own urban contexts.

No one volume can achieve everything. We have chosen to focus on key urban contextual themes, such as multilingualism, and on current policy developments, such as Every Child Matters, rather than on a complete coverage of the education system sector by sector, for example, the early years, primary, special, secondary, further, and higher education. Our approach has led to a major focus on schools, with higher education and pre-school provision being left for future volumes. We also recognise that we have focused on formal education and on state institutions. Writers on urban education have long recognised that this is only part of the picture. Informal and supplementary education, home educational practices, and relationships between schools, families, and communities are all vital, and perhaps increasingly important – parts of the urban educational landscape that we have not had room to cover here. Nor, truthfully, have we the knowledge and expertise; research on non-formal, non-institutional education still remains marginalised in academia and on the policy radar.

This remains, then, a partial set of essays on education in London, rather than a complete record. The contributions are deliberately diverse in coverage and in style. We trust that they will become a valuable resource and reference point, but our main hope is that they will inspire further research and debate to the future benefit of education in our great city, and beyond.

**Tim Brighouse and Leisha Fullick**
November 2007

# 1 The London context

Ruth Lupton and Alice Sullivan

## Introduction

In the last 20 years, London has undergone a dramatic transformation, and with it the opportunities and challenges facing London's learners and the education system that serves them. In the early 1980s young Londoners grew up in a city whose industries were in serious decline and whose population was shrinking. Post-imperial, post-industrial London had a downward trajectory, much akin to those of other large British, European and North American conurbations at that time and, for some, since. By contrast, today's young Londoners grow up in a city on the up: a global financial and cultural centre, with a booming economy and an increasing population. London has become a city of growth, wealth, diversity and rapid change, offering at the same time both great opportunity and great risk. In many ways, its strengths are also its weaknesses, its advantages also its threats. As a recent government report said, 'London's challenge is to resolve tensions arising from its intensity; great wealth with social inclusion; diversity with tolerance; openness to migration with security and public support; mobility with community; and population and economic growth with quality of place and quality of life' (PMSU 2004: 7).

In this essay, we describe this London context in more detail. We also provide an overview of London's education system and its performance in relation to these challenges. The essay aims to set the scene for the thematic essays which make up the rest of this book.

## London: growth and diversification

London's trajectory over the last 20 years is characterised by two key features: growth and diversification. Both are on a scale far exceeding that in other British cities and both are driven by global forces: the increasingly international nature of capital markets and the population movement across national and continental boundaries.

The increasingly global nature of business and financial investment, with its impact on Britain's manufacturing industries, has been one of the major causes of decline in Britain's industrial cities. For London, it has enabled a sustained period of economic growth, with growth in the financial and business sectors and associated services eclipsing manufacturing losses and effecting a remaking of the city's economy around high-end professional and managerial employment. The deregulation of the city in 1986 was the critical moment, enabling London to capitalise on its historic strengths as a financial and trade centre and to emerge as *the* premier international centre for foreign exchange dealing, international stock trading and fund management. Associated business services such as management consultancy, law and advertising have correspondingly grown, and these sectors between them have effectively replaced manufacturing as London's largest sector. By the end of the 1990s, one-third of workers were employed in these industries (Hamnett 2003). Other new sectors have also boomed, as London has built on its strengths in broadcasting and publishing, and developed, with Paris and New York, as a major centre for cultural and creative industries (Hamnett 2003).

The range of job opportunities available to Londoners has thus widened, and the proportion of people employed in professional or middle-class jobs has expanded. In London in 2001, 60 per cent (and in Central London 67 per cent) of jobs required post-compulsory education – professional and managerial occupations, skilled trades, associate professional and technical occupations – compared with 52 per cent in England as a whole. Lower skill jobs were less common in London. Of the 20 local authorities with the lowest proportions of workers in elementary occupations, 13 were in London, including some of London's richest boroughs like Westminster and Richmond-upon-Thames, but also some of its poorest: Lambeth, Southwark and Tower Hamlets (Green and Owen 2006). By comparison with other British cities, London's economy has become distinctively professionalised.

Over the same period, and largely because of expanding economic opportunity, the city has experienced population growth on a relatively rapid scale, in European terms. Since 1991, London's population has grown by about 600,000, to 7.4 million, an 8.8 per cent increase compared with 4.5 per cent for England and Wales (GLA 2005a). London is Britain's fastest growing region and its growth far exceeds that of the country's other major conurbations (Figure 1.1). Growth has mainly been in the working age population, and has been driven by a combination of natural change and overseas immigration (countered to a certain extent by increasing out-migration to the rest of the UK). Net inflows to London from overseas increased from about 16,000 in 1991–2 to over 100,000 in 2001–2 (GLA 2005b). Continued population growth is forecast, with an additional 800,000 people anticipated in the next ten years to 2016. To put this into perspective, growth on this scale is equivalent to adding the population of a city larger than Leeds to Greater London within its boundary.

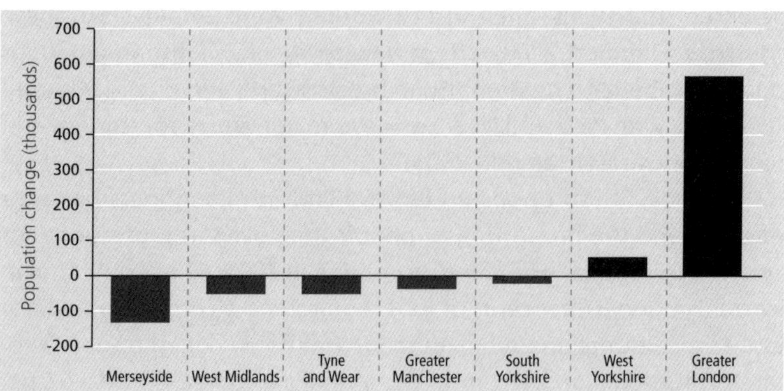


**Figure 1.1** Population change in England's major conurbations 1981–2000
*(Source: Planning for London's Growth)*

New international immigration, combined with the faster growth rate of existing minority ethnic communities and the greater rate of out-migration of white British households, has brought fresh diversity to a city whose historical position as a commercial and cultural centre and a seat of empire has always lent it an international character. According to the census in 2001, 40 per cent of London's population (and 50 per cent of Inner London's) was from an ethnic group other than white British. The largest single minority ethnic groups were 'other white' (8.3 per cent), Indian (6.1 per cent), black African (5.3 per cent) and black Caribbean (4.8 per cent). These headline figures obscure much of the rich diversity of London. Country of birth data identify over 2 million Londoners born outside the UK or Republic of Ireland, from 175 different countries (GLA 2005c). In 2001, the Greater London Authority estimated the number of refugees and asylum seekers at between 350,000 and 400,000, about one in 20 of the city's resident population (GLA 2001). Three hundred and sixty home languages are spoken in London schools (Baker and Eversley 2000).

Overall population figures also obscure substantial age differences. Among all under-18 age groups identified in the 2001 census, nearly half of the population (48 per cent) was from a minority ethnic group. In these age groups, black Africans made up 8–9 per cent of the population (compared with 5 per cent overall) and people of mixed heritage or other ethnic groups 11–14 per cent compared with 17 per cent overall. London's minority ethnic groups have younger population structures than the white British group. As the population ages, the city becomes naturally more diverse. Indeed, Table 1.1, showing data from 2006, shows that only 39 per cent of London's primary school pupils and 45 per cent of secondary pupils were white British. In Outer London, 50 per cent of secondary pupils were white British compared with 60 per cent of the whole population, and in Inner London, 26 per cent of secondary pupils compared with 40 per cent of the population.

**Table 1.1** Ethnic group of London pupils in state schools, 2006

| | Inner London | | Outer London | | Greater London | |
|---|---|---|---|---|---|---|
| | Primary % | Secondary % | Primary % | Secondary % | Primary % | Secondary % |
| White British | 22 | 26 | 47 | 50 | 39 | 42 |
| Other white | 12 | 10 | 9 | 8 | 10 | 10 |
| Indian | 3 | 3 | 7 | 9 | 5 | 7 |
| Pakistani | 3 | 3 | 4 | 4 | 4 | 4 |
| Bangladeshi | 11 | 11 | 1 | 1 | 5 | 4 |
| Black Caribbean | 11 | 11 | 5 | 5 | 7 | 7 |
| Black African | 17 | 17 | 9 | 7 | 12 | 10 |
| Chinese | 1 | 1 | 1 | 1 | 1 | 1 |
| Other and mixed | 20 | 18 | 19 | 13 | 17 | 15 |
| **Total N** | **127, 780** | | **295, 370** | | **423, 150** | |

*(Source: DfES Schools and Pupils in England 2006)*

This makes London schools very much more diverse than schools outside the capital. In England as a whole (including London), 81 per cent of secondary pupils and 78 per cent of primary pupils are classified as white British. The percentage of pupils in LA maintained schools whose first language is not English is considerably higher in both Inner London (51 per cent of primary pupils and 46 per cent of secondary) and Outer London (30 per cent of primary pupils and 26 per cent of secondary) than in England taken as a whole (12 per cent of primary and 9 per cent of secondary) (GLA 2005d).

## Unequal city

A major consequence of these patterns of economic and demographic growth is that Londoners have very polarised experiences of the city. London accounts for 20 per cent of national employment (SOCD), and far more in its key sectors. Interesting jobs and high salaries attract high-skilled workers. Gross median full-time weekly earnings in the London area are substantially higher than in Britain's other major cities (£629 per week in 2003 compared with £453 in Manchester, £439 in Leeds, and £402 in Newcastle).[1] In the city, remuneration packages have risen out of all proportion. The average city salary is approximately £81,000 (Hickman and Thornton 2006) with average starting salaries around £50,000 (*Management Issues* 2005) – huge salaries when we bear in mind that annual UK median full-time earnings are £23,000, with 90 per cent of workers earning less than £45,000.[2]

However, at the other end of the scale, low-skilled workers compete with commuters and migrant workers for a relatively small number of low-skill jobs. Qualified workers in London are more likely than they are elsewhere to 'bump down' into lower skilled jobs (Gordon 1999), and with over 200,000 non-UK workers in London as students, au pairs or on working holidays, employers find it easier to fill low-skill vacancies in London than they do almost anywhere else in the UK (PMSU 2004). The result is that worklessness rates in London are higher than in other major cities, even after controlling for workforce characteristics (PMSU 2004). Green and Owen (2006) calculate that nearly four per cent fewer Londoners are working (over 150,000 people) than would be expected if the Great Britain employment count applied at the local scale. Newham and Tower Hamlets have the first and third highest shortfalls in employment in the country. Moreover, in London, workless people are further from the labour market than anywhere else in the country. In boroughs such as Newham, Tower Hamlets, Hackney and Haringey, over a third of workless people of working age have never worked. This is a situation that presents major challenges for adult learning, as Fullick discusses in Essay 11.

A compounding factor in the polarising of living experiences in London is the cost of living. London is now one of the most expensive cities in the world in which to live, with housing costs being particularly high (UBS 2006). High housing demand and the inflationary impact of city salaries has made London's house prices rise significantly faster than the national average since the late 1980s (Nationwide House Price Index 2006). Crucially, also, prices have risen much faster than wages – three times faster since 1997 (GLA 2005e). At the time of writing, the average London home costs £292,450, 8.8 times the average salary, when most banks and building societies reckon that a mortgage of 3.5 times salary is affordable (LHF 2006). Four thousand homes worth more than one million pounds were sold in 2006 (Hickman and Thornton 2006). Even lower priced homes are unaffordable. The London Housing Federation (2006) estimates that to buy an average lower quarter property (at £177,000), a household would need an annual income of £48,000, well in excess of the average teacher's salary (£32,000). Despite very significant improvements since 2001, which have partly been achieved by subsidised housing schemes for teachers, London still has the highest vacancy rate in the country for teaching posts (1.2 per cent), roughly twice the national average, with some boroughs, such as Greenwich, Newham and Lambeth, twice as badly off (ONS 2006). Largely as a result of housing pressures, London's teachers are less well qualified, younger and less experienced than elsewhere in the country (London Challenge 2007).

Housing affordability difficulties are set to continue, with another 200,000 households projected by 2011 (GLA 2006a) and the average house price soaring to £400,000, outpacing wage increases (LHF 2006). With private rental costs reflecting the costs of buying, more people are forced to share housing, or to rely on subsidised (affordable) housing. In 2006, over 300,000 people were on waiting lists for affordable housing, while affordable homes continue to be sold through the Right to Buy scheme at a faster rate than they are being built (LHF 2006).

These housing trends have direct effects on the living conditions of lower income families. Twenty per cent of families in London (and 28 per cent of poor families) are in overcrowded homes, much higher than in Britain as a whole (GLA 2006b), and as pressures on affordable housing have increased, numbers of overcrowded households in the private sector have risen rapidly, doubling between 1998–9 and 2005–6 (Hills 2007). In 2006, 63,000 households were in temporary accommodation (LHF 2006). In addition, the combination of a competitive low-skill labour market and high housing and living costs means that many households just do not have enough money to live on. Rates of income poverty after housing costs for working age adults are the highest in Great Britain, and fully 34 per cent of London's children (and 51 per cent in Inner London) are in income poverty after housing costs are taken into account – again the highest in the country (GLA 2005f). High housing costs trap low-skilled workers on benefits, because they cannot earn enough to pay for their accommodation. High childcare costs, typically 15–30 per cent higher than elsewhere (PMSU 2004), add to the problem. The result is that parental employment rates are well below the national average and diverge from national trends, especially for minority ethnic groups, and for parents with low qualifications (GLA 2006c). Thus despite London's booming economy, children in London are much more likely to live in households where no one is working than their counterparts in other parts of Britain. Twenty-seven per cent of all London's children live in workless households (38 per cent in Inner London) compared with 14 per cent in the rest of the UK (GLA 2005g), impacting directly on child poverty and childhood experiences. High housing costs also contribute to polarisation. The cost of housing has a big impact on the resources of middle income families who choose to stay in London, while others in this bracket are forced to move to cheaper locations. London's 'middle' is depleted (Figure 1.2).

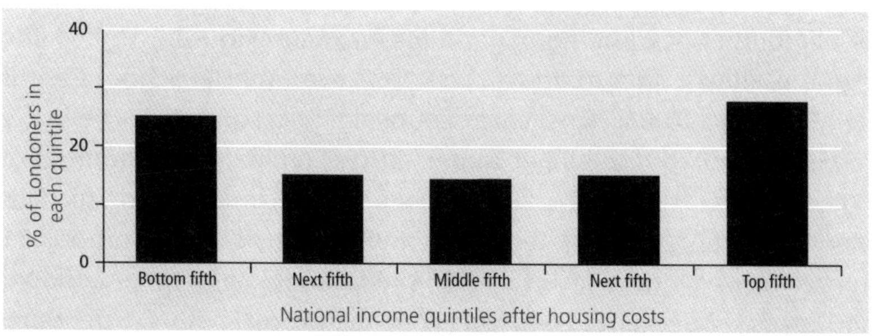


**Figure 1.2** London: a city of rich and poor
*(Source: PMSU 2004)*

London's increasing inequality is reflected spatially, exacerbating residential differences in a city that has always been marked by its 'cheek-by-jowl' pockets of poverty and wealth. On the one hand, pressure on social housing means that only those in the most urgent need are housed, leading to what is sometimes described as 'residualisation' of the social housing sector, as it is left to the very poor and those in the greatest difficulties. On the other hand, the very rich are increasingly able to pay to segregate themselves in exclusive neighbourhoods and, increasingly, gated communities. Indeed, in a city with a depleted middle, perhaps the wealthy see an increasing need to segregate themselves from the lower strata of society – the 'dangerous classes'. Income, benefits and deprivation data all show stark differences between boroughs, electoral wards and neighbourhoods. Parts of Central and South-west London are the richest in the country, while all of Hackney and Newham and most of East London, parts of Brent, Ealing, Hounslow and Hillingdon in West London and parts of Lambeth, Lewisham and Southwark in South London have incomes lower than the national average and higher rates of poverty and deprivation (GLA 2005f, h, i, j, k). Economically, socially and geographically, London is divided.

These divisions are directly experienced by London's children. Eligibility for free school meals (FSM) serves as one indicator of child poverty, with school students eligible for free school meals if their parents are claiming income support or other low income state benefits.[3] Note the important proviso that the 'FSM eligibility' measure is not a measure of eligibility but of being *eligible for and claiming* FSM (Hobbs and Vignoles 2007). According to the Pupil Level Annual School Census (PLASC) data in 2004, 36 per cent of pupils in Inner London were eligible for FSM, compared to 18 per cent in Outer London. These figures are not dissimilar to those of other large cities in England, such as Manchester (42 per cent), Birmingham (33 per cent) and Liverpool (31 per cent), which have levels of FSM similar to those of Inner London; and Leeds (17 per cent), Sheffield (17 per cent) and Bristol (18 per cent) that have levels similar to those of Outer London. However, all of these cities are significantly cheaper to live in than London. Thus the resources of families on state benefits are likely to be even more stretched than those of similar families elsewhere: note that FSM figures are significantly lower in London than child poverty rates after housing costs (51 per cent in Inner London). This means that we have to be very careful in making comparisons between the performance of schools with high FSM in London and elsewhere – their characteristics may not be as similar as at first appears.

Neverthless, FSM levels can help us to understand the patterning of poverty across London. Table 1.2, which shows the level of FSM among state school pupils in 2006, demonstrates the diversity of child poverty by borough. The Outer London boroughs of Kingston-upon-Thames, Sutton, Havering, Bromley and Bexley all had less than 10 per cent FSM, while the highest proportion of FSM pupils was found in Tower Hamlets (64 per cent), followed by Southwark (45 per cent) in Inner London. Note also relatively high levels of FSM in some affluent Inner London boroughs, such as Westminster and Kensington and Chelsea, where pockets of poverty exist alongside pockets of wealth, and where there are high rates of exit to private schooling among more affluent families.

**Table 1.2** Percentage of pupils in state secondary schools known to be eligible for free school meals, 2006

| | | % FSM | Number of pupils on roll |
|---|---|---|---|
| **Inner London** | Camden | 28 | 9,956 |
| | Greenwich | 28 | 6,857 |
| | Hackney | 39 | 11,659 |
| | Hammersmith and Fulham | 35 | 8,063 |
| | Islington | 38 | 3,514 |
| | Kensington and Chelsea | 30 | 8,050 |
| | Lambeth | 39 | 11,023 |
| | Lewisham | 28 | 18,304 |
| | Southwark | 45 | 10,247 |
| | Tower Hamlets | 64 | 14,381 |
| | Wandsworth | 23 | 10,436 |
| | Westminster | 30 | 8,401 |
| **Outer London** | Barking and Dagenham | 25 | 12,632 |
| | Barnet | 16 | 19,549 |
| | Bexley | 9 | 18,396 |
| | Brent | 23 | 16,418 |
| | Bromley | 9 | 22,486 |
| | Croydon | 16 | 18,718 |
| | Ealing | 31 | 15,196 |
| | Enfield | 19 | 22,160 |
| | Haringey | 37 | 11, 659 |
| | Harrow | 17 | 9,038 |
| | Havering | 9 | 16,594 |
| | Hillingdon | 17 | 17,085 |
| | Hounslow | 18 | 16,592 |
| | Kingston-upon-Thames | 8 | 9,579 |
| | Merton | 14 | 8,615 |

| | % FSM | Number of pupils on roll |
|---|---|---|
| Newham | 43 | 18, 304 |
| Redbridge | 15 | 20,649 |
| Richmond-upon-Thames | 14 | 7,165 |
| Sutton | 9 | 16,164 |
| Waltham Forest | 26 | 14,076 |

*(Source: DfES: Schools and Pupils in England: 2006)*

Underlying all of these patterns is an undercurrent of racial and ethnic inequalities. While people from all ethnic groups welcome London's diversity as one of its greatest strengths (PMSU 2004), it is not yet the case that all groups benefit equally from the city's advantages. Londoners from most minority ethnic groups are more likely to be workless, and less likely to be in high-earning jobs than white British Londoners or (usually white) migrants from other high-income countries. Their labour market fortunes are partly but not wholly explained by differential levels of qualifications (GLA 20051). Labour market disadvantage is compounded among families with children. Ninety per cent of white fathers in London work, compared with 78 per cent of minority ethnic fathers, and while lone mothers have comparable employment rates whatever their ethnicity, minority ethnic women in couples are much less likely to work than comparable white women (47 per cent compared with 67 per cent) (GLA 2006c). More than two-thirds of all children in Bangladeshi and Pakistani households in London (69 per cent) and half of all London's black children (51 per cent) are in poverty. Considered together, children from minority ethnic families in London comprise 41 per cent of all London's children but 52 per cent of all those living in poverty (GLA 2005g).

These patterns are further illuminated by FSM data. Table 1.3, for pupils at Key Stage 4 (KS4) (age 15), in 2004, shows the link between FSM and ethnicity, distinguishing between major minority ethnic groups. Pupils of Indian ethnicity and the white British were the least likely to be eligible for FSM (12 per cent and 15 per cent respectively). All other ethnic groups (including other whites at 26 per cent) were substantially more likely to be eligible for FSM. The worst-off group on this measure were Bangladeshis (68 per cent FSM).

**Table 1.3** Eligibility for free school meals (FSM) by ethnicity, 2004

| Ethnicity | FSM% | N |
|---|---|---|
| White British | 15 | 33,162 |
| White European and other | 26 | 6,317 |
| Mixed | 26 | 3,444 |
| Indian | 12 | 5,524 |
| Pakistani | 35 | 2,431 |
| Bangladeshi | 68 | 2,917 |
| Asian other | 24 | 1,763 |
| Black Caribbean | 27 | 5,606 |
| Black African | 42 | 6,571 |
| Black other | 30 | 1,352 |
| Chinese | 24 | 672 |
| Other | 41 | 2,718 |
| **Total** | **24** | **72,477** |

*(Source: Based on KS4 returns, PLASC 2004)*

Lower household incomes are of course reflected in housing circumstances, with minority ethnic households more likely to suffer from overcrowding (DCLG 2005) and to be priced out of the housing market (GLA 2005e). Thus the spatial distribution of ethnic groups plays a key role in the spatial distribution of worklessness, poverty and exclusion, as well as in creating the distinct cultural and retail quarters that Londoners celebrate. Some boroughs, such as Havering, Bromley, and Barking and Dagenham, remain predominantly white British, while Brent and Newham have a majority of minority ethnic groups (Figure

1.3). On the whole, London's poorer boroughs are also its most diverse. Low-income migrants have moved into areas of cheap housing and declining manufacturing, and their continuing disadvantage keeps these are relatively poor. Enabling more equal outcomes across ethnic groups is thus a key to creating greater spatial equalities of income and wealth.

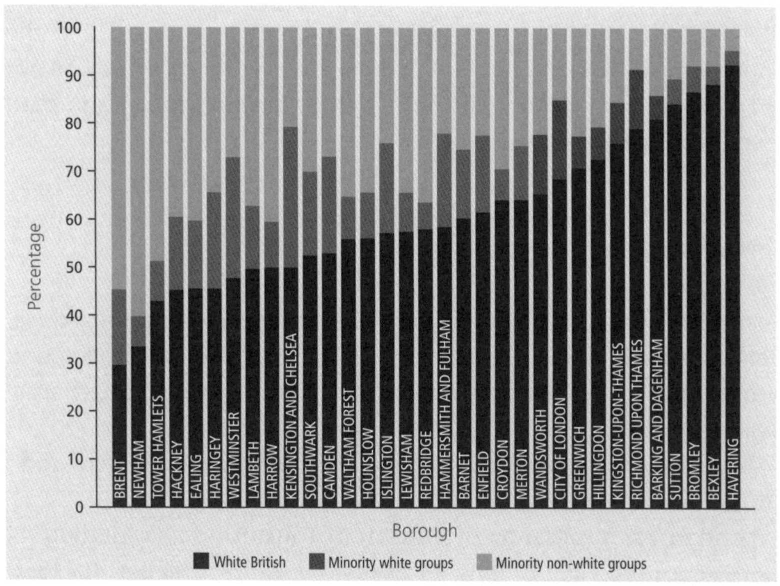


**Figure 1.3** Majority and minority ethnic groups by borough 2001
*(Source: 2001 Census Key Statistics Table KS06 ONS Crown Copyright)*

Distinct clusters of particular minority ethnic and migrant groups in particular boroughs, locales and neighbourhoods are also a feature of London: Bangladeshis in Tower Hamlets and Newham, Indians in Ealing, Cypriots in Enfield, Nigerians in Southwark, Jamaicans in Lambeth, to give just a few examples. These particular local demographies are important, imbuing areas with particular cultural or religious traditions, driving demands for particular local facilities and services, including translation services or prayer facilities, and partially explaining labour market patterns and household poverty rates (Green and Owen 2006). Nevertheless, what distinguishes London from many of the other towns and cities in Britain with large minority ethnic populations is its great mix. Single groups do not tend to dominate, nor is there evidence that ethnic group segregation is growing at the neighbourhood ward level (GLA 2006d). Even among the under-16 age group, there are few places where single minority ethnic groups are in the majority: only parts of Tower Hamlets (Bangladeshi) and the Southall area of Ealing (Indian). 'Ethnic enclaves' or 'ghettos' are not characteristic of London. The city's particular opportunity and challenge is its genuine diversity.

## London's education system

Bearing this broader context in mind, we now turn to London's education system. What is the pattern of educational provision in London and how well does the system appear to perform in relation to its particular urban context?

A first key point to note is the size and fragmentation of London's education system.

London has thousands of educational institutions, including 44 higher education institutions, 36 further education colleges, 401 local authority (LA) maintained secondary schools, 1,836 LA maintained primaries, as well as 18 city academies or city technology colleges (CTCs), several hundred independent schools, and numerous mother tongue or supplementary schools run by community organisations. Yet, as Brighouse and Fullick point out in the introduction to this book, the city has no overall strategic education plan. Greater London has never had a single educational body, even for the compulsory schooling sector.[4] The abolition of the Inner London Education Authority (ILEA) in 1990 removed even the Inner London strategic function, making it even harder than previously to identify common London education issues and to develop overarching or co-ordinated responses. In this essay we concentrate on provision and performance at compulsory schooling age; issues for older learners are addressed in Essay 11.

## Patterns of school provision

Perhaps not surprisingly, London has a particularly diverse range of schools. Most of the city, and all of Inner London, have a comprehensive system, with no selection at age 11. However, there is a high proportion of private schools. Over a fifth of England's 2,302 private schools are in London. In England as a whole, eight per cent of 15-year-old pupils attend private schools, compared to nine per cent in Outer London and 16 per cent in Inner London (DCSF 2006: SFR38/2006). These figures refer to the location of the school, rather than the residence of the pupil. This is important, because Inner London contains a large number of private schools, many of them old and well known, and the pupils may travel some distance to attend these schools. On the other hand, London pupils also attend out-of-London private schools. While it is difficult to calculate the exact numbers, we can be confident that the level of private schooling is higher in London than elsewhere in the country.

There is also substantial diversity within the comprehensive sector. A high proportion of England's city academies and city technology colleges are in London. London has 14 academies and four CTCs. It also has a relatively high proportion of religious secondary schools. Eighty-three per cent of England's maintained secondary schools are non-religious in character, compared to 77 per cent in Outer London and 66 per cent in Inner London. London has four Jewish schools and one Sikh secondary school, but the great majority of its religious schools are Christian (DfES 2006a). There is a small number of full-time schools organised by different linguistic communities – Spanish, Greek, Swedish, French – and a small number of international schools.

London also has a distinctive tradition of single-sex schooling within the maintained sector. In most of England, coeducation was introduced alongside comprehensivisation, and single-sex schooling within the state secondary sector declined enormously as a result. London, and especially Inner London, has resisted this trend to some extent. Single-sex schooling has remained popular for girls, especially among some minority ethnic groups. However, there has been less parental demand for single-sex schooling for boys. The result is that coeducational schools, especially in Inner London, have more boys than girls. In Inner London, more than half of all girls (52 per cent) attend girls' schools, fully four times as many as in the country as a whole, and 59 per cent of students in mixed schools are boys (Table 1.4).

**Table 1.4** Full-time students in maintained secondary schools of different gender mix

| | % of girls at girls' schools | % of boys at boys' schools | % boys in coeducational schools |
|---|---|---|---|
| England | 13 | 10 | 51 |
| Outer London | 33 | 24 | 53 |
| Inner London | 52 | 27 | 59 |

*(Source: Whatford 2005)*

The imbalance of provision is more extreme in certain boroughs. For example, Camden has four maintained girls' secondary schools, and only one boys' school. The most extreme gender imbalance in the co-educational sector occurs in Islington, where boys make up 71 per cent of the coeducational secondary school population (Whatford 2005, figures derived from Appendix P). Camden and Hackney have only about 40 per cent of boys in state schools at KS4 (age 15), suggesting that boys avoid single-sex schools either by going to school outside the borough, or going into the private sector. The impact of this gender imbalance on attainment outcomes has not yet been demonstrated in the UK. Israeli research suggests that a high proportion of boys in a year group is linked to worse academic outcomes for both girls and boys (Lavy 2007), while van Houtte (2004), using Belgian data, demonstrates that the larger the proportion of girls in a school, the higher the boys' achievement.

This rich pattern of schools, combined with the city's high population density and good public transport, enables choice for those with the cultural, social and economic capital to negotiate the system. In London, 99.6 per cent of secondary school pupils have three schools within 5km, compared with 78 per cent for the country as a whole, and perhaps not surprisingly, they are less likely to go to their nearest school – only a quarter do so, compared with a half elsewhere (Burgess *et al.* 2005a). Class and race intertwine in school choice decisions (Vincent and Ball 2006). While some white and black and minority ethnic (BME) middle-class parents welcome the positive diversity of London's schools, others feel torn between liberal predispositions towards diversity and the comprehensive principle, and concerns about their own children being held back by the presence of children whose mother tongue is not English or whose families lack middle-class orientations towards educational success. Residential patterns and school choice decisions certainly lead to wide differences, even within boroughs, in the social and ethnic composition of schools. In Camden, for example, three schools located almost adjacent to one another have FSM ranging between 15 per cent and 35 per cent, and English as an additional language (EAL) between 16 per cent and 31 per cent. Tower Hamlets has one school that is predominantly white British (67 per cent) at KS4, alongside three schools without a single white British pupil. The predominantly white British school is also the school with the lowest levels of FSM in the borough (23 per cent).[5] In Brent, schools vary between two per cent and 37 per cent white British pupils at KS4, and between 10 and 50 per cent FSM pupils. It is clear that London's school students have very different social experiences of schooling, perhaps more so than one might expect even given residential patterns. Recent research matching school and neighbourhood suggests that London's schools are slightly more segregated by race than are the areas in which they are situated (Burgess *et al.* 2005b), indicating some racial sorting in the process of school choice, but more evidence is needed to establish how much of a role choice plays in school mix, and on the extent to which mix matters either for pupil attainment or for social cohesion and racial integration.

## Patterns of achievement

London's schools are one of its least well-rated features, according to surveys of the city's residents (Ipsos MORI 2007), and for some time there has been a widespread popular belief that the city's schools are relatively bad. However, this view is no longer supported by the data. There have been very substantial improvements in London schools since 2000 (OFSTED 2006) and in 2005–6, they did relatively well both on measures of quality (inspection judgements) and on measures of academic performance. In 2005–6 59 per cent of London's secondary schools and 64 per cent of primary schools were judged good or better by OFSTED, compared with 49 per cent and 59 per cent respectively of schools nationally (*ibid.*). School performance data for 2006 shows that LA maintained schools in London had slightly higher results at GCSE (aged 15) than the national average, with 58.3 per cent of students gaining five GCSEs at grades A*–C in 2006, compared with 57.5 per cent for England as a whole. Nearly half of London schools were ahead of the national average in 2006, and none were below the national 'floor target' of 25 per cent. Inner London performance in 2006 (54 per cent) was slightly below the national average, but represents a massive improvement from 32 per cent in 2001. Nearly all of the Inner London schools that had particularly low GCSE performance in 2003 had improved by 2006, significantly more than in the country as a whole. Moreover, London's relatively better performance is sustained when we look at students whose five A*–Cs include the core subjects of English and mathematics, indicating that improvements have not been achieved by channelling students into 'easier' subjects.

Examination of value-added data demonstrates that this relatively good performance is not simply a product of more advantaged intakes, but reflects the progress that students make through school. Value-added data produced by the Department for Education and Skills (DfES) measures progress between KS2 (age 11) and KS4 (age 15).[6] Figure 1.4 shows value-added for London compared with the rest of the country, distinguishing students who are eligible for FSM from those who are not. It shows that both FSM and non-FSM students make more progress in London than in the country as a whole. London students are making more progress, on average, than those from elsewhere.

Moreover, what is particularly striking is the comparatively much better progress made by FSM students, particularly in Inner London. Inner London schools do relatively well for disadvantaged students. At least in terms of progress (although not to the same extent, as we shall see, in terms of attainment), they appear to override what we may think of as 'the poverty penalty': the familiar gap in progress between pupils from advantaged and disadvantaged homes. This is a significant achievement, although one that merits further investigation. We need to bear in mind that there is great diversity in the socio-economic characteristics of the families of both FSM and non-FSM children. The non-FSM group ranges from those just above the poverty line to the wealthy, and both FSM and non-FSM families vary in terms of characteristics such as parental education and family size and structure, which are known to be highly predictive of children's educational attainment. FSM is a crude proxy for families' educational resources. As Hobbs and Vignoles (2007) point out, FSM status is a better proxy for low parental income and employment, and to a lesser extent one-parenthood, than low parental education and social class.

These limitations of the FSM measure raise serious issues of interpretation, especially when we bring the interaction between ethnicity and FSM eligibility into the picture. The better performance of FSM pupils in Inner London is largely accounted for by variations in the performance of different ethnic groups. In general, in England as a whole, pupils from minority ethnic groups tend to make more progress between KS2 and KS4 than pupils from the white British group (although this is not the case, on average, for the Black Caribbean,

Black other, and mixed groups). In addition, the gap in value-added scores between FSM and non-FSM pupils is considerably larger for the white British than for any other ethnic group. Inner London has a high proportion of minority ethnic pupils, particularly from South Asian groups, and this may be one factor that pushes up the average value-added score, especially for the FSM group. When we remove ethnicity from the equation by focusing only on the white British group (Figure 1.5) we see a very different picture. White British pupils on FSM in Inner London still do better than similar pupils elsewhere in the country, but by a much smaller margin than in Figure 1.3. Those in Outer London do not. For these students, the 'poverty penalty' remains – those on FSM make less progress than those from better-off homes. Moreover, white British pupils who are not on FSM do worse in Inner London than elsewhere in the country.

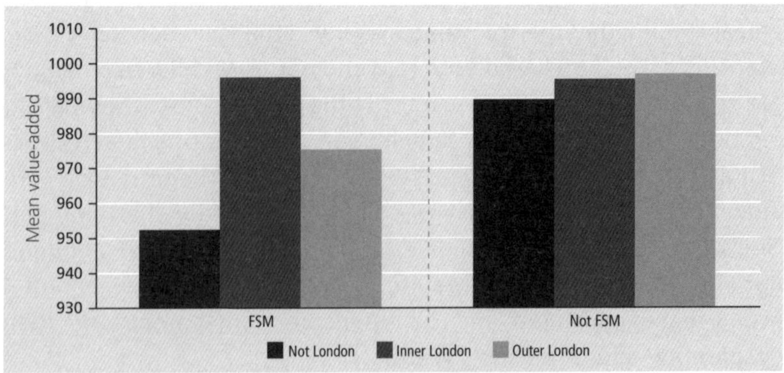


**Figure 1.4** Value-added KS2 to KS4 by FSM eligibility

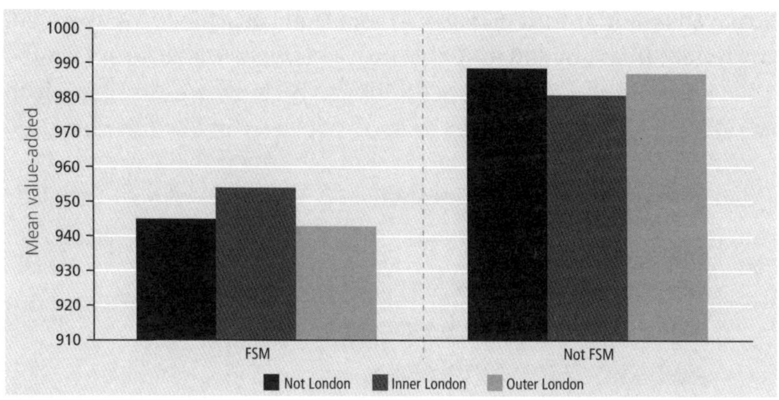


**Figure 1.5** Value-added KS2 to KS4 by FSM eligibility, white British only

Progress, then, is uneven among different ethnic groups, and the relationship between poverty (at least as measured by FSM eligibility), ethnicity and educational progress appears to differ from one ethnic group to another. The same is true of attainment. Despite recent progress, some groups remain well behind others. FSM students still lag behind non-FSM students at every stage of the curriculum (London Challenge 2007). There remain significant differences by gender and ethnic group. Figure 1.6 shows that pupils with Chinese (64 per cent), Indian (58 per cent), and other Asian (58 per cent) ethnicity, had on average about double the attainment level of the lowest attaining groups: Bangladeshi (34 per cent), black African (31 per cent), black other (27 per cent) and black Caribbean pupils (24 per cent). Pupils with Pakistani (43 per cent) white British (40 per cent) or white other (40 per cent) ethnicity, and those of 'mixed' heritage (39 per cent), occupied the middle of the distribution. The low attainment of many black Caribbean pupils is of particular concern, because this group is predominantly British born, and neither language nor recent migration is an issue. Only six per cent of these black Caribbean pupils have English as an additional language, compared to 98 per cent of the Bangladeshi pupils. The gender differential is also greatest in this ethnic group.

Within all ethnic groups, girls were more likely to achieve the five A*–C benchmark than boys. Black Caribbean girls were 1.6 times as likely to achieve the benchmark as black Caribbean boys, whereas white British girls were 1.2 times as likely to be successful as white British boys.

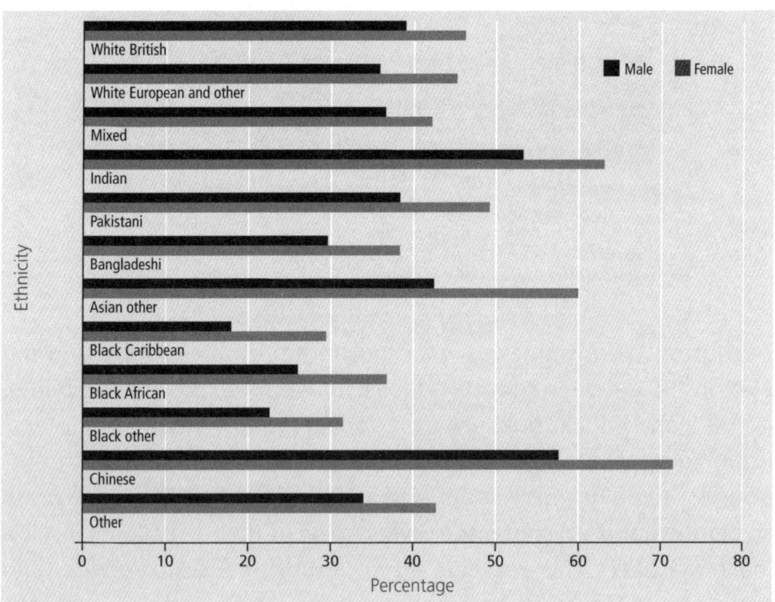


**Figure 1.6** Pupils achieving five GCSE passes at grades A*–C, including Maths and English, in 2004, by ethnic group and gender
*(Source: PLASC KS4 returns, 2004)*

The economic disadvantage of some minority ethnic groups no doubt explains part of this pattern, but the relationship is not straightforward. As Figure 1.7 shows, FSM pupils with Pakistani or Bangladeshi ethnicity do better, on average, than non-FSM pupils with black Caribbean ethnicity. The attainment gap between FSM and non-FSM pupils is much bigger in certain ethnic groups (notably the white groups) than others (notably Bangladeshis), a fact that may well reflect the breadth of the income distribution in these different ethnic groups, and the labour market penalties that mean that educational qualifications of parents (a key factor associated with school success) from certain minority ethnic groups are not reflected in levels of earnings (Heath and Smith 2003, Heath and McMahon 1997). Further investigation is needed to understand the significance of all these factors.

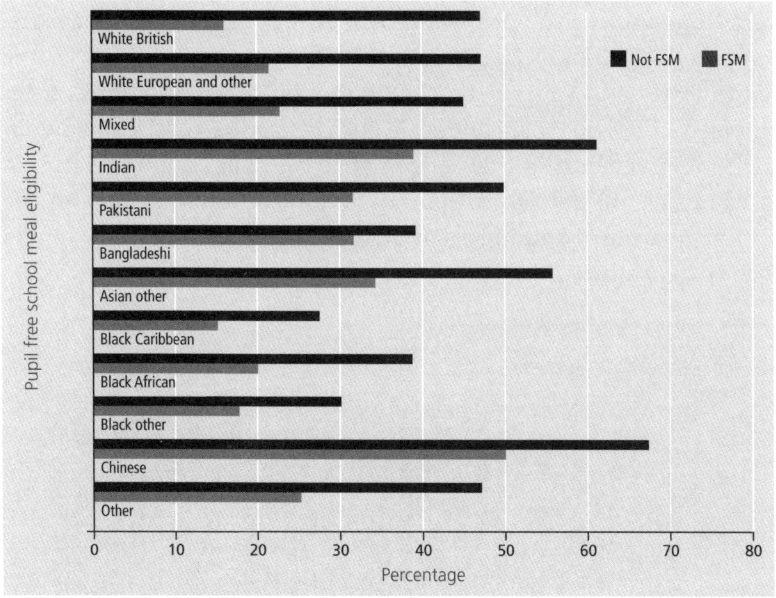


**Figure 1.7** Pupils achieving five GCSE passes at grades A*–C, including Maths and English, in 2004, by ethnic group and FSM
*(Source: PLASC KS4 returns, 2004)*

Finally, it is important to recall the size and diversity of London, and its fragmented educational governance. Patterns of progress and attainment, overall and by gender, socio-economic status and ethnic group, vary significantly across the capital. At KS2 (aged 11), for example, although the band of achievement is relatively narrower than at later stages, there is a substantial difference between boroughs. Hackney has the lowest proportion of students achieving the expected level 4 or above – 64 per cent for maths and 71 per cent for English. At the opposite end of the spectrum, in Richmond-upon-Thames, 85 per cent of pupils achieve this level in maths, and 89 per cent do so in English (Figure 1.8). At age 15, achieving five or more A*–C GCSE passes is a more demanding benchmark, and this reveals greater differences between boroughs (Figure 1.9), with the Outer London boroughs of Redbridge and Sutton achieving over 70 per cent on this measure, compared with under 50 per cent for Greenwich, Islington, Merton, Westminster and Southwark.[7] There remain substantial differences between schools in Inner London. Even in the context of the very significant improvements in the performance of Inner London schools in recent years, 40 per cent of Inner London secondaries were in the bottom quartile of attainment at GCSE in 2005, and only 16 per cent in the top quartile.

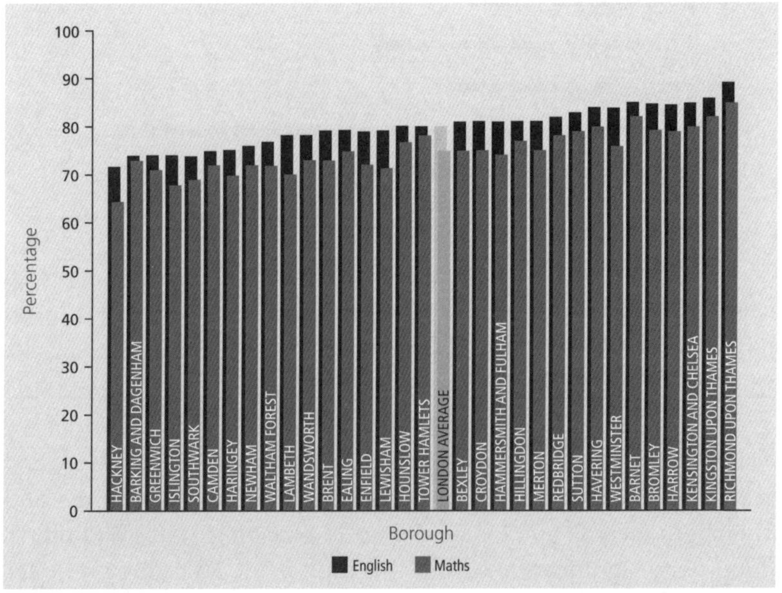


**Figure 1.8** Percentage achieving level 4 or above at Key Stage maths and English 2006 (ranked in order of English results)

*(Source: DfES http://dfes.gov.uk/inyourarea/)*

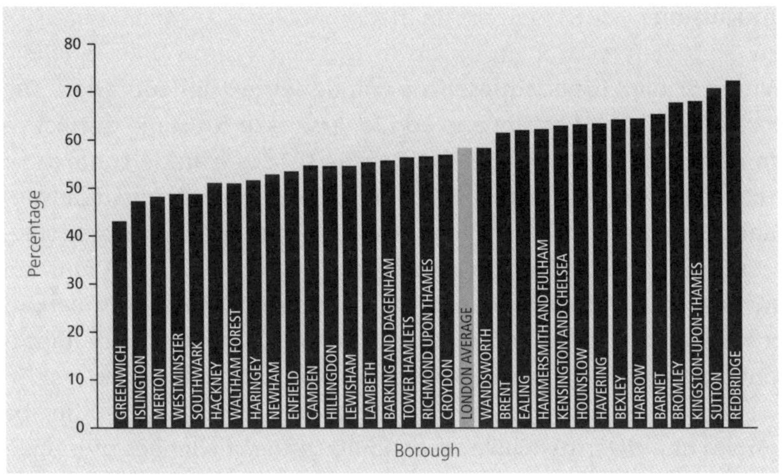


**Figure 1.9** Percentage achieving five GCSE passes at grades A*–C or equivalent by end of KS4, 2006

Data recently released by the London Challenge (2007) shows that not only do overall attainment patterns vary by school and borough, so too do the differentials between different groups of pupils. In Islington, there is virtually no attainment gap between FSM and non-FSM pupils, while in the Outer London boroughs of Sutton, Havering and Bexley, the gap is over 30 per cent. These are staggering differences, no doubt reflecting differences in family income and resources within and across FSM and non-FSM bands, different ethnic composition, and different rates of exit to private schools, as well as the interventions of schools themselves. They illustrate the complexity of the challenge for London in achieving equitable educational outcomes in a city of this size, diversity, and inequality.

## Conclusion

Within Britain, London presents a unique context for education. The characteristics of London and Londoners make for some distinctive opportunities and challenges for learners. They learn in contexts of cultural and linguistic richness but also of discontinuity and disadvantage. Beyond school and college, there is a vast array of job opportunities, and huge earning potential, but a high premium on qualifications and much competition. Starting out in the labour market, or staying at its lower end, is tough. Lifelong learning is more important than ever, but it is expensive to live and study in London.

London's education system must harness the opportunities of growth and diversity, while responding to the challenges of mobile students, students for whom English is not a first language, and students from workless families on low incomes and in inadequate housing, and to the challenges that London's labour and housing markets present for students in the HE sector and for the recruitment and retention of teachers at all phases. Perhaps most importantly, London's education system must do its part to counter social, economic and ethnic segregation, to offer inclusive and equal schooling and to build the values of tolerance and community that can help to heal London's divisions as well as to foster its continued growth. In this essay, we have looked at only a small part of this picture, with an overview of patterns of provision and achievement in compulsory schooling. Our analysis indicates substantial progress but also that a big challenge still remains to equalise access and achievement in education for all young Londoners, regardless of gender, ethnicity, social class or family income. The remaining essays in this collection explore this challenge, and others, that the London context presents, in greater detail, and point to ways forward in policy and practice.

**References**

Baker, P. and Eversley, J. (eds) (2000) *Multilingual Capital*. London: Battlebridge Publications.

Burgess, A., Briggs, A., McConnell, B. and Slater, H. (2005a) *Background Facts for School Choice in England.* Evidence to the House of Commons Select Committee on Education and Skills, January 2006.

Burgess, S., Wilson, D. and Lupton, R. (2005b) 'Parallel lives? Ethnic segregation in schools and neighbourhoods'. *Urban Studies*, 42 (7):1027–56.

Department for Children, Schools and Families (DCSF) (2006) *Statistics of Education: Schools in England*, SFR38/2006.

Department for Communities and Local Government (DCLG) (2005) *Housing Statistics 2004/5.*

Department for Education and Skills (DfES) (2006) *Schools and Pupils in England.* <http://www.dfes.gov.uk/rsgateway/DB/SFR/s000682/index.shtml>

Gordon, I. (1999) 'Move on up the car: dealing with structural unemployment in London'. *Local Economy* 14 (1):87–95.

Greater London Authority (GLA) (2001) *Refugees and Asylum Seekers in London*. London: Greater London Authority.

— (2005a) *Greater London Demographic Review 2004.* London: Greater London Authority. DMAG Briefing 2005/45.

— (2005b) *Focus on London's Demography.* London: Greater London Authority. DMAG Briefing 2005/17.

— (2005c) *London – the World in a City.* London: Greater London Authority. DMAG Briefing 2005/6.

— (2005d) *Statistics of Schools in London: Key facts 2001–2005.* London: Greater London Authority. DMAG Briefing 2005/41.

— (2005e) *Housing in London 2005*. London: Greater London Authority.

— (2005f) *Income Poverty in London 2003/4. Summary Data from the Households Below Average Income Series*. London: Greater London Authority. DMAG Briefing 2005/16.

— (2005g) *Child Poverty in London: Income and labour market Indicators: Summary of findings.* London: Greater London Authority. DMAG Briefing 2005/19.

— (2005h) *Paycheck 2005: An analysis of household income data for London*. London: Greater London Authority. DMAG Briefing 2005/29.

— (2005i) *Model-based Income Estimates (2001/02)*. London: Greater London Authority. DMAG Briefing 2005/42.

— (2005j) *Indices of Deprivation 2004: An analysis of London wards based on SOA ranks.* London: Greater London Authority. DMAG Briefing 2005/5.

— (2005k*) Benefits Data for London. No 1: Income support.* London: Greater London Authority. DMAG Briefing 2005/20.

— (20051*) Country of Birth and Labour Market Outcomes in London: An analysis of labour force survey and census data.* London: Greater London Authority. DMAG Briefing 2005/1.

— (2006a) I*nterim Household Projections*. London: Greater London Authority. DMAG Briefing 2006/21.

— (2006b*) Family and Children's Study 2004*. London: Greater London Authority. DMAG Briefing 2006/21.

— (2006c) *Parents and Work in London: An analysis of annual population survey data for 2004*. London: Greater London Authority. DMAG Briefing 2006/6.

— (2006d) *Simpson's Diversity Indices 1991 and 2001*. London: Greater London Authority. DMAG Briefing 2006/2.

Green, A.E. and Owen, D. (2006) *The Geography of Poor Skills and Access to Work*. York: York Publishing Services for the Joseph Rowntree Foundation.

Hamnett, C. (2003) *Unequal City: London in the Global Arena*. London: Routledge.

Heath, A. and McMahon, D. (1997) 'Education and occupational attainments: the impact of ethnic origins'. In A.H. Halsey, H. Lauder, P. Brown and A.S. Wells, *Education: Culture, Economy and Society.* Oxford: Oxford University Press.

Heath, A. and Smith, S. (2003) 'Mobility and ethnic minorities'. *New Economy* 10 (4):199–204.

Hickman, M. and Thornton, P. (2006) 'City bankers on spending spree as pay soars'. *The Independent* 28/10/06.

<http://news.independent.co.uk/uk/this_britain/article 1935925.ece>

Hills, J. (2007) *Ends and Means: The future roles of social housing in England.* CASE report 34. London: Centre for Analysis of Social Exclusion.

Hobbs, G. and Vignoles, A. (2007) 'Is Free School Meal status a valid proxy for socio-economic status (in schools research)?'. *Centre for the Economics of Education, Working Paper CEEP0084.*

Ipsos MORI (2007) *Annual London Survey 2006, Final Top Line results.* <www.london.gov.uk/mayor/annual_survey/2006/als-2006-toplines.pdf>

Lavy, V. and Schlosser, A. (2007) 'Does being with more girls in school improve students' human capital outcomes and behaviour?'. *Mechanisms and impacts of gender peer effects at school* NBER Working Paper 13292, August 2007.

London Challenge (2007) *London's Key Issues.* <http://www.dfes.gov.uk/londonchallenge/pdfs/KeyIssuesRev.pdf>

London Housing Federation (LHF) (2006) *London's Housing Timebomb. Affordability and Supply 2006–2011*. London: London Housing Federation.

Management Issues (2005) 'Talent shortage pushing up City salaries'. *Management Issues 21/6/05.* <http://www.management-issues.com/display_page.asp?section=research&id=2251>

Nationwide House Price Index (2006). <http://www.nationwide.co.uk/hpi/historical.htm>

Office for National Statistics (2006) *School Workforce in England (including pupil:teacher ratios and pupil:adult ratios), January 2006, revised*. National Statistics First release SFR 37/2006.

OFSTED (2006) *Improvements in London Schools 2000–2006*. London: OFSTED.

Prime Minister's Strategy Unit (PMSU) (2004) *London Project Report*. London: Cabinet Office.

State of the Cities Database (SOCD). <http://www.socd.communities.gov.uk>

UBS (2006) *Prices and Earnings: A comparison of purchasing power around the globe*. Zurich: UBS AG.

Van Houtte (2004) 'Gender context of the school and how the presence of girls affects the achievement of boys'. *Educational Studies*, 30 (4):409–23.

Vincent, C. and Ball, S. (2006) *Childcare, Choice and Call Practices*. London: Routledge.

Whatford, C. (2005) *Secondary School Places Planning in London.* London: London Challenge.

**Notes**

1. Data from the New Earnings Survey. Refers to the London urban built-up area, which includes parts of the surrounding Home Counties as well as the London administrative area.
2. Annual Survey of Hours and Earnings (ASHE) (2005), Table 1.7a.
3. Income-based Jobseeker's Allowance, Support under Part VI of the Immigration and Asylum Act 1999, Child Tax Credit (provided their income is below a certain level), or the Guarantee element of State Pension Credit.
4. In common with other cities, London's further education colleges lie outside local authority control.
5. We exclude small cells less than n=100 here.
6. The DfES value-added score takes the difference between a pupil's capped Key

Stage 4 (KS4) score and their Key Stage 2 (KS2) score. The capped KS4 points score is the points score for a pupil's best eight results at GCSE and equivalent. The difference between the capped KS4 score and the KS2 score had a range of -404 to +447. DfES conventionally adds 1,000 to this figure in order to yield a positive integer (to avoid the implication that some pupils have made negative progress). This gives a scale from 596 to 1,447. A score of 1,006 is interpreted by DfES as showing that a pupil has gained one more GCSE pass than would have been predicted based on their KS2 scores, while a score of 994 is interpreted as showing that a pupil has gained one less GCSE pass than expected. This interpretation has the rather odd implication that pupils on average do less well than expected.

7. The ranking of boroughs differs from that for KS2, with Richmond-upon-Thames falling to below the London average, and five boroughs achieving at lower levels than Hackney. Pupil mobility between boroughs and exit to the private sector may account for some of the differences between KS2 and KS4.

# 2 Global city school systems

Anne Sofer

## Introduction

One of the most noticeable things about the linguistic style of the public relations departments of metropolitan authorities across the English-speaking democracies of the world is its sameness. 'Global', 'redesign', 'twenty-first century', are bound to appear, along with 'knowledge economy', 'vibrant', 'diversity', and 'competition'. They also talk freely of visions, missions and challenges. As well as the common language, there is a common analysis of their situation, and of the solutions to the main problems.

The cities considered in this essay – London, New York City, Chicago, Sydney and Toronto – are the nerve centres of what Peter Hall and David Soskice have described as the 'liberal market economies' of our new world (Hall and Soskice 2001). Unlike the 'co-ordinated market economies' typified by the countries of continental Western Europe, they are based on openness, light regulation and relentless competition. The cities are all 'global' in the sense that they are the hubs of major world markets, important centres of finance and commerce, homes to successive waves of immigration, and surrounded by sprawling suburbs and dormitory towns. In the last half century they have experienced the rapid loss of manufacturing jobs accompanied by the equally rapid growth of service and professional jobs.

There is an energetic flavour to the promotion of their glamorous new downtown areas and conversion of industrial dereliction into waterside pleasure areas, as they compete internationally for the top spot for cosmopolitan coolness. But at the same time these cities also face the challenge of localised unemployment, chronic shortage of moderately priced housing, polarisation of rich and poor, and pressure on public services. They fear youth crime, ethnic tension and the loss of the middle class.

As far as education is concerned, the analysis of need and the remedies applied have now become thoroughly familiar. To maintain their position in a global economy, they believe they need safe and attractive city streets, abundant and diverse cultural life, good public services and a highly skilled workforce. The public education system in its traditional form, it is said, is not capable of contributing to this climate, or producing this workforce without more competition, new and innovative management techniques and dynamic leadership. More investment will have to be found for education, but this will only be effective – or acceptable to the tax payers – if there are rigorous systems of accountability. All these systems set detailed targets, administer frequent blanket tests and publish the results, school by school. Some more than others also have tough and public procedures for dealing with schools thought to be performing below a certain standard.

Although the rhetoric and the remedies may be similar, the schools and what happens in them are embedded in different histories, national cultures and political climates. As a result, there is at least one respect in which each city's system differs from the others. This essay examines the similarities and differences in an attempt to learn from them lessons that may be of benefit to London. It takes as a framework for discussion four frequently recurring themes: governance, quality, choice, and equity.

The four sections that follow draw examples and evidence from all five cities. Some of the basic facts and figures are set out in the table attached as Appendix A to this essay.

## Governance

### *Structures*

Governance is a difficult issue for large metropolitan areas. As one expert on the subject puts it:

> The search for an effective and acceptable form of metropolitan government is far from unique to London...other cities have struggled to define institutions and systems which balance the competing goals of economic growth, social cohesion and democratic accountability.
>
> (Travers 2004: 155)

The different cities discussed here have all made their own accommodations with one or other of these 'competing goals', but working within different national structures.

Structurally, London is unique. All the other cities are in countries with a federal structure, where the states (or provinces in the case of Canada), not the national government, hold the major responsibility for education. They control the curriculum, the structure of the system, budgeting, the certifying of teachers, and arrangements for school admissions. Management of the system is in the hands of local school districts.

At this point practice in the four other cities diverges. In Toronto there is a school board of 22 members, elected by geographical district, a single purpose authority with no structural connection with the mayor and city council. It is – at least in theory – non-political. Its members do not stand for office under party affiliations. It operates entirely within the policies and authority of the provincial government of Ontario, which provides the bulk of the budget for schools (see Appendix A).

New York City and Chicago both have histories of turbulent education politics, with the elected school board playing a major role. In recent years, however, the school board has been transformed into a small unelected body, appointed by and accountable to the mayor, who also is empowered to appoint the chief executive. This is not the normal pattern in the United States but is becoming a fashionable model for the bigger cities (Kirst 2004). It is the state government that adopts this arrangement, usually subject to close monitoring and renewal after a number of years.

The US federal government only contributes a small proportion of the education budget – mostly targeted towards disadvantage. However, President Bush's 'No Child Left Behind' Act (US Department of Education 2002) has increased the leverage of the federal government, making the publication of test results and an element of school choice a condition of grant, and requiring states to take action in relation to underachievement.

In Sydney, the local district administration consists of officials appointed by the New South Wales government: there is no locally elected input, and not even an identifiable separate district of Sydney (it is covered by four districts). The New South Wales cabinet minister in charge of education also holds the portfolio for industrial relations, and two other portfolios (Government of New South Wales 2007). By the standards of other countries, political oversight of a very large education system (one-third of Australia's school population) seems sparse, but this arrangement appears to be generally accepted. It is interesting that of all the city education systems under consideration here, this is the only one that has not been changed within the last 20 years.

All these cities, while being major players within their states, are contained within that larger and more powerful political entity. The states (or provinces) have comprehensive powers and responsibilities rooted in the national constitution, and are therefore capable both of standing up to national government, and of strategic integration across services. This may explain the fact that there appears to be far less concern in cities other than London about the need for 'joined up delivery'.

By contrast, the governance of London is a paradoxical combination of complexity, decentralisation and micromanagement from the national government. Tony Travers has described it as 'an extraordinary muddle of overlapping and often competitive institutions ... a rococo layering of government departments, regional offices, appointed boards (and their sub-divisions) city-wide elected government, the 32 boroughs and the City of London' (Travers 2004: 185). A closer look specifically at the education world would add to the complexities of local government structures and government agencies many additional rococo layers of ornamentation; notably individual school governing bodies, diocesan authorities, and children's trusts. It is unsurprising that in those parts of the London education system that urgently need better planning and co-ordination, particularly 14–19 and special educational needs, a lobby is developing for placing these powers with the mayor.

What saves the whole from descending into anarchy is the detailed control over the education system which the central Westminster government has taken to itself over the last 20 years, under both Conservative and Labour governments. There has been a level of hyperactivity at Secretary of State level, which is well illustrated below:

> Within two years (he) had issued 387 new regulations, 315 consultation papers and 437 notes of guidance. He had required every local education authority ... to complete seventeen separate plans, including plans for development, literacy, numeracy, communication, organisation, class size, lifelong learning, asset management, admissions, behaviour support, action zones, and even a 'plan for plans'. By 2001 Hansard reported that in a single year English schools received 3,840 pages of instructions (including one guidance note called a 'bureaucracy-cutting toolkit').
>
> (Jenkins 2006: 283)

It is this tight control by central government which sets the English system, and London within it, apart from the other systems described in this essay, and probably from most other national systems in OECD countries. The federal governments of the United States and Australia are both certainly claiming a larger role in education, and there are pressures for greater standardisation across those countries, but it is still the intermediate regional level of government that holds the major responsibilities for budgets, strategy and curriculum.

*School autonomy*

On one governance issue, however, there has been an international trend going beyond the English-speaking advanced economies. That is the trend towards increasing school autonomy. This has been documented by the OECD Programme for International Student Assessment (PISA), which found that 'increased autonomy ... with the objective to raise performance levels through devolving responsibility to the front-line and encouraging responsiveness to local needs, has been the main aim of the restructuring and systemic reform since the early 1980s'. It also reported that a greater degree of autonomy tended to be associated both with higher literacy levels and a more advantaged social intake (PISA 2005: 89).

There is, on the face of it, a contradiction between the widely held view that the English system of local management of schools has gone further in the direction of devolution than most others and the easily parodied approach to command and control described above by Simon Jenkins. In truth, however, the powers which the Westminster central government has taken over are those previously held by local education authorities. Other formerly local authority powers are now devolved to schools. For all the blizzard of central directives, individual schools in England do have some significant powers that their counterparts in other countries do not have – the appointment of all staff, for instance, and ability to vire within an overall budget as well as a capital budget. In a large minority of schools – and most contentiously, particularly in London where 217 secondary schools out of a total of 471 are their own admission authority – this extends to admission arrangements as well (a fact that is surely linked to the conclusions of the PISA 2000 report in relation to social intake, quoted above).

English schools even have the power, through a simple vote of the governing body, to convert themselves into 'trusts', independent of the local authority altogether. The fact that so few are rushing to do so probably indicates that most of them feel pretty independent already (at least from local government, less so from the national government). The vision, promoted by Tony Blair when he was prime minister, of local education authorities seeing themselves as primarily champions of children and parents rather than of schools and teachers, and as 'commissioners' of autonomous schools rather than managers of them, is at the same time radical in terms of international comparison and unsurprising in the English context.

This is of course a national, rather than a specifically London issue. But it does underline the point made in Essay 7 that the headteachers of London schools can sometimes feel overwhelmed by their responsibilities. Many London schools are in fragile and volatile neighbourhoods, and the problems that heads are daily presented with seem daunting to most ordinary mortals. Fewer candidates are coming forward for headship, particularly in such schools. It may be that the lack of a higher authority to fall back on is some part of the explanation. In both Sydney and Toronto, the local officials responsible for the school system support and control school management within the strong structures and policies of the state or province, in a way that recalls the situation that used to exist 20 years ago in London. There is also more evidence of active day-to-day involvement of the professional teaching unions in these systems.

New York City on the other hand is moving more towards the English system, by delegating more powers to the level of the individual school. The local education bureaucracy and the teacher unions tend to be regarded by political and business leaders as resistant to change, so greater school autonomy is seen as a solution. Significantly, however, it is to the school principal, not to an English-style governing body, that power is to be delegated; the city had a bad experience of racial politics and union intransigence when it experimented with 'community control' of schools in the 1960s (Ravitch 1988). 'Empowering the Principal' is the slogan that heads the list of the next phase of 'Children First' reforms proclaimed by New York City Education Chancellor Joel Klein in

January 2007 (New York City Board of Education 2007). It is the same new public management approach that has led to the belief in 'strong mayors' as the solution to the problems of urban school systems (Payzant 2004).

Similarly, Mayor Daley in Chicago is not about to delegate power to any local community body. This has already been tried in Chicago. The 1988 State of Illinois School Reform Act radically decentralised powers from the city's school board to local school councils, which consisted of elected parents (the majority), teachers and community members. The powers they were given – appointment of staff, control of budgets – were not dissimilar to those delegated to schools in England at the same time, but they were unusual in the United States. The defenders of this reform believe that improvements were already under way when, in 1995, Mayor Daley, with support from powerful groups within Chicago, convinced the newly elected Republican administration of the state that progress was too slow, and – with the city facing a fiscal crisis – persuaded them to give him control. Although the local school boards were preserved, many of their powers, and many of the protections that the teachers' union had had written into the previous reforms, were abolished. However, now a sort of 'earned autonomy' is being introduced, to a small minority of schools who are deemed to have improved sufficiently to be capable of it.

In both New York City and Chicago there is a strong move in the direction of creating new 'charter schools'. These are schools given a charter by the state to run independently. They are funded on the same basis as local public schools, but are not bound by local regulation or collective agreements. Some are run by not-for-profit organisations, others by private companies or quoted businesses. They are widely seen as the model for the academies and trust schools being introduced in English cities, though in the context of the English system they are not such a radical departure. Indeed, set in its international context, it is the peculiarly English institution of the individual governing body for every school, placing as it does huge powers in the hands of a purely local group of parents, teachers, and community members, which may be seen as the more radical form of school autonomy.

## *The place of religious schools*

In all these cities the role and status of religious schools have historically been issues with which the authorities have had major difficulties. (See, for instance, Diane Ravitch's history of New York City's public schools, *The Great School Wars* 1988.) The United States constitution, as currently interpreted, prohibits public funding of religious schools but in both New York City and Chicago there is a large 'parochial' sector running schools affiliated to different religious denominations, though by no means recruiting exclusively from them. Parochial schools charge modest fees, and have the image of stronger discipline and more traditional teaching than the public schools.

In Toronto the situation is different. In 1987 the Supreme Court of Canada ruled that separate Catholic schools were protected under the constitution, and their funding is now on an equal footing with the state sector. They are run by the Toronto Catholic District School Board, whose trustees are elected by all English-speaking Catholic electors. (The small number of French Catholic Schools in Toronto were separated in 1987 and placed under the jurisdiction of the French Catholic School Board.) Catholic primary schools are open only to Catholic children and the non-Catholic children of Catholic parents. Catholic secondary schools are open to all students.

In Australia, Catholic and other religious schools are, with independent schools, referred to as 'non-government schools'. In practice this means they are not controlled by the state governments, but are subsidised, on a sliding scale of student need, by both commonwealth (federal) and state governments.

In London, the status of the religious schools was settled by the 1944 Education Act. Unlike any of the other systems, they were brought within the local education authority's remit, although they retained control over the admission of pupils and the appointment of some staff, in return for a contribution to capital costs. (The required contribution to capital has been dropped, but the independence over admissions and appointments remain the same, with other local authority schools moving closer to their status in these respects.)

## Quality

Comparisons of the quality of education between countries are notoriously difficult and best left to the type of careful studies undertaken by OECD. These, of course, are nationwide and therefore usually not specific enough to highlight issues peculiar to big cities. The exceptions to this are those reports that deal with issues of equity, since these are most likely to be relevant to urban circumstances. Some of these reports are discussed in the section below.

It is also not possible to assess the quality of the systems by comparing their outputs to a national or regional average. This depends very much on how much of the middle-class residential areas are included within the metropolitan boundary. The English government statistics (possibly for historical reasons) distinguish between Inner and Outer London; but it is harder to access this distinction elsewhere.

### *Assessing quality*

What it is possible to comment on is the meaning given to 'quality', and the nature of the official curriculum, in these different systems. In all of them, but particularly in New York City and Chicago, quality is equated with academic achievement measured through test scores in maths and English, and graduation rates. Whether the improvement in test scores can be equated with an improvement in quality is still debated; critics, mostly from within the education profession, argue that it is only the result of relentless 'teaching to the test' and narrowing of the curriculum, particularly for socially disadvantaged students (see, for instance, Lipman 2002; Thomson 2002; Tymms 2004).

The extent to which test scores are available on a school-by-school basis varies – possibly an indicator of how far professional opinion has influenced policy makers in each country. The test scores of London schools, as with all English schools, are published annually in list form (rearranged in 'league table' order by the media); and in the two United States cities too, school-by-school test scores are publicly available. Of all the cities studied, Sydney's individual school results are the least accessible, although they are required to be reported to parents at the school level, and some district level data are available in the statistical appendices to the New South Wales Education Department's annual report.

Toronto takes a middle course – but one that is in practice the most informative to parents. Although a ranked list does not feature obviously in publicly available information, each school has an internet entry in standard form, with a description of the school's beliefs, course offering and extracurricular activities, as well as test results set against a state average; and contextual data, including the proportion of students who speak English at home, or who have special needs.

In England and in the two cities in the United States, school failure is publicly exposed. Whereas in England this is determined by an inspection report, in New York and Chicago it is judged primarily on quantitative indicators. A whole glossary of acronyms is needed to understand these: Adequate Yearly Progress (AYP), Annual Measurable Objectives (AMOs), Performance Index (PI), School Requiring Academic Progress (SRAP) and District Requiring Academic Progress (DRAP), and School under Registration Review (SURR).

The open publication of regular inspection reports, which set professional qualitative assessments alongside the quantitative data, and which can sometimes qualify the conclusions drawn from the figures alone, are not found outside England. However, independent judgements are available, particularly in the United States, from locally based and well-financed think tanks and academic institutions. In Chicago, for instance, there is 'Catalyst Chicago', an 'independent newsmagazine created to document, analyse and support school-improvement efforts in Chicago Public Schools'. It is published by the Community Renewal Society, established as an urban mission in 1882, working 'to create racially and economically just communities'. It provides a rich mix of authoritative data analysis and varied and perceptive opinion about what is happening in the schools. (The fact that it is affiliated to the Church of Christ – a congregationalist church – serves to remind an English reader that the role of religion in US political life does not necessarily conform to the stereotype.)

### *Graduation rates*

A key indicator of success in all systems is the high school graduation rate. This is weakest in England, where the idea that all young people should still be in some sort of full-time education to the age of 18, with the majority achieving a recognised qualification, is a relatively recent one. We are also out of line on the question of what an appropriate curriculum for this upper secondary phase should be. Even Australia (which is closest to the English system) has a broader definition. In New South Wales the Higher School Certificate is based on a minimum of four subjects including English.

In all the North American cities, the upper secondary curriculum requires the study of English, mathematics, the sciences and a subject embracing the history and geography of America, plus an international dimension, and there is a move at the state level to make the requirements progressively more demanding. For instance, New York State has agreed a timetable for introducing a 'Diploma with Advanced Designation' that includes a second science, and Illinois is insisting on a higher proportion of students' time to be spent on writing assignments. Despite this raising of the bar, graduation rates in all these cities are slowly improving.

### *Vocational education*

The proper place of vocational education in school is an issue of concern in all cities, but in all except London it is included as an option running alongside the academic requirements on all students, and contained within the umbrella of the graduation diploma. There is evidence of much effort having gone into the preparation of these courses; in New York City, for instance, 'career and technical education' covers a very wide range of courses that are claimed to be tied to industry standards. Thirty-eight per cent of New York City high school students are on these courses, but this proportion is down from 58 per cent in 1990. (In the rest of the state the equivalent figures are 19 per cent down from 35 per cent) (University of the State of New York 2006: 42)

This reducing popularity of school-based vocational courses, even at a time when the academic alternative has become more rigorous, should be giving the government in England pause for thought. It is as if the teenagers on the streets sense that in the neo-liberal market economies of the new global world, many of the vocational courses on offer may not give them as good a prospect of a worthwhile job as a more academic route. Paradoxically, however, some of the newer high schools which make a feature of a whole-school link with a particular vocation – the military academies in Chicago, for instance, or the Bronx School for Law, Government and Justice in New York City (see the section below on choice) – are hugely popular. But these serve only a tiny proportion of the population and it is questionable whether the intensive and high-quality work experience they offer could ever be made generalisable without a transformation of employers' attitudes.

### *Teacher quality*

Ever since the end of the Second World War, London has had recurring crises in recruiting and retaining teachers, often associated with the high cost of living (particularly housing) in this capital city. While the housing problem is worse than ever in the current decade, teacher shortages during the early part of the decade were not as crippling as they have been in the past, mostly as a result of better salaries and an effective recruitment campaign funded by the national government. However, the problem is by no means solved, and schools in most parts of London are heavily dependent on a constant flow of high-quality temporary teachers from British Commonwealth countries (including Australia and Canada). In the United States there are much more serious concerns about the quality of teachers in urban schools, in particular the high turnover and the proportion teaching subjects for which they are not qualified (Ingersoll 2004).

In neither Canada nor Australia, however, is this a preoccupation with urban educators. It seems that in these countries teaching has a higher status in society; it is certainly the case that the teachers have more professional autonomy. In Toronto, while the curriculum is set by the state, 'teaching and assessment strategies are left to the professional judgements of teachers, enabling them to address individual student needs and deliver the curriculum in a context that is locally meaningful' (Ontario Ministry of Education 2007). Teams of principals drawn from across the city sift and interview applicants for senior positions in schools.

### *Private schools*

Some observers might argue that the proportion of students whose parents choose private education is an indication of the quality of the public schools. It is certainly a figure which troubles those responsible for the reputation of the public system. But this issue is complicated by the differing status of religious schools in each of the systems and by social and historical attitudes. What is obvious, even from this brief survey, is that London is by no means atypical among global cities in having ten per cent or more of its parents choosing to opt out of state education (*see* Appendix A).

## **Choice**

The issue of choice overlaps with both quality and equity. Across all city systems there are debates about school choice. Does it drive up quality by introducing competition? Or does more choice merely widen inequalities? The fact that there is some evidence for both propositions has not stopped all the urban school systems under consideration here promoting choice as a positive feature.

Choice has to be seen in the context of the geography and demography of each city. Poorer families living in the sprawling south-western suburbs of Sydney, for instance, in practice may not have more than one accessible school, whereas a similar family living in Inner London will have several.

History is important too. In all of these cities, non fee-paying selective high schools, many with prestigious reputations, predated the introduction of a mass system of upper secondary education. In Toronto and London they have largely been incorporated within a comprehensive system. This has not happened in New York, Chicago or Sydney, where this element of choice is still available for a selected minority.

The London admissions system is unusual in that it is not based on formally defined catchment areas. All the other systems are based on the guarantee of a place in the neighbourhood school. The right to apply for an alternative has been grafted onto that system.

In the United States, parochial or independent schools are only available as alternatives to those who can afford the fees (although some experimental voucher systems and the provisions of the 'No Child Left Behind' legislation are beginning to erode that constitutional boundary). In densely populated cities, where housing is segregated by ethnic group (in the past often *de jure*, now *de facto*) the drawing of the catchment areas frequently became the subject of acrimonious legal disputes. Over the past decades, the idea of parental choice became a way out of these battles, appealing to parents of all races by apparently giving them freedom to escape local schools with poor reputations. To give the choice more meaning, and in an attempt to hold on to the whites and the middle class, over the last quarter century there has been an explosion of specialist or magnet schools, particularly at the high school level.

With the more recent spread of the idea of contestability in public services, choice has also come to mean a choice between schools run by the public authorities and schools run by independent groups or companies – hence the charter schools. Another newer development is the breaking up of large city high schools into small schools, a move that is being promoted and partly funded by the Gates Foundation.

The question of which children are benefiting from this increase in choice is an important one. Conscious of the accusations of selectivity levelled against them by their critics, most charter schools now deal with over-subscription by lottery. An analysis by Catalyst Chicago indicates that in that city at least the charter schools and more autonomous schools are recruiting an intake that is disproportionately poor and African American, and are succeeding better than other schools with a comparable intake, particularly in retaining students through to graduation. There are costs borne by other students, however, from restructuring. In particular, students from schools that have been closed because of poor performance are not finding their way into the newer types of school. They are disproportionately being placed in other schools with below average performance – the opposite to what was intended (Catalyst Chicago 2007).

In Australia, the right to choose a school other than that provided by the state, and to be helped by the state in paying for it, is embedded in law. This arrangement, which covers religious and independent schools, has been explained by the Ministerial Council on Education, Employment and Youth Affairs (a committee of the Commonwealth Minister of Education and the Ministers of all the states) as follows:

> Real choice in schooling cannot exist without effective and socially diverse government school systems ... When non-government schooling is recognised by government, and meets the particular requirements of individuals, families and communities, government funding should support this schooling on the basis of need ... (But) private contributions are important for ensuring viability.
>
> (MCEETYA 2002: ch. 3)

This is an example of what has been described as a peculiarly

Australian notion of a 'welfare assistance state', where government intervenes to help people help themselves (Thomson 2002: 27–28).

In Toronto, generally speaking, the system – both school board and Catholic – is non-selective, but a degree of diversity is introduced through specialist programmes, for example International Baccalaureat, ballet – within schools. The Toronto School Board's approach to choice is as positive as these other systems, but its language suggests a celebration of variety rather than contestability.

In Toronto there are also a large number of 'alternative schools' within the public system. These are described as offering 'something different from mainstream schooling'. Popular opinion may deem them to be targeted at those who for one reason or another are not welcome in other schools, but there is nothing in the official documentation to confirm this. They usually feature small size innovative and experimental programs and volunteer commitment from parents and other community members.

Admission to school is on the basis of catchment areas, except for the alternative schools and some of the specialist ones, but with freedom to apply to schools outside the area if there is space available.

This brief description illuminates the reality that the degree of choice for parents within the London system has always been greater than in other systems. This is a fact which English politicians, unfamiliar with the state education system in their own country, have sometimes been unaware of, particularly those who have enthusiastically adopted transatlantic remedies. While the introduction of specialist secondary schools is a more recent innovation, for at least the last 30 years London parents have been able to express a preference for a school which is Catholic, Anglican, Jewish or non-denominational, large or small, single sex or mixed, run by the local authority or a charitable foundation, within their own local authority area or outside its boundary; and the school has been obliged to offer a place if one is available. It is those last four words that are the key to all the frustration and disappointment on this issue, which is as strongly felt by London parents as those anywhere else. Simple logic dictates that if a school is oversubscribed, not every parent can have their first choice. In a political climate that promotes competition, pecking orders develop more strongly and more parents are disappointed. The key issue becomes not how many different types of school there are, but who decides, and on what criteria, priority for admission to those that are oversubscribed. While national governments over the last 20 years have been legislating for more and more schools to be set free to decide such things for themselves, pressure has been growing for a fairer and more transparent system – culminating in the admissions code arising from the 2007 Education Act (DfES 2007a). The next few years will reveal how effectively this works.

## Equity

Pressure for more equal opportunities in education, as in society generally, has been felt across the developed world over the last half century. Of the three categories within which this issue is usually discussed – gender, race and class – gender is the only one that has seen a transformation. Despite their historical position, girls are now outperforming boys in most subjects and in most countries, and those in the cities covered in this essay are no exception. This section therefore concentrates on the other two categories.

### *Resourcing*

Given the heterogeneity and socio-economic polarisation of most global cities, equity issues are particularly important. In England, Australia and Canada it has long been recognised that some groups in school populations – in particular those living in poverty, or newly arrived in the country, or speaking a language other than English – will need higher than average resources if they are to have an equal chance of succeeding. Resourcing systems in all these countries are weighted, either at regional or national level, to respond to these needs.

In the United States this is not always the case. With the heavy dependence on local school board funding enshrined in the US system, the suburbs have tended to have better resourced schools than the inner cities – a reality in both New York City and Chicago. The New York Board of Regents, which advises the state government, reported in 2006 that:

> On average, New York City served much larger percentages of students placed at risk by poverty, limited English skills and recent immigration than (...suburban districts). Nevertheless the City had more students per teacher, higher rates of teacher turnover, and less experienced teachers.
>
> (New York Board of Regents Report on the Status of the Schools 2006: Preface vi)

However, from 2007 the budget is to be increased by some five billion dollars over four years. Credit for this is variously claimed by the mayor and by a lobbying group, the Campaign for Fiscal Equity, which filed a constitutional challenge to the New York State's school finance system and won. In 2003, the court held that a 'sound basic education' as guaranteed by the New York State constitution, requires that all students have the 'opportunity for a meaningful high school education, one which prepares them to function productively as civic participants'.

In Australia, the unique and complex system of publicly funded 'non-government schools' (see above) results in a hefty public contribution to the independent sector, which may come as a surprise to anyone with an image of Australia as a relatively egalitarian nation. An analysis of the per capita income of such schools in New South Wales in 2005 indicates that funding for Catholic schools came 20 per cent from the state government, 50 per cent from the Commonwealth government, and 30 per cent from fees and donations. (This is an average – some schools would be much less dependent on fees.) In independent schools, which on average spent 30 per cent more per pupil, the profile was 12 per cent from the state government, 26 per cent from the Commonwealth government and 62 per cent from fees and donations (MCEETYA

2006). While the distribution of the taxpayers' money is supposed to be done on the basis of need alone, there are obvious concerns that this process sustains an unfair and selective system. But the popularity of non-government schools has been growing. In New South Wales, as in Australia as a whole, one in three students is in a non-government school, and – unsurprisingly perhaps – their performance outstrips that of the government schools. Sixty-eight per cent of non-government school students continue into higher or further education and only 7.5 per cent into unemployment. The comparative figures for government schools are 47 per cent and 19 per cent (MCEETYA 2006).

### *Equity outcomes*

The Programme for International Student Assessment (PISA) (2005: 92) has done some important work on this, analysing school factors relating to equity across a range of countries, and ranking them according to such indicators as between-school variance in standards, reading disadvantage of non-native students, and social class differences in performance. It is disappointing that England, despite a good position on quality (measured on average literacy levels), performs poorly on several of the equity measures, particularly in relation to the spread of the results and their correlation with social class. The United States and Australia do slightly better, while Canada is among the leaders. In recent years, since PISA results began to be published, educators in England have been aware of the extent of gap in achievement between the top and bottom, and a number of initiatives, described elsewhere in this book, have been launched. Part of the problem may be that the top has a tendency to improve faster than the bottom when schools become more effective. This perhaps implies the need for different targets (as have been introduced in some US cities) focused on the lowest achievers.

Another PISA publication, *Where Immigrant Students Succeed* (PISA 2006a), is a useful survey of first and second generation immigrant students in 17 OECD countries. It analyses the evidence from the PISA

2003 survey on education outcomes, including achievement at age 15, and attitudes to school. Unfortunately the sample does not include England – though some information from England is included in the section on second language teaching – but it does include Australia (and specifically New South Wales), Canada (and specifically Ontario) and the United States.

The report finds that although immigrant students in all countries are at least as positive in their attitude to education as their native born counterparts, immigrant students in many countries perform at a significantly lower level. Australia and Canada are in the small group of countries where this is not the case. Canada is also one of a small group of countries where second generation immigrants perform better than first.

The United States is in a large group of countries where more than 30 per cent of second generation immigrant students aged 15 have not reached PISA's 'level 2' in mathematics – a baseline level, reached by the great majority of native students, below which 'students are expected to face considerable challenges in terms of their labour market and earnings prospects, as well as their capacity to participate fully in society' (PISA 2006a: 8).

The report acknowledges that the background characteristics of the immigrant populations are a relevant factor. This is an important point for our purposes, given the policy differences between countries: Canada and Australia, in contrast to the United States, admit an immigrant group which has roughly the same socio-economic profile as the native population. Nonetheless, the report claims that this cannot fully explain the differences in performance.

Support in gaining fluency in the language of instruction is found to be important. Australia and Canada are identified as among the countries with 'relatively small achievement gaps between immigrant and native students, or smaller gaps for second generation students compared to first generation students ... (where) ... long-standing language support programmes exist with clearly defined goals and standards' (PISA 2006a: 11).

It is more difficult to reach useful comparative conclusions about non-immigrant ethnic minorities. The United States, Australia and Canada all have small indigenous communities which have yet to integrate fully into society and which sit heavily on the national conscience. Their educational achievement levels are monitored carefully but they are not a numerically significant feature of the big city scene. More significant are the large black populations – the descendants of slavery – in both the United States and England, and to a lesser extent Canada.

On both sides of the Atlantic there is a large literature on black underachievement, its historical roots and possible remedies, which it is impossible to survey within this short essay. In the United States this has been interwoven with the history of slavery, the civil rights campaign and protracted battles over integration. In both New York City and Chicago, where 'white flight' frustrated the hopes of integration this has been particularly contentious and bitter (Ravitch 1985; Lemann 1991).

Both these cities carry out extensive monitoring of academic performance by ethnic group. The New York City statistics show black and Hispanic students performing well below white and Asian students on virtually all measures and ages. A report on graduation and dropout rates from the Consortium on Chicago School Research indicates the same disparities. Only 39 per cent of African American boys graduated in 2003, compared to 51 per cent of Hispanics, 58 per cent of whites and 76 per cent of Asians. Furthermore

> Graduation rates are highest in ... areas with little poverty and a majority white population. A number of communities on the south side of the city showed significantly larger increases in dropout rates or declines in graduation rates than was typical for the city as a whole.
>
> (Allensworth 2005: 26)

This is a grim picture. Another publication from the same organisation explores the ambiguities felt by white professionals and the feelings of vulnerability and lack of social trust within the black community, both of which profoundly affect these outcomes (Payne 2005).

The quotation above raises the issue of segregation. Interestingly, the PISA report on immigrant students finds that there is not a significant association between the 'degree of clustering' in particular schools and the size of the performance gap. There is a world of difference, however, between living and being educated within the ethos of a newly arrived but aspirant immigrant community and the experience of life, such as that in the Chicago projects, stunted by many generations of poverty and segregation from mainstream society.

This brings us to the important issue of the connection between poverty, race and underachievement. This is explored more fully with data from across London in Essay 1. The statistics in Figure 1.7 of that essay, in particular, illustrate the complex interaction between ethnicity, class, poverty, and the historic position of each ethnic group. In general (though not in every case) there are greater differences within each group between pupils entitled to free school meals and those not entitled, than there is between one ethnic group and another. Also notable in this table is the fact that the achievement gap is greater in the case of the 'white British' group than any other, an indication that class differences still have deep roots in English society.

Lifting groups out of poverty is clearly related to improving their educational achievement levels, but it is also related to other factors – health, housing, and employment discrimination, to name the most obvious ones. In countries where more progress has been made on these issues, the extremes in achievement levels between rich and poor seem less acute. In Australia, for instance, 59 per cent of the lowest third by socio-economic status complete the twelfth year of education (equivalent to Year 13 in England), compared to 67 per cent of the top third (MCEETYA 2006)

Another interesting finding in Figures 1.6 and 1.7 of Essay 1 is the performance of the 'mixed race' group in London schools. Despite the concerns that are sometimes expressed over the potential for 'identity crisis' within this group, in academic terms at least these young people are achieving at similar levels to the white British group,and are less polarised. This is a fast-growing category – one that is less frequently cited, or perhaps even collected, in other countries. US visitors often observe that there seems to be more informal interaction between races in London than in US cities, where despite all the political effort to achieve integration during the decades following the *Brown v. Board of Education* Supreme Court decision in 1954, many segregated schools and neighbourhoods remain. The Mayor of London claimed in a magazine interview recently that there are only five wards out of a total of 625 in London with 80 per cent of residents from a non-white ethnic group (*Prospect* 2007).

## Conclusion

One recurring feature of this survey has been the theme of London's uniqueness. Despite all the similarities, many of its policies and practices stand out from the other four cities. What follows is an assessment of where this indicates strength or weakness – or merely difference – and what action should follow that assessment.

In terms of *governance*, it is clear that the current situation has weaknesses. A stronger regional body, with electoral legitimacy, is needed for planning and co-ordinating the general pattern of London's education. In terms of a joined-up delivery of local services for children, local councils need greater control and more operational independence from central government direction if the aspirations for children's trusts, and the agenda spelt out in the government's vision that 'Every Child Matters' are to become a realities.

The peculiarly English model of school autonomy, currently identified with an image of competitive zeal and 'heroic leadership', needs to be re-thought. Particularly in an urban setting, professional collegiality and mutual support between schools are extremely important.

In the drive for *quality* London can learn from experiments elsewhere, from the charter schools of New York City, the small schools of

Chicago and the alternative schools of Toronto. Many of these are new and innovative, but in most cases, ongoing independent scrutiny is available to indicate where they are succeeding or failing. Much can also be learnt from the pedagogic practice in relation to English as an additional language teaching in Canada and Australia, and for the greater attention paid to the professional voice in these countries.

The relative success of other cities' overarching graduation diploma in retaining upper secondary students is an indication that the proposals of the Tomlinson Report (DfES 2004) should be reconsidered. Genuinely high-quality vocational education, however, may be an elusive goal for all these cities. Parity of esteem between academic and vocational education is hard to achieve except in countries where employers' commitment to vocational training is widespread and highly institutionalised as in those of northern Europe, as PISA has found:

> The sharp differences between high-status academic programmes and low-status vocational programmes have been replicated in most countries, except for Germany, Austria and Denmark where dual systems combine school-based learning and serious work-based learning (or apprenticeships).
>
> (PISA 2006b:.26)

An analysis of 'Skill profiles in eighteen OECD countries' undertaken for the Hall and Soskice volume quoted in the opening paragraphs of this essay typified the vocational training system of all four of the countries studied here as 'weak' (Estevez-Abe *et al.* 2001: 170).

In relation to *choice*, London arrangements, for all their complexity, do in fact keep more types of schools within the same system and have probably encouraged more intercommunity mixing than any of the other systems. The frustration felt by parents on this issue (in London as elsewhere) owes much to the illusion implied by the word 'choice', which promises more than it can deliver. But the admissions system can certainly be improved, and the implementation of the new code needs to be closely monitored. London must treasure, preserve and if possible extend the heterogeneity of its neighbourhoods and ensure that this heterogeneity is reflected in its schools.

However, despite the increasing diversity of school governance arrangements, it should be noted that in some respects parents are not given as radically different choices in terms of the educational experience for children as are now available to parents in some other cities. For instance, parents in London cannot generally express a preference for a secondary school with fewer than 400 pupils, or a school that is not subject to the national testing regime, or a bilingual school – all choices that some parents may want, and that are now available to some parents in other global cities.

On the issue of *equity*, poverty and class remain the biggest problems, despite major efforts by the Labour governments since 1997 to change this situation. If there are lessons to be learnt from other global cities, those of Canada and Australia seem likely to offer better models than those of the United States.

## Postscript

In one of the closing episodes of *The West Wing*, the hugely popular Washington political soap opera, the new First Couple (the Hispanic Matthew Santos and his white wife Helen) are choosing a school in Washington for their two young children. They visit a string of private schools that have been recommended but are put off by their stuffy exclusiveness. Daringly, they decide to look for a public school – and find one. It is full of happy children's laughter and evidence of creativity; the female African American principal is upbeat and professional looking. 'What's your racial profile?' asks the President Elect. 'Forty-one per cent African American, 30 per cent white, 19 per cent Hispanic and nine per cent Asian,' comes the answer. 'And how many free lunch kids?' 'Eight per cent.' 'Isn't that very low?' asks the President Elect, wonderingly. 'The lowest!' replies the Principal with pride. The First Couple are clearly impressed and delighted. 'It's perfect,' they say to each other as they leave.

This whole vignette seems to be intended as an illustration of Matt Santos's genuineness as a man of the people, and a sign of hope for a new era in which a multiracial political class will be happy to identify itself with the public schools – but only up to a point. The script-writers have to be realistic after all – not if it means too much mixing with the poor.

Compare this with the sharp criticism addressed ten years ago to New Labour politicians who 'escaped' their local schools by choosing schools with a more middle-class intake on the other side of London. At that time, it was not considered appropriate for left-leaning politicians to insulate their offspring from contact with the urban poor, any more than it would have been to prevent them from mixing with children of other races.

This may now have changed. It seems likely that over the last 30 years London schools have played a major role in increasing tolerance and understanding, as well as genuine integration, between different races. Class remains a more intractable issue.

**References**

Allensworth, E. (2005) *Graduation and Dropout Trends in Chicago.* Chicago: Consortium on Chicago School Research. <http://ccsr.uchicago.edu>

Catalyst Chicago (2007) <http://www.catalyst-chicago.org>

Department for Education and Skills (2003) *Every Child Matters.* London: The Stationery Office.

— (2004) *14–19 Curriculum and Qualifications Reform: Final report of the working group on 14–19 Reform.* London: The Stationery Office.

— (2007a) *School Admissions Code.* <http://www.dfes.gov.uk>

— (2007b) *National Curriculum Assessments: Attainment by pupil characteristics in England 2005–6.* London: The Stationery Office.

Estevez-Abe, M., Iverson, T. and Soskice, D. (2001) 'Social protection and the formation of skills: a reinterpretation of the welfare state'. In *Varieties of Capitalism: the Institutional Foundations of Comparative Advantage.* Oxford: Oxford University Press.

Government of New South Wales (2007) *List of Current Ministers.* <http://www.parliament.nsw.gov.au/Prod/Parlment/Members.nsf/V3ListCurrentMinisters>

Hall, P.A. and Soskice, D. (2001) *Varieties of Capitalism: The institutional foundations of comparative advantage.* Oxford: Oxford University Press.

Ingersoll, R.M. (2004) 'Why do urban, high-poverty schools in the U.S. have difficulty staffing their classrooms with qualified teachers?'. Paper presented at the Institute of Education conference on Twenty-first Century Urban Education, December 2004.

Jenkins, P. (2006) *Thatcher and Sons: A revolution in three acts.* London: Allen Lane.

Kirst, M. (2004) 'Urban school governance in the United States: The trend toward mayoral control'. Paper presented at the Institute of Education conference on Twenty-first Century Urban Education, December 2004.

Lemann, N. (1991) *The Promised Land: The great black migration and how it changed America.* New York: Alfred A. Knopf; London: Macmillan.

Lipman, P. (2002) 'Making the global city, making inequality: the political economy and cultural politics of Chicago school policy'. *American Educational Research* 39(2).

Ministerial Council on Education, Employment, Training and Youth Affairs (MCEETYA) (2002) *National Report on Schooling, 2002.* <http.www.mceetya.edu.au>

— (2006) *National Report on Schooling in Australia, 2005.*

New York Board of Regents (2006) *Report on the State of New York Schools.* <http://www.nysedregents.org>

New York City Board of Education (2007) *Children First – the next phase.* <http://schools.nyc.gov/Offices/ChildrenFirst>

Ontario Ministry of Education (2007) *Frequently Asked Questions.* <http://www.edu.gov.on.ca>

Parker, S., Doodhart, D. and Travers, T. (2007) 'Interview – Ken Livingstone'.

*Prospect* Magazine (April).

Payne, C. (2005) *Still Crazy after All these Years: Race in the Chicago school system.* Consortium on Chicago School Research. <http://ccsr.uchicago.edu>

Payzant, T. (2004) 'Governance in the era of new public management'. Paper presented at the Institute of Education conference on Twenty-first Century Urban Education, December 2004.

Programme for International Student Assessment (PISA) (2005) *School Factors Related to Quality and Equity: Results from PISA 2000.* Paris: Organisation for Economic Co-operation and Development (OECD). <http:www.pisa.oecd.org>

— (2006a) *Where Immigrant Students Succeed.* Paris: OECD.

— (2006b) *Equity in Education Thematic Review,* Finland Country Note, 2006. Paris: OECD.

Ravitch, D. (1985) *The Schools We Deserve: Reflections on the educational crises of our time.* New York: Basic Books.

— (1988) *The Great School Wars.* New York: Basic Books.

Thomson, P. (2002) *Schooling the Rust Belt Kids.* Stoke-on-Trent:Trentham Books.

Travers, T. (2004) *The Politics of London: Governing an ungovernable city.* Hampshire, UK and New York: Palgrave Macmillan.

Tymms, P. (2004) 'Are standards rising in English primary schools?'. *British Education Research*, 30 (4) 2004.

University of the State of New York (2006) *New York – The State of Learning: Statewide profile of the State of New York.* Albany, NY 12234.

US Department of Education (2002) *No Child Left Behind,* Public Law 107–110, 107th Congress. <http://www.ed.gov/policy/elsec/leg/esea02/index.html>

**Appendix A** The cities compared (compiled by the authors from various sources)

| | London | New York | Chicago | Toronto | Sydney |
|---|---|---|---|---|---|
| School population | 1,150,000 (a) | 1,108,000 (b) | 421, 000 (c) | 270,000 (d) | 391,000 (e) |
| Minority ethnic % students | 52% (a)<br>21% Carribean/ African<br>17% Asian<br>8% Mixed<br>6% other | 86% (b)<br>33% African American<br>39% Hispanic<br>13% other | 92% (c)<br>49% African American<br>38% Hispanic<br>5% other | 58% (d.1)<br>28% Asian<br>14% Black<br>16% other | [see note e.1] |
| % students who speak a language other than English at home | 37% (a) | 53% (b. 1) | 37% (c. 1) | 49% (d) | 44% (e.1) |
| % private school | 10% (a) | 17% (b. 2 ) | 16% (c.2.) | 5% [Ontario] (d.2) | 22% Catholic<br>12% Independent<br>*[New South Wales]* (e.2) |
| Poverty data | 24% free school meals (a)<br>39% child poverty (a. 1) | 76% free/reduced lunch (b)<br>28% census poverty index (b) | 86% 'low income' (c.3) | 34% 'living in poverty' (d. 3) | 17% (e.3) |
| Graduation rates | 49% (a. 2) | 57% (b.3) | 54% (c.4) | 75% (d.4) | 67% (e.4) |
| School tax base: | | | | | |
| % National/federal | 97% (a. 3) | 11% (b.4) | 19% (c) | 2% | Gov. Cath. Ind. (e.5) |
| % State/regional | – | 49% | 37% | 98% (d.5) | 60% 20% 12% |
| % Local | 3% | 40% | 44% | – | – – – |

## Notes

### London sources

a) Statistics of Education, Schools and Pupils in England, January 2006.
a.1.) London Child Poverty Commission, 2006. This figure takes housing as well as other costs into account.
a.2.) London Learning and Skills Council. Learning and Skills Plan 2007–8. This is the estimated figure for 2007 of young people who have gained a 'Level 3' qualification by age 19.
a.3.) All funding for the direct operation of schools is provided by the government from central taxation, by way of the Dedicated Schools Grant, which is passed through the local councils. In addition, local councils raise money for such things as school transport, inspection and administration from the council tax, which is itself supported by government to the tune of approximately 75%. I am grateful to Tony Travers of the London School of Economics for his explanation of this highly complex arrangement, and his estimate of the proportions.

### New York sources

b) New York State Education Department. Report to the Governor and Legislature on the status of the State's schools, 2006.
b.1) This is the US census figure for the New York City population over five years of age who speak a language other than English at home.
b. 2.) This figure is calculated by subtracting the number of students enrolled in the New York City public schools from the US Census Bureau estimate of total school enrolments in New York City.
b. 3) New York City Education Department. Press release, May 2007. (This figure is for those students reaching the level set by the State after four or five years of high school, i.e. by age 19.)
b. 4) New York City Department of Education. Financial Status Report, 2006.

### Chicago sources

c) Chicago Public Schools. Office of Research, Evaluation and Accountability, 2007.
c. 1) This is the US census figure for the Chicago population over five years of age who speak a language other than English at home.
c. 2.) This figure is calculated by subtracting the number of students enrolled in the Chicago public schools from the US Census Bureau estimate of total school enrolments in Chicago.
c. 3) 'Low Income' is defined in the Illinois School Report Card as
'students coming from families receiving public aid, living in institutions for neglected and delinquent children, being supported in foster homes with public homes, or eligible to receive free or reduced-price lunches'.
c. 4) Consortium on Chicago School Research. Report Highlights 'Graduation and

Dropout Trends in Chicago', January 2005. (This figure is for students graduating by age 19.)

**Toronto sources**

d) Toronto District School Board. *(Note: There are additionally 90,000 students in the fully state funded Toronto Catholic District School Board system.)*
d.1) M. Ornstein 'Ethno-Racial Inequality in the City of Toronto' 2000.
d.2) Ontario Ministry of Education.
d.3) Campaign 2000. Report Card on Child Poverty in the City of Toronto, 2003. This figure is based on the national Low Income Measure – 50% of the median family income adjusted for family size.
d.4) Toronto District School Board 'Our Children, Our Schools' 2007. (This is the figure for students gaining the Ontario Secondary School Diploma by age 19.)

**Sydney sources**

e) Government of New South Wales. *A New Direction for NSW: State Plan 2005. Statistical Compendium, Table 2.9. Profile of NSW Government School Students by Region and Equity Group.* The figures quoted are calculated by adding together the four regions of Northern Sydney, South Western Sydney, Sydney and Western Sydney. Together they account for 53% of the school population of NSW.
e.1) The New South Wales Government reports student data by 'equity group'. The significant ones for the purposes of this table are 'Priority Schools Funding Programme' (PSFP) – i.e. students counting towards this status which confers entitlement on schools for extra funding, and 'Language Background Other than English' (LBOTE). 'Aboriginal' is the only ethnic category reported, and this is only 2% in Sydney.
e.2) Ministerial Council on Education, Employment, Training and Youth Affairs (MCEETYA). *National Report on Schooling in Australia, 2005, Table 4.*
e. 3) See note to e.1) above. This is the 'PSFP' figure. Interestingly this poverty indicator is lower for Sydney than for New South Wales as a whole – but the range between areas within Sydney is very large: 0.5% in wealthy Northern Sydney, and 32% in South Western Sydney. The range in 'LBOTE' (see above) is not nearly as large.
e.4) MCEETYA. *National Report on Schooling in Australia, 2005. Table 34.* This is the figure for 'Year 12 completions' (Year 12 is the last year of high school). To make this figure comparable with that quoted by other cities those students who obtained an equivalent vocational qualification by age 19 would need to be added. This would probably increase it to around 75%. (Figures are only available for the 20–24 age group.)
e.5) The figure of 40% for the Commonwealth Government's support to the New South Wales Government's budget comes from the New South Wales Treasury's 2006–7 Budget Statement, Chapter 8. The other figures in this box are derived from *National Report of Schooling in Australia, 2005 (MCEETYA), Table 23.*

# 3 The London Challenge – a personal view

Tim Brighouse

It is not my purpose to rehearse issues covered elsewhere in this book. Lupton and Sullivan set the broader contextual points about London; Sofer has analysed the comparative governance arrangements in different large cities. The essays from Bubb and Earley, and Emery and Riley will describe how the London Challenge was launched and how, within its general context, the school leadership strand and the provision for teachers' development have developed.

The contribution of this essay is to flesh out some of the thinking which led to the London Challenge, to describe in particular some of the strands not covered in other essays and then speculate about the effectiveness of the London Challenge and its impact, and on the implications for policies for urban education.

As Lupton and Sullivan have pointed out, London has much in common with other large cities with international ambitions both in Europe and elsewhere. Whereas once it could claim to be pre-eminent and unique as the capital city of a great empire, it now sees a few other peer cities as its competitors for the leading position, whether it be in finance, or as the European travel hub for the aviation industry, or in entertainment, including the arts and sport, or in providing the location for the staging of great events. It hosts the national headquarters of almost all the major trades and professions, to be at the apex of recognition in any of which you probably have to live and work in London. Moreover and of special importance in an age of information technology and creativity when change is accelerating and education therefore is seen as so important to a developed nation's continued economic wellbeing, London is also the home to 90 per cent of the country's journalists and broadcasters.

All this is not to say that London does not have things in common with other very large UK cities such as Birmingham, but it is to recognise that the schooling system in London faces even more complex problems and challenges.

When New Labour came to power in 1997 with Blair's declared priority of 'Education, education and education' there were no plans for urban education in general or in London in particular.[1] Nor did they consider the issue of 'faith' schools in the context of the fact that it was an important issue for urban education.[2] Neither of these featured in the 17 priorities for education announced by Blair in the months leading up to the 1997 general election. One of these priorities was to focus on 'standards' not 'structures' and led them in practice to set up within the DfES a Standards and Effectiveness Unit (SEU) which became the powerhouse for galvanising an attempted transformation of standards of school collective and pupil individual attainment outcomes. School examination and test result league tables were retained and extended in scope. OFSTED, led by a controversial and tough chief inspector, not only tightened school inspections[3] but began local education authority (LEA) inspections, which were to lead to the naming of failing LEAs and the outsourcing of their education functions. Under the leadership of the SEU, the DfES assumed an unparalleled role of directly managing the educational reform programme. Moreover, there was an expansion of the use of specific grants (central government directly financed grants with explicit conditions) through 'standards funds'. It was through this mechanism that the government introduced training materials and advisory staff for what were called 'literacy' and 'numeracy' hours.

In short, the new government had more than enough to do affecting general policy both in education and elsewhere. They did not spend time concerning themselves with things they did not recognise as pressing priorities. Both urban education and the shape of London's educational system fell into that category. So far as the shape of the system was concerned, they did not recognise that there were sufficient shortcomings in the Balkanisation of strategic control through 32 London boroughs and the City of London to justify change. After all, since the heyday of the ILEA further and higher education responsibilities had been taken from local government and handed over to the funding councils for further and higher education respectively. Moreover there was much local political pride, doubtless evident to MPs, in many of the London boroughs in 'their' schools. So although the new government in 1997 introduced a strategic pan-London elected authority – the Greater London Authority (GLA) – and elected Mayor, powers of education were not within their remit.

By the beginning of 2001 and their election for a second term, however, New Labour had become increasingly interested in urban education in general and London's schools in particular. It had soon become apparent to them that most pupils were being educated in urban schools where standards of pupil outcomes were comparatively very poor. The Excellence in Cities (EiC) initiative therefore had been launched in 1999 and provided significant extra resources to partnerships of secondary schools in a few specified areas within six metropolitan areas. Some of the boroughs in Inner London were beneficiaries of this scheme, which focused on four strands: extra provision for gifted and talented pupils; learning mentors for pupils who were struggling with school and consequently in need of greater personal attention; 'exclusion' centres attached to groups of schools and based on a school site for pupils who were unable to handle their behaviour within school; and the building of city learning centres (CLCs) which would contain state-of-the-art information communication technology (ICT) facilities which were to be made available to pupils and adults throughout the school year, both within and beyond the school day. Through targeted standards funds, schools with high degrees of socio-economic disadvantage, within and beyond the EiC areas, also benefited from substantial grants to combat school exclusion and provide extra educational experiences for pupils on free school meals through what were called 'pupil credits'. So there was a recognition – backed by funds for combating educational disadvantage – which had only one UK historical parallel. In the 1960s a similar attempt had been launched in the old West Riding and other urban LEAs: the so-called Educational Priority Areas scheme.[4]

After the general election of 2001 and on the back of the EiC programme that she had launched as Minister for Schools, the incoming Secretary of State Estelle Morris, a Birmingham MP and a former teacher in an inner city school, needed little persuading therefore that inner city education was different and required extra and different approaches if school standards were to be transformed. She also knew that London secondary schools needed particular attention. While she was Schools Minister she had to deal with adverse OFSTED reports that led to the outsourcing of most of the educational functions of Southwark, Haringey, Waltham Forest and Islington, and the setting up of an independent learning trust for Hackney. Moreover, the chronic issue of staff shortages especially among teachers[5] had entered an acute stage. Finally, and most importantly, parental choice for children's secondary school, which had always been a vexatious issue in metropolitan areas, had become politically embarrassing in London, partly because school failure was now more public but also because in the capital there were many more church-aided and specialist schools, which exercised their right to have idiosyncratic and partly selective admission arrangements. Coupled with an excellent public transport system and over 400 schools across the city, these features created in London an annual fevered and often frustrated parental search for their preferred secondary school. The attention given to the issue was doubtless the greater because almost all MPs have residences in London as do many journalists and broadcasters. What are widely dubbed the 'chattering classes' were prone to regale each other over the dinner table with tales of school failure or success and their relief or concern that their offspring attend a 'good school'.

Whatever the precise combination of reasons – and Estelle Morris herself has said that the percentage of youngsters leaving the state system for private schooling at the age of 11 was also a decisive factor[6] – the announcement of an initiative for London secondary schools was made in the spring of 2002. I retired as Chief Education Officer of Birmingham that summer and successfully applied for the post of London Schools Commissioner later that year. The offer of the appointment came one day before the resignation of Estelle Morris as Secretary of State. Her replacement, Charles Clarke, wrote the foreword to the prospectus for the programme *The London Challenge; Transforming London Secondary Schools* and included the following passage, which sets out well the origins and intentions of the scheme:

> This great city needs and deserves a truly world-class education system, which serves every community and enables every person in the city to fulfil their own individual creative potential. That is what the proposals published in this document are intended to achieve.
>
> London already does have some world-class universities, some world-class colleges and some world-class schools. It has some world-class teachers and some world-class educational facilities. And the educational performance of London's schools has improved significantly in recent years. Fewer than 11% of children in inner London achieved 5 good O levels in 1987 – more than 40% achieve the equivalent now.
>
> But there are still far too many schools which are failing to inspire and lead their communities and far too many areas where educational aspirations are low. Too many parents are anguished and fearful, rather than proud or confident, when choosing their child's secondary school. And there are far too many who feel that either expensive private education or lengthy journeys across the city from home to school are the only satisfactory answer.
>
> This situation is unacceptable and it is the reason why we are determined to establish an education system which is truly world class everywhere in London. That system has to be founded more on creativity and diversity which is the city's strength, rather than uniformity. It has to provoke and challenge rather than accepting mediocrity. And it has everywhere to stimulate excellence and establish world standards. In short the exhilarating achievement which characterises some London schools must become the trademark of all London schools.

> Though the Government is allocating more resources to London, and we are prepared to allocate still more, I do not fundamentally believe that London's educational problems are problems of resources. It is much more about significant and radical reform that will mobilise the vision and leadership of the London educational community to achieve educational excellence. We need to make a visible and radical break with the past to transform aspiration and create a culture of achievement.
>
> To that end the proposals we set out today have three essential components:
>
> First we have to focus on the two areas of London where we consider the problems to be greatest. These are the north London group of three local authorities (Haringey, Hackney and Islington) and the south London group of two (Lambeth and Southwark). In these areas we need to establish an educational organisation and systematic drive for excellence which rewards success and does not tolerate failure. We have to develop a diverse system of academies and specialist schools which ensures that parents have a choice between excellent alternatives.
>
> Second we have to work exceptionally closely with schools which are failing to reach acceptable standards and to take whatever decisions are necessary to raise the quality of these schools, so that their local communities can have full confidence in what they can achieve.
>
> And third we must strengthen, across the whole of London, the standing of London's education. We must celebrate and enhance the quality of London's teachers and create better educational opportunities for students. We will create a new and better deal for students, teachers and headteachers – so that London becomes seen as a highly attractive part of the country in which to study and teach.
>
> (DfES 2003: p. 4)

The frequent use of the phrase 'world class' bears out the current preoccupation in the developed world with producing ever higher standards of educational outcomes in a quest to be economically competitive, and in the knowledge that unskilled jobs are disappearing and that those that remain are increasingly filled by immigrants.

Of course, work had already started on almost all the aspects mentioned in the launch document. Moreover, debate among politicians and civil servants revealed those issues that were seen as of overriding importance and others which were off limits. Among the latter, as I discovered when I raised it at a meeting with the Prime Minister, the Secretary of State and the Prime Minister's Delivery Unit (PMDU), was the question of school admissions. I saw the way these secondary admissions operated in London – with many quasi-selective schools setting their own entry criteria – producing a set of secondary schools that collectively resembled not so much a marketplace of individual competing shops that parents could choose to use, but more a hierarchy of private clubs ranging from the Carlton Club at one extreme and the East Cheam Working Men's club on the other. It seemed to me that in practice such an arrangement tempted heads to seek to make their schools attractive to ambitious middle-class parents, as a means of securing a reputation for success and conversely making the task of those schools at the wrong end of the league table more difficult. It also meant that those secondary aged children who arrived in London from poorer backgrounds, both elsewhere in the UK and abroad, were less likely to secure a school place of any sort. In one London borough at that time, the number of such children out of school was thought to be 500, which led some to speculate that there might be as many as 5,000 to 6,000, at a conservative estimate, across London. This issue, however, was not given priority. Nor was the tension between giving individual schools more power and the need to have some sort of plan for the strategic placement of the new schools that would be needed across London, as the overall population was estimated as likely to increase by over 700,000 in the decade that lay ahead. There was, too, the need to accommodate the creation of academies either by allowing them to be new schools or to replace those schools perceived to be failing and serving a socio-economically deprived area – in effect a variant on an earlier half-abandoned policy of Fresh Start. One other matter was raised at the meeting called to discuss the draft prospectus, namely the suggestion that more London secondary schools should have a sixth form. This was also something that could be questioned for a number of reasons. On that occasion I voiced one by explaining that we were already short of minority subject teachers (e.g. physics and maths) and that we should solve the immediate problem before exacerbating it.

Notwithstanding these points of concern, the London Challenge was duly launched in the way set out above. Its management rested with a small group of young, energetic, and talented civil servants with an exceptionally able leader, Jon Coles. The political leadership came from the Minister, Stephen Twigg, and I was expected to provide the professional lead. I considered that to do that effectively required me not to be seen by teachers and headteachers to be in the politicians' pockets – a stance that had served me and the politicians well in local government. I was theoretically not full time. So with agreement from civil servants and Stephen Twigg I therefore chose to remain based at the Institute of Education.

Although it was neither in the prospectus nor seen as one of the key indicators against which the PMDU would judge the success of the Challenge, we all agreed that the real question was one of a changed climate or culture. Put simply, we needed more outstanding teachers and headteachers in London if the pupil outcomes were to be improved. Of course there were many such committed professionals already in the capital's schools – indeed it was they who provided the glue which held the fragile system together – but we needed more of them. We therefore felt the need both to inspire those already in post who had the potential to improve, and to attract new staff to work in London. We were unlikely to achieve that unless schools and their staff felt supported. This changed message, predominantly of belief in and support for individual and collaborative expectations for and among schools, was at variance both with the negative reasons for the initiative and with the negatively inclined mantra of 'challenge'(or 'pressure with support'). It was also at variance with messages of 'zero-tolerance' of failure, which was the hallmark of the 1997 New Labour government's educational message and well understood and supported by the tabloid press. I believed strongly that a much more successful approach would be to express support for ever higher expectations, which would find a resonance with the best teachers, and to talk as if these were widespread and inevitable while simultaneously dealing with deficiencies, shortcomings, and failures expeditiously and, as far as possible, in private and where deserved, with dignity. After all, teachers and headteachers knew only too well that such an approach was a recipe for success within their schools. Certainly it had served me well and had proved successful in Birmingham, another large city where I had been Chief Education Officer.

It was my purpose therefore to emphasise the moral as well as the economic purpose of education both by referring to a passage of prose[7] that had inspired the 1944 Education Act and by referring to those moments when teachers succeed in unlocking the minds of even the most disadvantaged of youngsters in their charge and therefore contributing to cracking the cycle of disadvantage.

We all declared that the true measure of the success or otherwise of the London Challenge would be by making comparisons not merely with the rest of the country or with comparable cities and also whether we could be the first place to show that schools could crack the cycle of disadvantage.

We also knew that agencies beyond the school needed to share this endeavour, so much of the time of Stephen Twigg, Jon Coles and myself, in the early days of the London Challenge, was taken up in individual visits to schools and boroughs to listen, observe, and learn, and to convey a consistent message. We then compared notes afterwards and ensured that actions taken were consistent with the message and were tweaked to take account of individual needs according to context. Both Jon Coles and I attended bimonthly meetings of the Association of London Chief Education Officers without whose help we knew we would fail. We also spoke to the collective body for the 32 London boroughs – then called the Association of London Government – the Mayor and the GLA, as well as the recently created Connexions companies[8] and the new Learning and Skills Councils. Besides these there was also the need to keep the diocesan authorities and the teacher associations creatively involved. The complexity and incessant need for communication can thus be seen to have been challenging to the successful running of the programme.

The practicalities of the London Challenge involved the four themes – the London teacher, the London leader, the London school, and the London student – referred to earlier. In implementing each we were anxious to give priority to the five boroughs identified as containing the areas of most challenge.

Of the four themes, the first priority was clearly the 'London teacher', not least because without their successful daily efforts there was no chance of significant improvement. In this the London Challenge started with some disadvantages.

## The London teacher

It has already been noted that teacher supply and retention has always been a chronic and sometimes acute feature of London schools, particularly those facing the greatest challenges. Reliance on young teachers from overseas, especially Australia, New Zealand and South Africa, has been a continuing feature of London's schools, this despite the fact that there is a disproportionately large number of Initial Teacher Education (ITE) training places in London. By 2002, however, the problem was by any standards more acute than it had been for many years and certainly since the days of the ILEA, whose demise meant the problem was more intractable, for two reasons. First, there was the obvious point that each of the 32 boroughs had a separate – and often competing – programme for recruiting teachers. Second, and more subtly, retention of teachers suffered from the absence of a pan-London authority; many teachers and headteachers regretted the abolition of the ILEA whose major strength lay in its professional support for schools and teachers. It was this element, as I soon discovered on taking up the role of Commissioner, that was the source of most concern not merely for professionals in Inner London but in the outer boroughs too, whose leading teachers had also made use of the resources available to staff through the network of vibrant teachers centres maintained by the ILEA. It also attracted inspectors and advisers of the very highest quality, partly because to be part of the ILEA inspectorate was seen then to be at the very leading edge of one's chosen career. It has sometimes been said that the ILEA was an excellent place for a teacher to be, though not quite as good a place to be if you were a school pupil. Whatever the validity of the second part of that statement, it seemed crucial to its chances of success that this sense of shared endeavour and of belonging to a great enterprise with a commonly held moral purpose had to be revived for and among London staff, along with clear signs of better professional support. At every meeting of teachers and heads, therefore, it was essential to emphasise the purpose of the London Challenge in terms which would resonate with committed teachers and heads.

The supply of teachers was an urgent priority. Pragmatically and serendipitously, 2003 was the first year of a venture borrowed from the US called 'Teach First'. Aimed at the best graduates from the Russell group of universities, Teach First was a programme designed to attract those who intended a long-term career in business and commerce into first doing two years in the inner city as teachers committed to making a contribution to changing the world for the better. The scheme involved an intensive five-week induction course during the summer after graduation, to be followed with school placement and salary payment just below that which a newly qualified teacher would receive, but with a teaching commitment similar to a newly qualified graduate teacher. During their two years on the programme the Teach First participants received additional mentoring and support, after which they would in theory enter their chosen business career. In practice about 50 per cent of approximately 150 recruits annually have chosen to continue in teaching. Although the contribution of this scheme to the 35,000 secondary school teachers needed in London at any time is numerically small, its significance is disproportionately greater. It is not simply that the placement of these high-quality graduates was in secondary schools where recruitment was most difficult, it is also that in the longer term it seems as though we have set in train a supply of future school leaders. It can also be hoped that we have seeded in those who resume their original career intent in the business world, a concern for inner city schooling that may influence their future actions in support for or even a return to the schooling system.

Meanwhile the London Challenge sought to support the efforts of the many high-quality PGCE providers in London and to persuade those pursuing a PGCE elsewhere in the country, but interested in teaching in the inner city, to come to London. The cost of housing in the capital has always been a disincentive to young teachers continuing their careers after a few years in London, so part of the London Challenge was to make full use of the key workers' housing scheme whereby £50,000–£100,000 of interest-free loan support could be made available to those who satisfied certain criteria and wished to buy a house in London, where house prices are so expensive that they are beyond the financial reach of many in public sector employment

Other steps have been taken to attempt to recreate the professional networks that were such a strong feature of ILEA. Regional centres for maths and science have been created, and extra support marshalled for other subject areas. Most significant, however, in the attempt to feed the intellectual curiosity of hard-pressed inner city teachers has been the introduction of a Chartered London Teacher (CLT) scheme. Backed by the College for Teachers' royal charter, CLT provides certified recognition of the extra professional development undertaken by successful teachers in the multi-faith, multi-lingual, multi-racial capital city. Put simply, the case for the CLT rests on the assumption that to be successful, an inner city teacher needs more and some new knowledge and skill than is necessary for his/her counterpart in mono-cultural and more affluent areas. The successful completion of the CLT qualification requires teachers to accumulate and demonstrate learning under the broad headings of pedagogy, subject knowledge, whole school issues, race and community (i.e. cultural understandings that aid pupil learning), and barriers that exist and have to be overcome with teachers' help to ensure some pupils can learn. Bubb and Earley describe elsewhere the detail of the scheme and how success is validated. For a teacher, the hope is that in addition to the £1,000 token for successful completion there would be a greater likelihood of their taking their continuing professional development seriously. So, too, was there an expectation that the schools themselves would give more attention to professional development as a whole school issue, essential to school improvement, and that their staff would subsequently take advantage of the rich array of postgraduate courses and opportunities available in the many higher education institutions in London. By April 2006 over 38,000 teachers had enrolled on the CLT course.

Finally, extra resource was provided to the Institute of Education, as the main professional provider of teacher education, to create a centre for leadership in teaching and learning.

Of course, there are other things that could, and should, be done if the improvement that these measures have produced in staffing for London is to be maintained. Salaries in the capital need to be constantly reviewed in order to avoid a chronic issue from becoming acute from time to time. But there are also other steps to be considered such as concessionary public transport and subsidised access to cultural venues and events in London for school staff.

In short, teachers and teaching have been the London Challenge's top priority and have received the most extra expenditure; it is arguably so far its most successful element.

## The London school leader

In the UK the influence of headteachers has always been seen as an essential element of school success. The 1988 reforms, at least at secondary level, made their importance seem even greater, as substantial power over budgets and appointments was transferred from the LEA to the school. Unsurprisingly, therefore, the London Challenge focused on school leadership, especially among those schools that had found success hard to come by and then sustain over any reasonable period. Through the already established London Leadership Centre at the Institute of Education, the National College for School Leadership[9] commissioned extra targeted programmes for leadership with the additional resource provided by the London Challenge. Directed by a serving headteacher seconded for the purpose, the programmes contained four main elements.

First, the 'Leadership from the Middle' courses would, it was hoped, address the weakness in departmental and head of year posts in schools that OFSTED identified as a particular London problem. Second, bespoke residential courses were made available to the leadership teams of challenged schools in the hope that they would strengthen their collective determination and capacity to improve. The third element was a general offer to broker two or three school visits for any newly appointed middle or senior school leader, ideally between the date of their appointment and their first day in post. This initiative was based on the theory that too often leaders were conditioned by the necessarily narrow experience of their few previous posts and that, therefore, there would be merit in widening its range.

The fourth element, however, was to prove most effective, namely the training and subsequent focused deployment of 'consultant heads'. Within a year or two, a particular variant and extension of this scheme enabled 'Keys to Success' schools (see below) to obtain prolonged support from what, in effect, were 'Teaching Schools'. It is an initiative which led the government, through the National College for School Leadership, to adopt it as an essential ingredient of secondary schools 'in special measures'.[10]

## The London school

The London school element of the London Challenge prioritised attention for those schools at the bottom of exam league tables. They often had a long history of social challenge and difficulty that manifested itself in acute staffing shortage and effectiveness problems, and consequently in chronic low morale. Whether in special measure or not, these were schools often dubbed by the media and politicians as 'failing' and not places to which responsible parents would send their children. The odds were stacked against such schools, not least because the admission practices of other schools were often *de facto* selective in some way or other. This meant that not only were such schools seen as 'schools of last resort' but also they were the recipients of pupils excluded or counselled out of other more successful schools. They were also schools described as having 'high mobility': that is to say they had places, which the more popular schools did not, for children who, for whatever reason (e.g. children of refugees or usually poorer parents who were moving from one area of social housing to another) move school in mid phase. Their pupil population was therefore unusually transient.

Since we had set ourselves the moral task of demonstrating that it was possible in London to crack the cycle of disadvantage, we reasoned that it was demonstrably counter-productive to blame the victim – in this case the schools which had the biggest task in breaking the link between poverty and educational performance. If they could do it, we argued, any school should be able to do the same. The back of our self-imposed task would be broken. We therefore dubbed the schools Keys to Success and set about the complex task of helping them. Of course, each Keys to Success school faced subtly different circumstances and we were determined not to fall into the trap of prescribing one solution for all. First, we recruited eight part-time school improvement advisers whose task would be to broker extra appropriate support for the half dozen or so Keys to Success schools for which they were responsible. They were to do this after appropriate consultation with the LEA and in the light of the particular diagnosis of the school's problems. The quality, competence, and credibility of these advisers proved to be crucial. In every case they were attempting to help a change in the culture of the school from a resigned acceptance that 'things would always be like this' and anyway 'what more can you expect from kids from backgrounds like this?' to one where there was a sufficient determination to believe that an ever-strengthening 'achievement culture' was not just possible but was going to happen. Of course, to this approach was added the powerful ingredient of variable amounts of extra resource involving, as appropriate, short-term extra leadership staff, regular help from Advanced Skills Teachers,[11] extra tutorial support for year 10 or 11 pupils, new ICT equipment designed to expedite that school's capacity to make the best of the new learning technologies, consultant heads, short-term support and expert advice to solve a long-standing blockage in school organisational practice, and sometimes the removal of parts of the leadership team.

This small group of advisers has needed great diplomatic skills to deal with the various parties with a legitimate interest in the schools (e.g. LEA, diocesan authority, teacher union) in addition to a capacity to diagnose and then help the schools in question to grow their capacity and energy. The best of these advisers – and they have all been of high quality – have demonstrated the value of the role of 'critical friend' to a school and may have influenced the launch in 2005 of a national strategy designed to provide every school with a 'school improvement partner' whose role it will be to enable all schools to sustain an upward trend in pupil attainment results.

Their work was supplemented by occasional conferences for teams from the schools involved and by publications designed to illustrate what we called 'high leverage–low effort' interventions in school improvement[12] and that might have application nor merely in Keys to Success schools but more widely.

During the first five years of the London Challenge more than 70 schools have been involved in some way in the Keys to Success programme in what we have dubbed either a 'light touch', 'maintained' or 'intensive' way. Some schools have left the programme as 'alumni'.

The encouragement of schools to learn from each other, both through the Keys to Success programme and more generally, has been helped by the publication of *Families of Schools*. Its importance is hard to overestimate. Put simply, this document contains performance data, subject by subject and overall, of all secondary schools in London. Each school is allocated to a particular 'family' according to the prior attainment at entry and the socio- economic circumstances of their pupils. The school can see that the other schools in their 'family' have broadly similar starting points. What the school can then see is how it performs relative to others, both in terms of 'rate of improvement' (i.e. the momentum for each age cohort of pupils to achieve higher scores than its predecessor) and in absolute 'points per pupil'. Since, as has been pointed out above, separate subject performance is comprehensively set out, every school can learn from another in some aspect of performance, especially if it is combined with Fischer Family Trust analysis.[13]

The 'Family of Schools' approach, introduced in the second year of the London Challenge, has since been extended to primary schools.

Under the heading of the 'London school' one more point deserves notice, namely the issue of school place planning and the extent to which this would involve academies. The original prospectus was clear: there should be 60 academies, either as replacements for existing schools or as new schools. Some London boroughs embraced the concept of academies. For example, Hackney's Learning Trust was unequivocal in seeing the academy route as being a relatively quick and effective way of transforming the perception and the reality of secondary school failure. Others were less enthusiastic.

The understanding anyway was that if a school was not responding to the Keys to Success intervention, or at the inception of the London Challenge was failing irredeemably, academy status would follow. In effect such a path was a variant, albeit with brand-new buildings, new governance, and some new staff, of the Fresh Start approach which the first Blair government had attempted and then abandoned.

Two final points need to be made regarding the planning of school places. The expected increase in population of more than 700,000 by 2015 demanded that some calculation should be made of the need for new schools. To do this a pan-London exercise was commissioned and carried out. It revealed an enormous cross-borough boundary movement of pupils, a result of the London County Council and ILEA legacy, which paid more attention to the historical pattern of parents choosing to use public transport to find a school for their children than the need to encourage local neighbourhood provision. To avoid the real danger that the separate decisions of individual boroughs about the need for new schools might collectively not make sense – indeed, could result in the closure of other schools further away from the providing borough – it was recommended that an annual pan-London review be undertaken and that the placement of academies should be planned within that context. Finally, there is no escaping the fact that in London, as with all densely populated large cities, secondary schools are necessarily going to be on constricted sites. It has to be said that some decision-making by individual boroughs during the first five years of the London Challenge seems to have made that chronic problem worse.

## The London student

The fourth and final discrete element of the London Challenge was the student for whose benefit it was launched in the first place.

A 'Student Pledge' was launched, which outlined a minimum set of experiences which it was hoped every secondary aged pupil should enjoy in or out of school. The thinking behind this initiative was that London, as a long-established capital city, is home to disproportionate 'common wealth' in the form of buildings; these include buildings of historic interest, theatres, art galleries, museums, concert halls, sports facilities and stadiums, which are the home to great events and spectacles. London is also the place where those at the top of their profession, craft or business need to spend at least some of their working life. There are also over 40 institutions of higher education. In short, the enrichment opportunities for young people are enormous. But so too is the poverty that blights the lives of some of them. The Student Pledge represented a symbolic way of describing our collective determination to make sure that all youngsters should enjoy what the 'good enough' middle-class parent could and would ensure that their teenager would experience. Efforts were made to open the doors of providers, to fund some provision and to encourage schools to sign up to the Pledge.

Additionally, extra resource was provided to the London Gifted and Talented programme which had been set up under EiC.

The implementation of the four strands – teacher, leader, school and student – had a particular focus on five London boroughs which at the outset of the Challenge were perceived to be facing some of the most challenging social problems with thus far too little sign of success. These were Haringey, Hackney, Islington, Southwark and Lambeth.

## The outcomes of the London Challenge: an attempted evaluation

At one level – in headline terms – it is easy to set out the outcomes of the intervention. Tables 3.1 and 3.2 at the end of this essay reveal some statistics showing the extra staff and their stability, pupil exam outcomes at age 16 and other key indicators. Indeed, it is worth emphasising that for the number of high- or low-performing schools, the improvement in London has been significant compared with other places. Moreover, the average performance at 16 is now higher than the national average. So far as we know, this is not the case in any other large city (except Birmingham) either in the UK or across the developed world. Statistical analysis also shows that compared with elsewhere, London secondary schools perform better for every decile of students when they are classified in socio-economic terms.

At another level, OFSTED has carried out an inspection and its findings are similarly positive, particularly about the strategy, leadership and management of the London Challenge and notes that 'schools have improved dramatically'.[14]

Both the perceived successes and the apparent limitations of the London Challenge are reflected in the announcements (May and June 2007) that the Challenge is to be continued on a scaled-down basis for another three years and in the extension of a similar programme to two other metropolitan areas, namely the Black Country boroughs of Dudley, Walsall, Sandwell and Wolverhampton, and the ten boroughs of Greater Manchester. The two new challenges are to have a primary element from the start – one for London was only introduced in 2006.

Other key non-negotiable ingredients are the use of a 'Family of Schools' data set to encourage inter-school learning, the leadership programmes involving the National College for School Leadership, differentiated and expert support for Keys to Success schools and the identification and improved performance of underachieving groups of pupils.

Both the London extension and the new city challenges will also focus on those schools with low proportions of youngsters achieving five or more higher grades (GCSE or equivalent), including maths and English.

Apart from the successes identified here and by OFSTED, it is reasonable to claim that the London experience has increased our understanding and knowledge of improving schools in challenging circumstances and how to disseminate what appears to be successful practice.

Of course, as the London Challenge enters its extension phase, secondary schools are facing new priorities such as the 'Every Child Matters' agenda, the determination to make every school an extended school and the government's wish to promote 'personalisation'. All of these changes, as well as those affecting local authorities (where Directors of Children's Services have replaced Directors of Education and the term 'local education authority' is no longer used in statute nor in practice) reflect an increased emphasis on the duty of care discharged by the school. School improvement services are provided by School Improvement Partners (SIPs) answering to the DfES-run National Strategies rather than to the local authority, even though they will continue to be held accountable for the performance of their schools. There are also local 'progress pilots'[15] and a major reformulation of the national curriculum at Key Stage 3 (KS3). For London schools, too, there is the chance to take full advantage of the upcoming 2012 Olympics with its celebration of competitors who will all be keenly aware of their PBs ('personal bests'), so close in concept to the best form of teaching and learning with its emphasis on formative and ipsative assessment. Small wonder that some sort of strategic overview and capacity for London was thought necessary, when the track record of the 32 London boroughs continues to prove so variable.

Perhaps the other major change facing secondary schools, the 14–19 agenda (see Essay 10 by Grainger *et al.*) highlights one of the weaknesses not addressed by the London Challenge, namely the tensions in a marketplace of schooling that promotes choice and diversity by establishing a set of largely autonomous and competing schools. The implementation of the new diplomas cannot be successful unless schools and colleges form themselves into 'collegiates'; and this will not happen successfully unless there are financial and accountability incentives for groups of schools to co-operate.

So the questions and doubts remain. Will the academies, with their new-found independence, choose to operate outside local partnerships, for example for 14–19? Will the presence of an academy lead to the decline and eventual closure of a successful local school or the decline in the viability of a more distant school as the traditional pattern of travel for school preference changes? In short, will the lack of co-ordinated school place planning lead to the right schools being in the right place for the expanded population? Will the inflationary pressures on London's house prices lead to another crisis in the supply and retention of school staff, especially teachers? How well will London cope with the impending 'succession for headship' problem?

These and other issues mean that the extension of the London Challenge is essential to make good the lack of any overarching strategic education body for London. But these doubts and unsolved issues, which perhaps will always be a feature of cosmopolitan school provision, should not obscure the very real achievements of London secondary schools in recent years.

**Table 3.1** London results, Key Stage 4 (London Challenge figures)

| | **1997** | **2006** | **Change 1997–2006** |
|---|---|---|---|
| 5 good GCSEs | London 40.4%<br>England 42.5% | London 58.3%<br>England 57.5% | London 18%<br>England 15% |
| 5 good GCSEs inc English and maths | London 31.1%<br>England 35.6% | London 45.8%<br>England 45.3% | London 14.7%<br>England 9.7% |
| No. of schools below 25% at GCSE | 95 | 0 | |
| No. of schools achieving over 70% 5 good GCSEs | 36 | 126 (almost 1 in 3) | +90 |
| No. of teachers | 56,800 | 63,500 | 6,700 |
| No. of support staff | 18,980 | 42,140 | 23,160 |

**Comments**

- London secondary schools are improving faster than nationally: London is ahead of the national average at five A*–C at GCSE for the third year running, and ahead of the national average including English and maths.
- Inner London results have improved by 22 per cent since 1997.
- Almost one in three London schools achieved outstanding GCSE results in 2006.
- No London borough is now below 41 per cent five A*–C at GCSE. In 1997 two-thirds of London boroughs (19) were achieving below this level.
- London is narrowing attainment gaps faster than the national average (including African, Black Caribbean and FSM pupils).

- 16,300 more pupils getting five good GCSEs (A*–C) compared to 1997.
- 14,100 more pupils getting five good GCSEs including English and maths compared to 1997.

**Notes**

1. Meeting with Estelle Morris and David Blunkett in Education Office, Margaret Street, Birmingham: November 1996.

2. Meeting with same at same venue in March 1997.

3. Under the Conservatives in 1993 the decision had been taken to publish OFSTED reports. On election the Blair government decided to 'name and shame' secondary schools which were still in 'special measures' (i.e. failing). This was to herald a much tougher emphasis on what was dubbed 'zero tolerance' of failure.

4. Educational Priority Areas (EPAs) were launched in the wake of the 1967 Howden Report on Primary Education. See Smith, G. 'Whatever happened to Educational Priority Areas?'. *Oxford Review of Education* 13 (1).

5. Inner London has always suffered disproportionately from the supply of teachers. In the early 1970s the problem was so acute that it was often the case that a primary school would start the school year with one set of staff and complete it with another. By 2001 a similar crisis in supply was occurring.

6. Conversation with Estelle Morris in December 2003 when she confided that one of the clinching arguments for launching the London Challenge was confusion between 13 and 30 as percentages of parents who sent their children to private schools. It is worth noting that such figures as existed were based on the number of private school places in a given area, not on the number of residents in that area who sent their children to these schools. So for example Exeter and Oxford also have very high figures – higher than London – but that reflects only the number of private school places in those cities.

7. According to R.A. Butler's autobiography he was influenced heavily by the writings of Archbishop William Temple and in particular one passage of his speeches and writings that described the purpose of education as 'raising people from what they are to what they might become' and resting that purpose on the need for social justice and political freedom. The passage concludes, 'There exists a form of mental slavery which is as real as any economic form. We are pledged to destroy it. If you want a just society you must have educated people.'

8. One of the first acts of the Blair government was to remove 'Careers services' from local authority control and reconfigure them as independent 'not for profit' companies. In London there were five. It was to prove to be a short-lived venture, as by 2006 the decision had been taken to return the companies to local authority control.

9. The National College for School Leadership was another ingredient in the Blair government's efforts to give priority to transforming educational standards in schools. It took over new qualification standards and courses for new and existing headteachers and supplemented these with other courses and programmes intended to raise the quality of leadership throughout schools.

10. In 2006 the National College introduced a scheme of 'national leaders in education' (NLEs) who were to be headteachers with a track record of contributing to the success of the wider educational system as well as running their own school successfully. The model of what was called 'mooring a successful school alongside a school in special measures' was based on work pioneered within the London Challenge by Ravens Wood School in Bromley and its headteacher George Berwick who eventually became the leader for the leadership strand of the London Challenge while still running his school.

11. The 'Advanced Skill Teacher' (AST) was another innovation of the Blair government's education transformation programme. The intention of the AST, which was introduced soon after the election, was to keep exceptional teachers in the classroom by increasing their salaries and securing their release on one day each week to teach alongside teachers in other schools.

12. These interventions are called 'Butterflies' after the chaos theory. DfES published a book of 'Butterflies' of small but effective interventions in London schools and followed it up with a set of ICT 'Butterflies'.

13. The Fischer Family Trust is a charitable foundation established by Mike Fischer, one of the founders of Research Machines plc. It has pioneered analysis of pupil progress and performance in schools in a way that has allowed schools to focus in a much more precise way on subject teaching of groups of youngsters who appear not to be fulfilling their potential.

14. OFSTED December 2006 'Well Done London' 04327–2006 POS-EN.

15. 'Progress pilots', launched by the DfES in 2007, build on the work of the Fischer Family Trust. Put simply, schools are invited to improve to the norm the progress of pupils who between Key Stage 2 (KS2) and Key Stage 3 (KS3) are either static in their achievement or actually losing ground.

# 4 Comprehensive schooling and social inequality in London: past, present and possible future

Sandra Leaton Gray and Geoff Whitty

London has undergone a dramatic transformation in the last 20 years, both in relation to population growth and increasing disparity of wealth. Moreover, as a large international city with a complex educational history, the capital is sometimes seen as presenting a unique problem for policy makers in terms of contemporary social, political, and educational change. However, some of the ongoing problems surrounding education in London could also be attributed to tensions that exist between conflicting aims within any educational transformational process and in any geographical area. For example, the purpose of education has been seen variously over the years as: transmitting knowledge; providing opportunities for growth; removing 'hampering influences' or 'broadening horizons'; developing the capacities of the individual; giving culture to the individual; or training future citizens (Russell 1932: 29; Miliband 2006: 16).

Urban education provides a territory where these aims are contested more hotly than in other educational arenas. As London is a particularly large urban conurbation, with a particularly diverse population, the effect is exaggerated. Indeed, Grace described the city as 'providing the most dramatic context in which conflicts become visible' (1984: 34). Another issue is that Parliament itself is based in London and policy makers and media commentators observe (and sometimes experience)

London education at first hand. This seems to influence the debate significantly, resulting in a situation where education policy in England is in many senses London-centric, and therefore essentially urban in nature. Furthermore, London has often been a testing ground for new initiatives, as indeed it is at the present time. A key question now is whether we are in fact gradually moving towards a post-competition era in maintained secondary education. First, we need to provide some historical context.

## A brief history of secondary schooling in London

The 1944 Education Act was the first to use the term 'secondary education' and it did not include references to different types of school for older children. There was a significant reorganisation of education at this time, and it was brought more fully under state control, with secondary education becoming free rather than fee-paying. These changes reflected the national mood from the inter-war period, demonstrating a desire to move away from elementary provision until the age of 14, towards the provision of secondary education for all pupils aged between 11 and 14, allowing for greater equality of opportunity and social mobility (Fogelman 2006).

The actual reorganisation that followed the 1944 Act drew on thinking in the Spens Report (Consultative Committee of the Board of Education 1938) and the Norwood report (Committee on Curricula and Examinations 1943) to establish a tripartite system of secondary education. On the basis of testing at 11 plus, children were selected to attend a grammar school, a technical school (in a few places), or a secondary modern school. This supposedly meritocratic system reflected Labour party policy at the time, endorsed by Prime Minister Attlee, although some Labour party members already preferred alternative systems.

In this respect, Middlesex paved the way by creating some multilateral secondary schools with grammar and secondary modern streams within the same school. The use of the term 'comprehensive' to describe schools dated from Circular 144/47, although many advocates would have preferred the term 'common' or 'single' school (Morris 2004). By the 1960s, there was a reduction in resistance to the growth of comprehensive education in Britain, which meant that numbers increased, particularly after the issue of Circular 10/65 by Harold Wilson's first Labour government. This asked all English local authorities to submit plans for the reorganisation of secondary education in their areas, although there was no legislative requirement to implement changes. Table 4.1 below indicates the numbers of different types of schools in the Greater London area between 1965 and 1985.

**Table 4.1** Number of different types of school in Greater London area, 1965 to 1985

| Year | Comprehensive | Grammar | Secondary Modern | Technical and other | All maintained secondary schools | Direct grant | Independent |
|---|---|---|---|---|---|---|---|
| 1965 | 77 | 141 | 202 | 57 | 477 | 11 | 331 |
| 1970 | 197 | 155 | 244 | 79 | 675 | 22 | 414 |
| 1975 | 387 | 89 | 74 | 39 | 589 | 21 | 350 |
| 1980 | 483 | 19 | 30 | 28 | 560 | 19 | 350 |
| 1985 | 436 | 15 | 22 | 18 | 505 | Reclassified as independent schools | Data unavailable |

*(Sources: Department of Education and Science (1965)* Statistics of Education Part One *(London, HMSO); Department of Education and Science (1970)* Statistics of Education Vol One – Schools *(London, HMSO); Department of Education and Science (1975)* Statistics of Education Vol One – Schools *(London, HMSO); Department of Education and Science (1980)* Statistics of Schools *(Photocopy supplied by DES); Department of Education and Science (1985)* Statistics of Education – Schools *(London, HMSO))*

In 1965, as a result of local government reorganisation, the London and Middlesex County Councils were brought together with parts of Surrey, Essex, and Kent to form the Greater London Council. The 20

Outer London boroughs became local education authorities in their own right, and the Inner London Education Authority (ILEA) was created from the remaining boroughs, covering the same area as the original London County Council.

Within days of the Conservatives taking power nationally in 1970, Margaret Thatcher, as Edward Heath's Education Minister, repealed Circular 10/65. Ironically, though, more grammar schools were probably abolished during Thatcher's term of office than under any other education minister. By 1974, when there was a return to a Labour government, 62 per cent of children nationally attended comprehensive schools. During this period, there was continuing active resistance to comprehensivisation from some state grammar schools, including St Marylebone Grammar School in ILEA, which fought hard to maintain its grammar school status but was eventually closed in 1981. Another national policy under Labour at this time ensured that selective secondary education was increasingly confined to the private sector. When faced by the government with the choice in 1976, most direct grant day schools chose to become completely independent rather than joining the local maintained system and taking a comprehensive intake, effectively increasing the proportion of children educated by the private sector[1] at secondary level.

After the Conservative party returned to power in 1979 with Margaret Thatcher as Prime Minister, their first change to education was the introduction of the Assisted Places Scheme in 1980. This allowed academically able children to opt out of the state system and attend independent schools, paying means-tested fees in order to do so. This enabled many London day schools to take more free and partial fee-paying pupils even if not on the scale they had done when they were direct grant schools. However, the scheme was dominated by middle-class parents of limited financial means, shown by the fact that many of the mothers of children accessing places had been educated privately or in selective schools themselves. It was difficult for gifted children from working-class families to access this type of education, as there was little if any support during the application process (Edwards *et al.* 1989).

In 1986, the Conservative government introduced city technology colleges with business sponsors, the forerunners of today's academies. Then, as part of the 1988 Education Reform Act, we saw the creation of grant maintained schools – schools that opted out of local authority control to be self-managing and funded directly by the government. The specialist schools initiative started in 1994 with technology colleges. The opportunity to apply for specialist status was initially restricted to voluntary aided and grant maintained schools, which by definition gave them more autonomy than other maintained schools, including acting as their own admissions authorities. They were also allowed to select a proportion of their pupils by aptitude, although few of them actually chose to do so.

In Inner London, the fragmentation of provision, governance, and admissions was exacerbated by the abolition of the ILEA in 1990. Beforehand, children in the ILEA area had been allocated to three broad ability bands with a view to achieving balanced intakes. Although there were some criticisms of the effectiveness of the policy, particularly as it was applied in voluntary aided schools, it was generally felt to be a useful way of mitigating a tendency towards academic and social polarisation. However, most of the Inner London boroughs abandoned this approach and, in the context of the 1988 Education Reform Act, adopted choice policies that seemed to enable affluent parents to 'colonise' the best state schools either through the effects of the property market or their utilisation of cultural capital. Market forces were further encouraged by the Greenwich Judgement of 1989, which established that maintained schools could not give priority to children simply because they lived within the LEA's administrative boundaries.

From an organisational and logistical point of view, the jostling of parents in their attempt to secure places in popular schools has caused substantial problems for many London local authorities in placing children. The combination of a degree of selection with new types of secondary school has also made self-selection on the part of some of the more affluent parents easier than in the past. Although the election of New Labour to government in 1997 might have been expected to introduce a greater degree of equity into the system, Tony Blair's own enthusiastic espousal of market forces made this difficult to achieve. The remainder of this essay looks at the legacy for London schools of the Blair government and the possibilities for the future.

## Choice and diversity

Policy makers continually claim that there has never been more choice in secondary schooling for parents, and that diversity leads to school improvement and consequently greater social equality. However, the evidence for this is contentious at best. Here we explore New Labour's record on choice and diversity and give specific consideration to the role of specialist schools and academies.

### *The rhetoric and reality of school choice*

Bruce Liddington, appointed as New Labour's Schools Commissioner during the passage of the 2006 Education and Inspection Act, has suggested that the English secondary school system is developing as a 'Spectrum of Diversity' – a range of schools of different types from which parents will be able to choose freely according to their children's needs (Specialist Schools and Academies Trust 2007). The current categories of state schools from which London parents can choose include community schools, voluntary controlled schools, voluntary aided schools, foundation schools, trust schools, academies, and city technology colleges. Most but not quite all secondary schools are now also specialist schools. The problem with the Commissioner's vision is that, of course, not all schools – and not even all types of school – are equally desirable in the eyes of parents and not all parents are equally well placed to gain places for their children in the most desirable ones.

One of the major problems with school choice policies is that advantaged schools and advantaged parents are able to seek each other out (Whitty *et al.* 1998). This seems to be exacerbated by the fact that some but not all schools are their own admissions authorities.[2] For example, Tough and Brooks (2007) found that faith/voluntary aided schools that are their own admissions authorities are ten times more likely to be highly unrepresentative of their surrounding area than schools where the local authority is the admissions authority. The figure for non-religious schools that are their own admissions authorities is six times more unrepresentative. This suggests that some schools may have an unfair advantage in the recruitment of pupils. While this concern was evident in the controversy surrounding the recruitment practices of voluntary aided schools within ILEA in the 1980s (Williams and Murphy 1979), since the introduction of open enrolment after 1988 it has been generalised to a wider group of schools. This was an area of significant concern for the Education and Skills Select Committee in its review of the Blair government's 2005 schools White Paper, and its report to government prompted some significant concessions on admissions policy, specifically by strengthening the standing of the admissions code and insisting that all schools have to act in accordance with it rather than merely to have regard to it (Education and Skills Committee 2006; DfES 2005a; DfES 2007a).

Prior to the introduction of the new school admissions code, schools were often accused of using questionable admissions practices, either overt or covert, to skew their intakes. Some specialist schools are permitted to select up to ten per cent of their intake according to pupils' aptitude for the subject, although few carry this out. Aptitude is not strictly defined, even in the new Admissions Code, but it is regarded as having the ability to benefit from teaching in a particular subject or demonstrating the capacity to succeed in that subject (DfES 2007a). This definition is clearly open to considerable interpretation and may have led to what Dunford (2006) has described as 'semi-selectivity'. This entails attracting pupils who are more likely to perform at higher levels, for intellectual or social reasons, such as being 'pro-school' children generally supportive of the ethos of the school. Techniques used included drawing the admissions boundaries in a particular way so as to exclude large areas of public housing, or taking account of pupils' primary school reports when deciding whether to admit them. A few schools omitted specific references to admissions criteria involving medical or social needs, such as looked after children, or pupils with statements of special educational needs (SEN), even though these categories are legally required to be the first two criteria for selection in oversubscribed schools (West and Hind 2003). Again, this is likely to have adversely affected disadvantaged families in particular and it is to be hoped that such abuses will be significantly reduced by the impact of the Education and Inspection Act and the new Admissions Code.

For London parents in particular, the claim that they have real choice is also undermined by the fact that 32 per cent of 11-year-old children are rejected from their first choice of secondary school – compared with 15 per cent in the rest of the country (Centre for Educational Research 2005). There is also a difference between the likelihood of success on appeal in London as opposed to England as a whole. London parents are more likely to appeal secondary school places, and if they do appeal, they are significantly less likely to win than in the rest of England, as can be seen in Table 4.2, confirming the arguments made by Pennell *et al.* (2006) and the Greater London Authority (GLA) (2005).

**Table 4.2** Comparison of secondary school admissions appeals in London and England

| | **London – appeals as a % of total admissions** | **England – appeals as a % of total admissions** | **London – % likelihood of success of appeals** | **England – % likelihood of success of appeals** |
|---|---|---|---|---|
| 2002–2003 | Data not available | 9.9% | 16% | 34% |
| 2003–2004 | 10% | 6.7% | 15.5% | 35.2% |
| 2004–2005 | 13% | 9.3% | 16.9% | 35.7% |

*(Source: DfES Admission Appeals for Maintained Primary and Secondary Schools in England, 2002–3 to 2004–5)*

Unfortunately, the recent admissions reforms have not yet been mirrored by reform of the appeals system, which may limit their effectiveness.

### *Diversity and school hierarchies*

Sir Peter Newsam, former Education Officer of ILEA, once categorised English secondary schools into a hierarchy of school types, ranging from super-selective independent or state grammar schools through genuinely and partially comprehensive schools to what he called 'sub-secondary modern' schools (cited in Chitty 2002). This classification has recently been updated in Braswell's model in which a small number of independent schools are at the top of a pyramid, with fully selective grammar schools immediately underneath, followed by a larger number of partially selective schools (voluntary, specialist, single sex, foundation) and finally the largest group, consisting of all ability schools, such as community comprehensives and secondary modern schools, at the bottom of the pyramid (Braswell 2005).

In London, we can look at this hierarchy in relation to the recent London Challenge publication *Families of Schools* (DfES 2005b), which groups institutions into 27 'Families of Schools' according to various indicators, including prior levels of pupil attainment at Key Stage 2 (KS2), and the proportion of pupils entitled to free school meals (FSM). If one reviews the graph 'Families of Schools, Percentage of Pupils eligible to receive a Free School Meal in 2003 against Average Prior Attainment 2001–2003' (DfES 2005b: 9), one can contrast the performance of schools at the top and bottom ends of the graph but also see the relative social homogeneity of schools that might be perceived to be at the top and bottom ends of current classification systems.

The top two families of schools in performance terms are also clearly the groups with the lowest eligibility for FSM. They have Key Stage 3 (KS3) scores of approximately 29 or above, but have FSM take-up rates of two to ten per cent. The bottom two families on the other hand have KS3 scores of 24 or lower, and have FSM eligibility rates of 35 to 75 per cent, which is a much wider spread, and suggests significantly less social homogeneity than the top group. Social homogeneity is certainly not the only criterion for classifying schools and parental choice patterns. However, there is a general pattern of increasing social deprivation being associated with decreased academic attainment. It is likely that those advantaged parents who are more likely to make active choices tend to migrate to the better performing schools where possible, thereby reinforcing this effect (Gewirtz *et al.* 1995).

We can then look at the data in relation to the number and proportion of school types within each family of schools. In Figure 4.1 below , we see that groups containing schools with higher proportions of students eligible for FSM or with low prior attainment tend to have a majority of community schools. Community schools tend to be in the minority in the more advantaged families of schools. Thus the lower down the achievement and social inclusion scale, the more community schools a family of schools is likely to include as a proportion of its total.

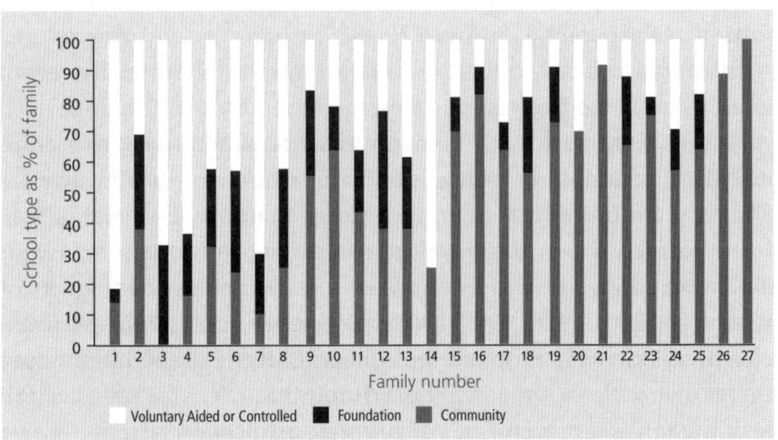


**Figure 4.1** School type as a proportion of London 'Family of Schools'
*(Source: Department for Education and Skills (2005b))* [3]

The reasons for these patterns require further exploration, but there is other evidence that pupils eligible for FSM, and low-achieving pupils, are over-represented in community schools. A recent study of religious voluntary aided and controlled secondary schools in London by Allen and West (2007) found 17 per cent of pupils at faith schools are eligible for FSM compared with 25 per cent at non-faith schools. Similarly, faith schools had 20 per cent of the lowest ability pupils compared with 31 per cent in non-faith schools. Intakes of faith schools were also found to be significantly more affluent than the neighbourhoods in which they are located.

### *Specialist schools*

Although specialist schools are often cited, along with faith schools and foundation schools, as abusing the admissions system, where they now fit into the hierarchy of schools is not entirely clear. From its beginnings in 1994, the specialist schools programme has grown from 42 technology colleges to a movement encompassing 75 per cent of maintained secondary schools by 2006, giving a total of 2,380 schools with a range of specialisms. In London there are 335 specialist schools and academies out of a total of 401 secondary schools at the time of writing, which represents 84 per cent of the city's total.

Specialist status can now be obtained in technology, science, engineering, maths and computing, business and enterprise, humanities, language, arts, music, combined subjects, sport, and special educational needs. The selection of the specialist subject is often somewhat arbitrary and can be contingent on the prior choices of other maintained schools in the area (Gorard and Taylor 2001). Most specialist schools are currently required to raise £20,000 to £50,000, depending on the size of the school, in sponsorship from local businesses, charities, or other private sector sponsors. In return, specialist schools receive preferential funding from the government and an enhanced per capita allowance for each pupil.

It is not clear how far apparent improvements in pupil outcomes in specialist schools can be attributed to preferential funding, or favourable selection procedures, rather than specialisation or increased diversity and choice as such (Jesson 2002; Mangan *et al.* 2007). But given the number of specialist schools there now are, specialist status in itself probably no longer confers significant status within a notional hierarchy of schools (Exley 2007). However, additional foundation or voluntary aided status does arguably still provide such advantages (Castle and Evans 2006; Tomlinson 2001).

## *Academies*

Despite the uncertainty surrounding the relationship between diversity and standards, the government has turned to new structures as a means to generate further improvement. As former Prime Minister Blair said in a speech to the Specialist Schools and Academies Trust in 2006:

> At first, we put a lot of faith in centrally driven improvements in performance and undoubtedly without that, we would never have got some of the immediate uplift in results. But over time, I shifted from saying 'it's standards not structures' to realizing that school structures could affect standards.
>
> (Blair 2006)

Originally designated city academies, academies are probably the prime example of New Labour's commitment to structural reform through the development of yet more new types of schools. Academies are independent state schools in the mould of Margaret Thatcher's city technology colleges, intended to increase choice and diversity locally and have a positive effect on standards, usually by raising achievement levels in underperforming schools. Two hundred academies were due to be open or in development by 2010 (National Audit Office 2007) but this figure is set to rise to 400 (Blair 2006). Academies are partly sponsored by business or private philanthropists, with up to five per cent of the overall capital costs of the academy being met via sponsorship.[4] In return for a relatively small overall investment, sponsors are permitted unprecedented levels of influence over staffing arrangements, curriculum planning, and admissions processes. They constitute an important strand of the London Challenge strategy for improving school standards in the capital.

In some cases, this formula appears to have been successful in terms of its initial academic outcomes. In a study undertaken on behalf of the DfES, a sample of 11 academies improved at an average rate of five per cent between 2002 and 2004, whereas nationally schools improved at a rate of three per cent. Schools in the same local authorities as the academies only improved at a rate of two per cent during this time (PriceWaterhouseCoopers 2005). They have also improved more rapidly than their predecessor schools and, at KS3, the results of academies are comparable with more conventional Fresh Start[5] schools (National Audit Office 2007).

Nevertheless, official statistics show that there is considerable variation among academies nationally. This is similar to the situation of specialist schools and it is equally difficult to ascertain where they, as a group, fit within the hierarchy discussed above. Haberdashers Aske Hatcham College in New Cross had a 94 per cent success rate at GCSE level in 2006, for example. On the other hand, some academies seem to have performed poorly. For example, at Capital City Academy in Willesden just 17 per cent of pupils were awarded five GCSEs at grades A to C in 2005, compared with 29 per cent in 2004, and a national average of 54.7 per cent.

This variability in educational outcomes continues to be a cause of significant concern, although it is claimed that the achievement gap between the best performing and the worst performing academies is starting to narrow. If so, this is a noteworthy achievement as, despite frequent claims to the contrary, most academies seem to accept high numbers of pupils with SEN and in receipt of FSM (Chamberlain *et al.* 2006). However, while academic standards might appear to have been raised for disadvantaged pupils, in some schools this may have been the result of other factors.

For example, there have been reports that the number of exclusions in academies has been higher than in similar schools within the same local authority. During the academic year 2004–5 the West London

Academy in Ealing excluded 1.95 per cent of its pupils, compared to 0.49 per cent for similar schools within the same local authority (LA). The City of London Academy in Southwark excluded 0.83 per cent of pupils as opposed to 0.27 per cent for similar schools in the same LA (Garner 2007). As a consequence of this, academies have been accused of disrupting local school systems (Hatcher and Jones 2006).

Furthermore, a very recent report by PriceWaterhouseCoopers (2007: 83) claims that some of the improvement in pupil performance in academies 'can be explained in terms of the fact that the social and educational profile of pupils entering academies is improving'. This suggests academies may now be acquiring something of a cachet among middle-class parents, thereby edging out the poorer pupils who were expected to gain most from them. This is a danger which had been flagged up by Gorard (2005). According to the PWC report, the number of pupils from deprived backgrounds in the 24 academies it studied (or the schools they replaced) actually fell from 42 per cent in 2002 to 36 per cent last year. At one academy, the number of pupils eligible for FSM fell from more than 50 per cent to just 12 per cent.

The report's authors urge the government to investigate whether the freedom that academies have over their own admission policies serves to exclude poor children. In particular, their report said that a system of 'fair banding' may be acting against the interests of children from poorer areas, a point emphasised in the *Daily Mail* report on the study (Clark 2007). At first sight, the findings of the report are disturbing in that they seem to support the view that schools that are their own admissions authorities exploit their freedom to recruit affluent and more biddable pupils. On the other hand, if the improvements in examination results were partly down to changes in the social mix of children, this is consistent with broader evidence that the presence of high-achieving and well-motivated pupils can impact positively on the performance of the whole school. As Maden (2002: 336) puts it, successful schools tend to have 'a "critical mass" of more engaged, broadly "pro-school" children to start with'. If improvement has been brought about in some academies by their use of ability banded admissions, this may point to the benefits of a wider reintroduction of banding, but on an area-wide rather than individual school basis in order to ensure a more equitable distribution of children of different abilities across all the schools in an area.

This approach would also help to integrate the academies better within local systems of schooling and reduce the fear that they will merely undermine other struggling schools. The recent announcement by the Brown government that local authorities will have more of a role in the planning of new academies and that more emphasis will be put on bodies such as universities in sponsoring academies (and the ending of the requirement that they contribute £2m in sponsorship) may signal some softening of the privatised and competitive model that has been emphasised hitherto (Ball 2007). However, a TUC report offers a mixed verdict on the performance of academies to date, and points out that there has so far been little collaboration between academies and neighbouring secondary schools, even though it was one of David Blunkett's original objectives (Rogers and Migniuolo 2007).

## Towards a post-competitive secondary school system in London?

A growing awareness of the difficulties in encouraging collaboration among London secondary schools within a competitive market resulted in the development of the pan-London co-ordinated admissions scheme in 2005. This sought to address some of the worst effects of the fragmentation and atomisation of secondary school provision in London that had developed since the 1988 Act. It also presaged wider changes in policy on admissions.

The London Challenge is another example of an initiative that has played a role in addressing the negative side of market-based policies, although its overall brief was more extensive and, as we have seen, included the creation of new academies (DfES 2007b). Overall, it was highly consistent with the New Labour emphasis on standards, and recognised the importance of concerted collective efforts to raise achievement among those schools and children that were languishing in the context of diversity and choice. In his essay in this book, Tim Brighouse describes this as trying to be the first place to show that schools could 'crack the cycle of disadvantage'.

This approach does now seem to be having a tangible impact. For example, national performance data show that between 2003 and 2006, the national rate of improvement in the number of pupils achieving five or more GCSE passes with grades A*–C at age 15 was 6.7 per cent, whereas in London it was 8.4 per cent and in 'Keys to Success' schools in London it was 12.9 per cent (DfES 2007d). This last group of schools are those in London facing the biggest challenges and in greatest need of additional support. Each school receives bespoke solutions, through diagnostic work and ongoing support (DfES 2007e), a carefully crafted process that has been described in detail earlier by Brighouse. Such support may well be necessary to counter the negative effects of school choice mechanisms if the social class achievement gap is to be reduced overall.

Early evidence suggests that such measures are effective. Not only are these 'Key to Success' schools improving at a faster rate than the norm, the attainment gap for disadvantaged children in London is narrowing faster than elsewhere and is narrowing fastest in these particular schools. Using the entitlement to FSM as a proxy for economic disadvantage, data provided to us by the DfES show that attainment for this group of pupils within 'Keys to Success' schools has risen by a larger amount than the non-FSM pupils (13.1 points compared to 12.3 points for the latter between 2003 and 2006).

There are also some new developments in terms of school structures, which may have the potential to move the emphasis away from competitive markets, and towards collaborative, post-competitive co-operation among schools. This might prove to be the ingredient that enables improvements in education to reach all pupils, rather than just pupils in a limited range of schools.

## *Trust schools*

Trailed in the 2005 White Paper and introduced amid considerable controversy, trust schools are felt by the government to provide a new way in which schools can achieve sufficient flexibility and freedom to transform standards, for example by having autonomy from local authorities in managing buildings and resources. In an announcement in September 2005, Secretary of State Alan Johnson outlined plans for 28 trust 'pathfinder' projects, through which the government would aim to develop a better understanding of how trusts might work in practice. At the time of writing, there are two 'pathfinder' trusts in London.

Potentially, there are four types of trusts (DfES 2006a). A single school may opt to become a trust school and indeed some voluntary aided and foundation schools already have trusts. Second, a single under-achieving school may be given a trust as a means of re-launching the governing body and recruiting a new leader. Third, it is possible to have collaborative trusts running groups of schools or linking a secondary and a local primary school, giving an 'all-through' model of education to minimise the difficulties of secondary transfer. Finally, it is possible to have a nationwide trust, such as the United Learning Trust, which was created to manage a number of faith-based academies throughout the country.

There is a risk that the first two types of trust may result in the relative isolation of individual schools from local provision. This has been the case with earlier forms of autonomous schools, such as city technology colleges and, as we have seen, academies (Whitty *et al.* 1993; Rogers and Migniuolo 2007). Additionally the reduction in the influence of the local authority raises questions about accountability, as there are few apparent controls over governing bodies of trust schools. These issues and other similar ones may account for the reluctance of education professionals to engage with the process. Indeed, a recent poll of 505 secondary headteachers and deputies suggested that only 5 per cent are actively considering trust status for their schools, despite inducements of £10,000 to encourage schools to become involved (Association of School and College Leaders 2007).

Nevertheless, the other types of trust may have greater potential to contribute to the improvement of the system as a whole. In his announcement in 2006, Johnson suggested that the government would be particularly interested in collaborative trusts, though not to the exclusion of other types. Within the trust model, schools can work together with outside organisations, such as charities, businesses, and universities, as a way of extending collaboration.[6] Trusts therefore may offer some scope to address social inclusion issues through formalised collaboration arrangements and, in so doing, may usefully become linked to other initiatives, such as federations and extended schools.

### *Federations*

Federations (or collegiates, as they were called by Tim Brighouse when he was Director of Education in Birmingham) seek to encourage collaboration rather than competition among schools. In his capacity as Commissioner for London Schools, Brighouse saw federations as a potential way of addressing the huge inequalities among London schools. At the most formal end of the spectrum, a hard governance federation is a pair or group of schools with a formal agreement to work together to raise standards, promote inclusion, find new ways of approaching teaching and learning, and build capacity between schools in a coherent manner, according to the DfES (2006b). Schools in a hard governance federation would share a governing body. A soft governance federation would involve schools having separate governing bodies, but there would be a joint governance/strategy committee with delegated powers. In a soft federation any joint governance/strategy committee would not have delegated powers. Finally, of course, it is possible for schools to form an informal, loose collaboration in which they meet on an *ad hoc* basis.

The first formal federation in London was that between Haberdashers Aske Hatcham College in New Cross and Haberdashers Aske

Knights Academy in Bromley. These schools are part of the Haberdasher's Aske Foundation, which also includes Haberdashers Aske Boys' School in Elstree and Haberdashers Aske School for Girls in Elstree. The first two schools in the list are academies, and therefore not fee paying, whereas the latter two are independent schools which charge fees. However, in formal terms, the federation is formed between the first two schools.

Federations may go some way towards allowing weaker or more recently founded schools to benefit from the experience of more successful schools, as in the case of the federation above, which involves an existing school (Hatcham College) collaborating with a newly founded one (Knights Academy). There may be scope within London for using similar federations as a kind of educational test-bed for school improvement. This would be achieved by encouraging schools in more affluent areas to link with those in areas of relative deprivation. This could be one answer to the problem of ensuring equality of access whilst allowing schools to have their own separate admissions processes.

### *Extended schools*

The final and arguably most important new structure currently being rolled out is that of extended schools. These are another fairly recent innovation, although to a certain extent grounded in existing practice, and appear to be underpinned by social justice arguments. In theory, they provide pupils with equality of access to reliable and affordable before and after-school care, parenting and family support, a varied range of activities including study support, sport and music clubs, swift and easy referral to specialist services such as speech therapy, and community use of facilities including adult and family learning and ICT. By 2010, all children will be entitled to have access to this type of provision at school, according to government guidance (DfES 2007c).

Extended schooling is usually grounded in the idea of a school serving its own locality, using local services, rather than drawing pupils or services from further afield. The provision of social care and collaboration with external health and welfare organisations lays a good foundation for learning. The opportunity to take part in extra-curricular activities fulfils the role of providing a window onto different cultures and experiences, whilst extending the capabilities of the individual. Finally, the important community role of the school encourages pupils and teachers to look outwards to see education in a broader life context.

More generally, the influence of broader social factors on schooling has been increasingly recognised through the 'children's agenda', and paying more attention to this is going to be essential if we are to make real progress in tackling educational inequalities. Teachers will need to use their professional skills in collaboration with social welfare organisations to develop more diverse, responsive, and comprehensive provision for the pupils in their care. This will also involve moving away from the tendency to pathologise social groups or situations towards a more cohesive model for urban education that anticipates needs rather than responds to them. A wide-ranging approach of this type is more likely to improve educational standards than simply addressing schooling itself (Hewlett 2006), and it also recognises Caroline Benn's argument, that the struggle to develop genuinely comprehensive education goes well beyond the issue of selection at 11 plus (Whitty 2004).

The three-year official evaluation of extended schools concluded that they improve GCSE results more quickly than the average. The number of pupils getting five good GCSEs at extended schools rose by five percentage points between 2005 and 2006 – compared to a national average of 2.5 points. The researchers particularly highlighted the benefits of 'full service' extended schools for children eligible for FSM and suggest that they make a 'real difference' for poorer families by providing stability and improving their chances of learning. Encouragingly, the study thus found that the gap in performance between pupils eligible for FSM and those who were not had narrowed (Cummings *et al.* 2007).

However, the Scottish experience suggests that the extent of funding will be crucial to the future success of extended schools (Sammons *et al.* 2003). If the reality is that socially disadvantaged children spend substantial periods of time outside normal school hours 'parked' in an institutional environment not designed for that purpose, staffed by poorly paid and poorly trained carers, the benefits are likely to stall. What needs to be embedded within any model of extended schooling is an understanding of the holistic nature of the child, evident throughout the school day. Nutrition, healthcare, and social welfare support all play a role. Thus, the cost of effective extended schooling is likely to be substantial, and it is unlikely that this cost can be recouped by charging all parents for services at market rates. If there is to be equality of access for children of all social classes, this is an important matter that needs to be addressed and the government has so far offered a £265m subsidy over the next three years to help children from disadvantaged backgrounds benefit from extra-curricular activities (DfES 2007f).

## Conclusion

These trends are not yet sufficient to suggest that education policy in general or London education in particular has decisively broken with the Thatcherite and Blairite legacies of neo-liberal marketisation. Nevertheless, there are some early signs that the new government under Gordon Brown is more willing than the Blair regime to move social justice and social cohesion issues up the agenda – and, at the time of writing, there is even talk of an 'egalitarian project' in the Brown camp (Wilby 2007). Also, the Director-General for Schools, within the newly created Department for Children, Schools and Families, has recently questioned whether hitherto New Labour policies have been 'sufficiently granulated to focus on lifting the disadvantaged as well as the advantaged children' (Stewart 2007). Particularly for those of us who have been arguing this case for some time, this is indeed welcome (Mortimore and Whitty 1997).

However, one of the major challenges confronting policy makers is that policies that address one aspect of the problem may impact negatively on another. For example, the emphasis on local support for families that is embedded in the extended schools approach can come into tension with the need to provide schools with a social mix. It may therefore be that the call for a 'good local school for every child' (Education Alliance 2006) will best be met by a combination of extended school provision in the locality and federation with other schools with different types of intake. This would, though, require changes in the way in which schools are judged – moving to collective performance indicators rather than merely individual ones and paying as much attention to the contribution of schools to the social inclusion and cohesion agendas as to the standards agenda.

Finally, equity in secondary schooling in London will require attention to the elephant in the room, the role of the very significant independent sector. Although government policy is encouraging greater collaboration between individual state and independent schools,[7] assisted perhaps by the new charities legislation, a broader approach to the relationship between the two sectors is surely desirable. This would involve revisiting the issue that was behind the ill-fated attempt in the mid-1970s to force direct grant grammar schools to join the mainstream system or go independent. One visionary proposal, in which private schools effectively withdraw from 11–14 provision but make a major contribution for all pupils post-14, was offered by Sir Peter Newsam when he retired as ILEA Education Officer in the mid-1980s. While this proposal did not find favour and probably would not do so today, the current changes in the 14–19 landscape may offer an opportunity for similarly visionary thinking on the part of the government, the London authorities, and representatives of the two sectors.

**References**

Allen, R. and West, A. (2007) 'Religious Schools in London: School Admissions, Religious Composition and Selectivity?'. Paper presented at the British Educational Research Association annual conference, Institute of Education, University of London, 5–8 September.

Association of School and College Leaders (2007) <http://www.ascl.org.uk/default.aspx?id=NewsItem&cmnID=4287> (Accessed 2 April 2007).

Ball, S.J. (2007) *Education Plc: Understanding private sector participation in public sector education*. London: Routledge.

Blair, A. (2006) 'Education is the most precious gift'. Speech at Specialist Schools and Academies Trust Conference, 30 November.

Braswell, S. (2005) 'Choice and social segregation in education: the impact of open enrolment on the social composition of English secondary schools.' Unpublished DPhil thesis, University of Oxford.

Castle, F. and Evans, J. (2006) *Specialist Schools – what do we know?* London: Research on State Education.

Centre for Educational Research (2005) *Evidence to the Education and Skills Select Committee Inquiry into the Schools White Paper*, House of Commons, Education and Skills Committee.

Chamberlain, T., Rutt, S. and Fletcher-Campbell, F. (2006) *Admissions: Who goes where? Messages from the statistics.* Slough: NFER.

Chitty, C. (2002) 'The right to a comprehensive education', Second Caroline Benn Memorial Lecture, Goldsmith's College, 16 November.

Clark, L. (2007) 'Academy schools '"turning away poorer pupils"', *Daily Mail*, 20 July.

Committee on Curricula and Examinations (1943) *Curriculum and Examinations in Secondary School.* London: HMSO [Norwood Report].

Consultative Committee of the Board of Education (1938) *Report on Secondary Education with Special Reference to Grammar Schools and Technical High Schools.* London: HMSO [Spens Report].

Cummings, C., Dyson, A., Muijs, D., Papps, I., Pearson, D., Raffo, C., Tiplady, L. and Todd, L. with Crowther, D. (2007) *Evaluation of the Full Service Extended Schools Initiative: final report*. Research Report RR852. <http://www.dfes.gov.uk/research/data/uploadfiles/RR852.pdf>

Department for Children, Schools and Families (DCSF) (2007) *Schools and Pupils in England: January 2006*. London: DCSF.

Department for Education and Skills (DfES) (2005a) *Higher Standards, Better Schools for All.* London: DfES [White Paper].

— (2005b) *Families of Schools.* London: DfES.

— (2006a) *Trust Schools.* London: DfES. <http://findoutmore.dfes.gov.uk/2006/02/trust_schools.html> (Accessed 21 March 2007).

— (2006b) <http://www.standards.dfes.gov.uk/federations/what_are_federations/?version =1> (Accessed 6 November 2006).

— (2007a) *School Admissions Code.* London, The Stationery Office.

— (2007b) <http://www.dfes.gov.uk/londonchallenge/> (Accessed 27 April 2007).

— (2007c) <http://www.teachernet.gov.uk/wholeschool/extendedschools/ teachernetgovukcoreoffer/> (Accessed 29 April 2007).

— (2007d) *Secondary Schools (GCSE and equivalent) Achievement and Attainment Tables 2006.* <http://www.dfes.gov.uk/performancetables/schools_03.shtml> <http://www.dfes.gov.uk/performacetables/schools_06.shtml> (Accessed 30 April 2007

— (2007e) <http://www.teachernet.gov.uk/wholeschool/london/schools/ keystosuccess/> (Accessed 30 April 2007).

— (2007f) Press Release: 'Building on achievement, meeting new challenges' <https://www.dfes.gov.uk/pns/DisplayPN.cgi?pn_id=2007_0126> (Accessed 24 July 2007).

Dunford, J. (2006) 'Comprehensive schools: continuing the success story'. In Hewlett, M., Pring, R. and Tulloch, M. (eds) (2006) *Comprehensive Education: Evolution, Achievement and New Directions.* Northampton: University of Northampton.

Education Alliance (2006) 'A good local school for every child: will the Education Bill deliver?' Conference held at the Institute of Education, University of London, 25 March.

Education and Skills Committee (2006) The Schools White Paper: Higher Standards, Better Schools For All. First Report of Session 2005-06 Vol 1. (HE 633-1).

Edwards, T., Fitz, J. and Whitty, G. (1989) *The State and Private Education: An evaluation of the Assisted Places Scheme.* London: Falmer.

Exley, S. (2007) 'Specialist schools and the post-comprehensive era in England: promoting diversity or perpetuating social segregation?' Unpublished DPhil thesis, University of Oxford.

Fogelman, K. (2006) 'A brief history of comprehensive education in England and Wales'. In Hewlett, M. Pring, R. and Tulloch, M. *Comprehensive Education: Evolution, achievement and new directions.* Northampton: Northampton University Press.

Garner, R. (2007) 'High expulsion rates "massage" academies' results', *The Independent*, 29 January. <http://education.independent.co.uk/news/article2193671.ece> (Accessed 21 February 2007).

Gewirtz, S., Ball, S. and Bowe, R. (1995) *Markets, Choice and Equity*. Buckingham: Open University Press.

Gorard, S. (2005) 'Academies as the "future of schooling": Is this evidence based policy?'. *Journal of Education Policy* 20(3) May: 369–377.

Gorard, S. and Taylor, C. (2001) 'The composition of specialist schools in England: track record and future prospect', *School Leadership and Management*, 21(4): 365–381.

Grace, G. (1984) *Education and the City: Theory, history and contemporary practice.* London: Routledge.

Greater London Authority (GLA) (2005) *Evidence to the Education and Skills Select Committee Inquiry into the Schools White Paper.* House of Commons, Education and Skills Committee.

Hatcher, R. and Jones, K. (2006) 'Researching resistance: campaigns against academies in England'. *British Journal of Educational Studies* 54(3): 329–351.

Hewlett, M. (2006) 'Defining comprehensive schools'. In Hewlett, M., Pring, R. and Tulloch, M. (eds) *Comprehensive Education: Evolution, achievement and new directions.* Northampton: University of Northampton.

Jesson, D. (2002) 'Progress of pupils in specialist and other schools from Key Stage 2 to GCSE'. In Jesson, D. and Taylor, C. *Value Added and the Benefits of Specialism.* London: Technology Colleges Trust. <http://www.schoolsnetwork.org.uk/content/articles/337/bookforweb.pdf> (Accessed 24 July 2007).

Maden, M. (ed.) (2002) *Success Against the Odds Five Years on*. London: RoutledgeFalmer.

Mangan, J., Pugh, G. and Gray, J. (2007) 'Examination performance, specialist status and school expenditure in English secondary schools: a dynamic panel analysis'. Paper presented at the British Educational Research Association annual conference, Institute of Education, University of London, 5–8 September.

Miliband, D. (2006) 'A social democratic settlement'. In Hewlett M., Pring, R. and Tulloch, M. (eds) *Comprehensive Education: Evolution, achievement and new directions.* Northampton: University of Northampton.

Morris, M. (2004) 'The Route to My Comprehensive'. In Benn, M. and Chitty, C. *A Tribute to Caroline Benn: Education and democracy.* London: Continuum.

Mortimore, P. and Whitty, G. (1997) 'Can improvement overcome the effects of disadvantage?' *Perspectives on Education Policy No 9.* London:Institute of Education.

National Audit Office (2007) *The Academies Programme.* London: The Stationery Office.

Pennell, H., West, A. and Hind, A. (2006) 'Secondary School Admissions in London'. *Clare Market Papers No 19.* Centre for Educational Research, Department of Social Policy, London School of Economics and Political Science.

PriceWaterhouseCoopers (2005) *Academies Evaluation: Second Annual Report.* London: PriceWaterhouseCoopers.

— (2007) *Academies Evaluation: Fourth Annual Report.* London: PriceWaterhouseCoopers.

Rogers, M. and Migniuolo, F. (2007) *A New Direction: A review of the school academies programme.* London: Trades Union Congress.

Russell, B. (1932) *Education and the Social Order.* London: George Allen and Unwin.

Sammons, P., Power, S., Robertson, P., Elliott, K., Campbell, C. and Whitty, G. (2003) *New Community Schools in Scotland – Final Report: National Evaluation of the Pilot Phase.* London: Institute of Education.

Specialist Schools and Academies Trust (2007) <http://www.specialistschools.org.uk/uploads/documents/Sir%20Bruce%20Liddington%20-%20Schools%20Commissioner_443.ppt#440,4,SpectrumofDiversity> (Accessed 6 March 2007).

Stewart, W. (2007) 'Poor are neglected in rush for results', *Times Educational Supplement*, 20 July, p. 1.

Tomlinson, S. (2001) 'Education Policy, 1997–2000: the effects on top, bottom and middle England'. *International Studies in Sociology of Education*. 11(3): 261–277.

Tough, S. and Brooks, R. (2007) *Fair Choice – Choosing a Better Admissions System*. London: Institute for Public Policy Research.

West, A. and Hind, A. (2003) *Secondary School Admissions in England: Exploring the extent of overt and covert selection.* London: Research and Information on State Education. <http://www.risetrust.org.uk/admissions.html> (Accessed 24 July 2007).

Whitty, G. (2004) 'Developing comprehensive education in a new climate'. In *A Tribute to Caroline Benn: Education and Democracy*. London: Continuum, p. 97

Whitty, G., Edwards, T. and Gewirtz, S. (1993) *Specialisation and Choice in Urban Education: The city technology college experiment.* London: Routledge.

Wilby, P. (2007) 'Why education remains the priority', *New Statesman*, 14 May, p. 14.

Whitty, G., Power, S., and Halpin, D. (1998) *Devolution and Choice in Education: The school, the state, and the market*. Buckingham: Open University Press.

Williams, P. and Murphy, T. (1979) 'Dual system – end it or mend it'. *Teaching London Kids,* 14: 3–7.

**Notes**

1. Currently 10 per cent in London as opposed to 7 per cent nationally across England. The figure for Inner London is 14 per cent and for one Outer London borough it is as high as 30 per cent (DCFS 2007).
2. About half of London's 400 secondary schools are their own admissions authorities.
3. We are grateful to Ruth Lupton for her assistance in compiling this figure.
4. In future, however, contributions will go towards endowments for the schools.
5. A school is given a 'Fresh Start' when it is experiencing serious difficulties. It is closed and reopened on the same site under the normal school reorganisation procedures.
6. At a trust schools conference in February 2007, Barnardo's, Dyslexia Action, New College Durham, City College Plymouth, the Universities of Sunderland and Northumbria, and the Tribal Group were all announced as having put themselves forward as potential partners.
7. The Haberdashers' example in this essay suggests how this policy may be linked into the idea of federations.

# 5 Does Every London Child Matter? The new agenda for children in London

Janet Mokades

## Introduction

This essay provides a picture of London's children and the context in which they are growing up in the early twenty-first century. Expanding provision for children and developing more holistic approaches to children's needs have been particular features of education and social policy in the UK since the late 1990s. It has resulted in the development of an ambitious national programme of whole system reform of services for children popularly called 'Every Child Matters', after the title of the seminal 2003 Green Paper 'Every Child Matters: Change for Children'. This essay will outline the genesis, history and scope of the Every Child Matters (ECM) policy and will identify those features of the London context that make it a policy of particular relevance to the city. It will examine the impact to date of Every Child Matters on outcomes for London's children and young people, particularly education outcomes. It will identify particular issues arising from its implementation. It will detail some risks and some gains. Finally, the essay will consider whether the ECM programme, as laid out by central government, is sufficiently robust to carry and fulfil the weight of expectations that it currently bears in the London context and will try to map out what might be the next stage of its development as far as London is concerned.

This essay is a personal view arising from many years of experience of working in education in London, as a practitioner, as a member of Her Majesty's Inspectorate (HMI) and as an adviser to the Department for Education and Skills (DfES). My reflections in this essay have been informed by a number of reviews and surveys I have undertaken in London, and by my many discussions with senior staff across London who are concerned with the issues raised in this essay.

## London's children – the context

In the first essay in this book Lupton and Sullivan have provided considerable detail on London's children and what, if anything, distinguishes them from children elsewhere in the UK. London is currently home to 1.61 million children under the age of 18; 29 per cent of all households in London have at least one dependent child and their most distinguishing feature is their diversity. Two-fifths of London's children belong to a black, Asian or minority ethnic group and nearly one-third of them speak English as an additional language (EAL). One-fifth of inner London's children are Muslim (GLA, 2004a). This diversity is allied to another distinguishing feature – the high level of inequality in life chances and outcomes they experience. The Mayor of London's *State of London's Children Report* states:

> The diversity and inequality, which so clearly characterise London, are even more apparent in relation to London's children. Indeed, London's children can be understood to be unique, both in terms of their diversity in relation to children nationally, and in terms of the specific inequalities, challenges and issues which they, their families and their communities face. London's children have themselves highlighted what they see as some of these challenges, including housing, the environment , mobility, racism, bullying and criminality.
>
> (GLA 2004a)

The conditions in which many children and young people live is a significant factor in London. Overcrowding, temporary accommodation, high housing costs that trap low-skilled workers on benefits, and mobility resulting from housing difficulties all have a significant impact on the wellbeing and life chances of children and affect their access to education, health and social care services.

Many children are growing up in very poor housing conditions. Overall, 29 per cent of London children live in overcrowded households. In Inner London, the figure is 41 per cent. London has a higher proportion of dwellings in 'poor neighbourhoods' than the England average and nearly one-quarter of London's social housing is in this category (GLA 2004a). Such neighbourhoods tend to be blighted by generalised decay, and children and young people react strongly against this. More than half of the young people in the Greater London Authority's (GLA) Young Londoners' Survey were troubled by traffic pollution, litter, dumped waste and rubbish, graffiti and dumped cars, and thought they were major problems in London (GLA 2004b).

Affordable housing is in exceedingly short supply and the level of homelessness is a major problem. Just over half of the households accepted as homeless in 2003–4 were families with children. Furthermore, the number of households with children living in temporary accommodation is higher than the number accepted as homeless. In addition, there are the unofficial homeless, many of whom have children. Older young people in London are over-represented among the homeless. Over 500 young people are given shelter by the London charity Centrepoint every night (GLA 2004a). A significant number of these are young runaways, including runaways from care, and repeat runaways.

As well as poor physical conditions, many children face considerable personal and social difficulties. The numbers of looked after children in London averaged around 12,000 in the period 2003–5 (GOL 2006). Looked after children are those who are, for a variety of reasons, not with their families and have been taken into local authority care. Booming London housing markets make it extremely difficult to secure sufficient affordable foster placements in London. Capable potential foster parents are constrained by lack of space. Thus many looked after

London children were in the recent past accommodated long distances away from their home areas; however, presently London has more children placed ten miles or less from their home than across England as a whole – 80 per cent in London, 70 per cent in England (GOL 2006). Hard-pressed London boroughs have found it difficult to fulfil their obligations to these children and ensure that their education is good and their wellbeing assured. Many such children have ended up in struggling schools, because that is where places have been available. Historically they have fared very poorly in terms of educational achievement and life chances generally, and many end up in the criminal justice system. However, attainment of looked after children in London is currently slightly higher than across England (GOL 2006) and the data also shows that offending by looked after children in London is lower than across England (*ibid*). London is a magnet for people from all over the world and a significant number of London's children and young people are from refugee or asylum seeking families. Reliable current figures are hard to come by, but the Mayor of London's *Children Report* stated that, 'Local Education Authority (LEA) data suggest that six per cent of London's children are refugees' (GLA 2004a). There are now some local authorities in London where a significant proportion of looked after children, particularly in the older age range, are unaccompanied asylum seekers. There are also increasing numbers of unaccompanied asylum seeking young people – 63 per cent of all looked after unaccompanied asylum seekers in England are registered in London (GOL 2006).

There are important distinctions to be made between London's settled diverse population and recent arrivals. Much of what is quoted in the first esssay of this book refers to the settled population. By definition, many of the recent arrivals are not included in the official statistics. In London there is a whole twilight zone of people who are here illegally or tenuously, who are highly mobile and whose relationships with public services are likely to be erratic.

Mobility is a hugely significant feature of London and has a major impact on many of its children. It is esimated that the number of people moving in and out of London every year is nearly 250,000 and this excludes mobility within London. In some boroughs the population turnover is over 35 percent annually (LSE 2007).

A study by Dobson, Henthorne and Lynas identified a number of categories, such as:

- International migration: labour/career cycles; refugees; settlement; students
- Internal migration: labour/career cycle; life cycle
- Housing/environment: schooling: travellers
- Institutional movement: exclusions; voluntary transfers; private/state school
- Individual movement: looked-after children; family fragmentation.

(Dobson *et al.* 2000 )

As the above classification shows, mobility in London is not restricted to those whose status is unclear. There are also children whose families move from borough to borough or who relocate in or out of London from another part of the country. There are new arrivals from the European Union accession countries; there are young people who finish foster placements outside London, or who come out of secure units or young offender institutions and return to London. Some may live in hostels or with friends and some have no real fixed abode. This kind of mobility hinders learning and often means that after age 16 these young people are not in any kind of employment, education or training.

Buried among these figures are huge amounts of human upheaval and suffering. Among the international migrants, there are children and young people arriving from war zones and places of terrible instability. There are people who bring with them unfamiliar cultural practices and beliefs. Thus there is a group of children and young people who appear and disappear in London schools, whose whereabouts are extremely difficult to keep track of and whose safety and wellbeing it is hard for public authorities to guarantee.

There are other negative factors affecting the lives of many young people in London, of which bullying is one of the most important. In the 2004 GLA *Young Londoners' Survey*, more than half (54 per cent) of the young respondents thought that bullying was a problem in their local neighbourhoods; 61 per cent cited bullying as a problem at school, and 46 per cent saw this as a problem on public transport (GLA 2004b). The Mayor's *Report* states that, 'Bullying and racism are closely related and may be more commonly experienced by young refugees and asylum seekers and young people from black and minority ethnic (BME) groups. Many young Londoners also experience disparagement on account of their sexual orientation, religion or gender' (GLA 2004a).

Racism in London is a complex phenomenon and the Mayor's *Report* may be unduly simplistic in its view. In particular, in the complex post-code street politics of young people, there are distinctions to be made between the experience of recent arrivals and that of British-born young people of minority ethnic heritage. Nonetheless, racism clearly is a very significant contextual factor in the lives of many London children and young people, as discussed by McKenley in Essay 8 of this book.

Bullying is a continuum. At its most extreme end it shades into violence and crime. Predictably, crime is another key London issue. Young people, typically young men, are major perpetrators and victims. The links between truancy, exclusion from school and juvenile offending are well established. So too are those between functional illiteracy and offending. Youth crime covers a wide spectrum: much of it is petty theft, often of mobile phones, while a significant proportion is drug related. What hits the headlines and is the greatest source of public concern is gun and knife crime, which is often gang based.

While violent crime in London on the whole is reported as falling, crime involving young Londoners, especially those from BME groups is on the increase (*London Bulletin* 2007). In 1998 a special police operation entitled 'Trident' was established with the mission of helping to bring an end to a spate of shootings and murders among young black Londoners, but it has had limited success. According to the *London Bulletin* (issued by London Councils, an organisation representing all London boroughs), 'the number of murder and shooting victims under the age of 20 dealt with by Trident is on the increase; from 31 in 2003 to 79 in 2006' (*London Bulletin* 2007). The *Bulletin* also reports on evidence that black boys are pressured into becoming gang members, and that they, as well as their victims, are currently of a younger age than ever before. Over the last five years the number of gang members below the age of 16 has more than doubled. Around 3,000 young Londoners are members of 169 London gangs known to the police. These gangs are directly linked with the majority of violent crime in London (*London Bulletin* 2007). The summer of 2007 was particularly shocking, with three teenagers killed in separate incidents in the space of just 11 days, bringing the number of such murders beteen January and August 2007 to eight.

The London Youth Crime Prevention Board (LYCPB) was launched in May 2007 with the aim of preventing such crime through better partnership between the police, local authorities and community groups (London Councils 2007).

These contextual factors, by no means comprehensive, give some indication of how the health, social care, recreation and education needs of London's children are complex, diverse and demanding. And, of course, they are underpinned by the key factor of poverty. As shown elsewhere in this book, London has the highest child poverty rate, after housing costs, of any region in the UK. Thirty-eight per cent of London's children are living in poverty compared with an England average of 29 per cent (GLA 2004a). For many of these children and young people, particularly those who emerge from 11 years of compulsory education without qualifications, the future looks very challenging indeed.

Tackling the way in which a range of complex social and economic problems impact on the educational outcomes and life chances of children is the key social policy issue for London. We know that good education outcomes bring substantial and long-lasting benefit to those who achieve them and is thus an important way of improving the life chances of the most disadvantaged (Reed and Robinson 2005), but we also know that despite the marked improvements in school performance in London described elsewhere in this book, the links between lower socio-economic groups and poor education outcomes remain strong. It is in this context that an integrated policy for children and young people which tackles all aspects of a child's life that impact on their educational outcomes has most resonance for London.

## The Every Child Matters policy

So where does Every Child Matters come from and what can it do for London's children? The catalyst that led to the development of the Every Child Matters strategy was a government-instituted independent inquiry into the murder of a young child (Victoria Climbié) by her carers (Laming 2003). This report catalogued the failure of a range of agencies to co-ordinate and communicate information about the welfare of a vulnerable child and to prevent her death. It highlighted the imperative for improved integration, communication and accountability across all services for children to prevent such an occurrence ever happening again. The report, and the government's response to it (DfES 2003) prompted an unprecedented debate about services for children, young people and families.

Following the debate and consultation, a new Children Act became law in 2004. It established the elements of a new framework for developing more effective and accessible services, focused around the needs of children, young people and families. The Act instituted a ten year national programme for change. The changes were designed to establish a comprehensive and integrated approach to supporting children, young people and families. Clearly defined outcomes for all children and young people were at the heart of the change process. The Act defined five outcomes for all children – to be healthy, to stay safe, to enjoy and achieve through learning, to make a positive contribution to society and to achieve economic wellbeing. These outcomes were seen to be interdependent and they recognised the important relationship between educational achievement and wellbeing. Children and young people learn best when they are healthy, safeguarded from harm, and are more broadly engaged.

Since 2004 there has been a concerted drive to develop common processes to underpin joint working, to integrate front line services, to develop integrated approaches to planning and commissioning the full range of services for children, and to develop clearer governance and accountability arrangements for services for children. There has also been a drive to remove the legal, technical, and cultural barriers to information sharing between agencies and to facilitate more effective communication between every agency with responsibility for children. A clear framework of accountability at national and local level has been established, with the appointment of a director in every local authority responsible for services for children and a requirement for local authorities to lead and work in partnership with others to achieve the safeguarding and the wellbeing of all children in their local area. Inspection agencies and regimes have been redesigned to reflect the focus on the child and the required joint approaches. National qualifications and occupational standards have been reviewed and integrated workforce planning has been developed with a view to achieving a more flexible, skilled and effective workforce.

New governance arrangements have developed in many areas through the establishment of children's trusts, where local authorities working with partners in health, social services, and the police among others, are required to find out what works best for children and young people in their area and to act on it. They are expected to involve children and young people in this process, listen to their views and act on them. In addition, in March 2005, the first Children's Commissioner for England was appointed, to give children and young people, particularly the most vulnerable, a voice in government and in public life and to promote their involvement in the work of organisations whose decisions and actions affect them.

In London, as elsewhere, this has meant major structural, political, managerial and operational change. At the time of writing, most London local authorities have merged their education and children's social services operations into children's services departments, headed by a Director of children's services and overseen by a designated lead elected member. Partnerships have been established with strategic health authorities and primary care trusts (PCTs) and with the police and the Youth Justice Board (YJB) and with other agencies to ensure the safeguarding of children; better preventive measures; and the delivery and management of the full range of services for children and young people.

Some partnerships are now so well established that they share premises, appoint shared staff and pool some funding. Children's trust arrangements in some areas are now engaging in high-level strategic planning, commissioning and policy making for their areas.

The process of bringing partners together has been difficult in some respects and in some parts of London. While structural change within local authorities has largely been accomplished, there is still the challenge of cultural change. How much of the latter there has been and at what levels is hard to assess. Gauging the extent to which educationalists still think education, and social services staff still think social care, is difficult. Creating a workforce that owes allegiance to neither camp but takes a holistic view is, realistically, a medium- to long-term project.

In some areas, partnership with PCTs has been bedevilled by structural and financial factors. The geographical areas for which PCTs were responsible were not necessarily the same as those of local authorities. Both they and the strategic health authorities have been subject to wave after wave of reorganisation. In addition, some London PCTs have had large financial deficits. Services for children are a small part of their remit, and their performance with regard to them is not central to the criteria on which they are judged and held accountable. Thus there has been little incentive for them to focus on this area of their work. Nonetheless, there are areas where strong and effective partnerships between PCTs and local authorities for children's services are in place.

Every Child Matters has represented a major change in the policy environment in London. The joined-up agenda that it promotes impacts fundamentally, not just structurally, on education, social care, and health. As far as education is concerned it has meant, in theory at least, a significant shift of focus. Before 2004 education at national, local authority and school level was firmly focused on the standards agenda. Setting, enforcing and meeting achievement targets were perceived as the key tasks of schools and local education authorities. Government policy, through a variety of measures, had long encouraged schools to concentrate almost exclusively on driving up examination and test scores. This policy was now having to live side-by-side with the new requirement for schools to act as the hub for delivery of other services to children and parents, and to consider a range of outcomes for the whole child and not just his or her educational outcomes.

For London, with its plethora of social problems, there were many in education who welcomed the ECM agenda and saw it as a powerful means to counter disadvantage. London was seen as prime territory for the development of a policy with a strong focus on the needs of each and every child, particularly the most vulnerable, and in addition it was seen as precisely what was required in the London context as a means of enhancing the capacity to learn and thus to raise standards

As well as being concerned with educational outcomes, most London local authorities and schools are also concerned on a daily basis with poor school attendance, exclusion from school, substance and alcohol abuse, domestic violence leading to children being taken into care, teenage pregnancy, mental health issues, and youth crime. Their impact on what children achieve in school is huge. In the London context, the Every Child Matters approach was seen as having huge potential in mitigating the impact of poverty on children's educational achievement and life chances.

## Developments in London

It is still early days for ECM implementation, and improvements in outcomes cannot yet be evidenced fully across the board. Nonetheless, across London there is evidence of some improvement in aspects of all five outcomes. It is stronger for some outcomes than others, in particular, as documented elsewhere in this book, in educational achievement. That is at least partly because there are comprehensive and well-established systems of data collection and analysis in the field of education.

It is certainly clear that some of the policy initiatives and programmes that are underway across London are already improving processes. Local authorities are working much more closely than in the past with their partners in health, in the criminal justice system, and the voluntary and community sectors. Substantial changes have already taken place within local authorities as education, social care and, in some cases, other services come together in new services frameworks. Authorities generally are improving systems so that they can identify and offer better support to vulnerable and needy children and families at transitions and other key points, thus avoiding the need for more intensive interventions later on. The development of better processes should lead to better outcomes in the long run.

In the area of child protection there are signs that the new Local Safeguarding Children Boards (LSCB) which, following the 2004 Children Act, replaced Area Child Protection Committees, are becoming much more central to the work of many councils with key people such as headteachers and housing staff much more closely involved. Many boards have well-developed subgroups to drive forward particular aspects of the safeguarding agenda. For example, some have performed specific safeguarding work with faith communities, including African churches and mosques. Countering domestic violence is a central part of safeguarding work in many boroughs.

Another important area is teenage pregnancy where figures have historically been high among certain groups and among looked after children. 'London accounts for 16 per cent of all under-18 conceptions in England ... It is the region that has made least progress in reducing teenage pregnancy rates and has the highest proportion of areas which have seen increases in these numbers' (<www.younglondonmatters.org/the-strands/>). Although some authorities and schools do well in supporting teenage parents and retaining them in education, premature parenthood too often spells the end of education and a significant worsening of life chances. Much effort is now going into reducing the figures, with agencies working much more closely together on prevention. There is evidence of success in some areas with rates reducing. Joint working with primary care trusts (PCTs) on sexual health, the identification of high-incidence areas and a concentration on high-risk young people are key features of successful strategies. So too is targeted work, often through male youth workers, with potential young fathers.

Another area where figures have been historically very high in London is in the numbers of children in care. A major drive within the ECM agenda has been to reduce the numbers of children coming into care and this is beginning to bear fruit. There is evidence that numbers are beginning to reduce through such mechanisms as family group conferencing, social workers in schools pursuing preventive work and projects countering alcohol and substance misuse. Where boroughs have been successful in recruiting more and better social workers they have been able to give families more and better support and to give children who do come into care the prospect of their own assigned social worker. This has helped to reduce the numbers of children coming into care.

There has also been a concerted drive in London to reduce multiple placements for looked after children. The single most damaging aspect of looked after children's lives in the past has been the lack of stability due to constantly moving placements that have disrupted their development and wellbeing. Local authorities are now putting a great deal of thought and effort into improving placement stability and things are improving. In some authorities, high-risk placements are being subjected to particular scrutiny and multi-agency support is being commissioned for them. Wherever possible children are now being placed closer to home thus minimising the disruption of placements at a long distance from home. Children with complex needs in particular have historically been housed outside of London. Some areas have developed or are developing new in-borough residential accommodation for these children, to keep them closer to home and reduce costs.

Authorities are also working hard to increase their pools of in-borough or close-to-borough foster carers. Simultaneously, they are developing ways of increasing the understanding and skills of existing and new foster carers. In part, this is to enhance the wellbeing of looked after children and to ensure that they do better in school. In part it is because, as the thresholds for taking children into care shift upwards, more of the children coming into care have complex and challenging problems and this makes foster caring a more complex task. Better prepared foster carers are also expected to increase placement stability. A particularly welcome development is the training and accrediting of foster carers, and incentives to training in the shape of higher pay for those who gain accreditation.

Looked after children are also getting healthcare that is better targeted to their needs and more accessible. More are having regular health and dental checks. In some areas, multi-agency teams or family planning trained nurses work with looked after children on a range of issues including teenage pregnancy. This is helping to reduce the numbers who become pregnant. Arrangements between local authorities and primary care trusts in some areas have ensured that looked after children can rapidly receive help and treatment from child and adolescent mental health services (CAMHS). Some boroughs have secured CAMHS services for young people placed outside the boroughs.

Rates of offending among looked after children have been high in the past. Recent data appears to show that things are improving in this area also. However, this may not be presenting an accurate picture. There are significant issues in data not being recorded, and levels of offending by all children are higher in London than the England average.

While it is difficult to draw conclusions from the data (GOL 2006) there is some evidence that in some areas where there is a concerted drive to ensure looked after children receive good individual care and attention as well as good multi-agency support, fewer are offending or re-offending.

When we come to educational attainment, there is still a mountain to be climbed. Educational attainment by looked after children has historically been exceedingly low when compared with that of their peers. Within this overall picture, the 2003 Social Exclusion Unit (SEU) report, *A Better Education for Children in Care* pointed to significant variations in the care population. The SEU found that children in stable foster care placements within their own local authority for a long time were likely to do better at school (SEU 2003). Hopefully the drive in London to increase placement stability and to get more London looked after children into local foster care should ultimately support improved attainment.

Some London authorities now work with multi-agency teams to produce good personalised plans for their looked after children. Some have priority places for looked after children in their chosen schools and have non-exclusion policies for them. One authority offers dedicated teacher assistance in its care homes. School attendance by looked after children has improved in places where consistent efforts have been made to ensure children are in school.

The SEU report also noted that 'low educational attainment is an important contributor to the high levels of social exclusion faced by care leavers' (SEU 2003). In order to prevent young people who leave care from ending up not in education, employment or training (NEET), many authorities have assigned dedicated workers to them. The proportion of 16–18-year-olds in the NEET category in the London central area was 8.4 per cent in November 2006 (Learning and Skills Council 2007). Some councils are employing their own care leavers in a range of capacities. Increasing numbers of looked-after children are staying in education and moving on into higher education. In some areas, a considerable proportion of these young people are unaccompanied asylum seekers.

The recent government focus on improving attainment by looked after children, the new ECM requirements and hard-edged targets have put pressure on local authorities and schools to improve their performance for these children. The DfES review *Care Matters: Time for Change* found that 'despite high ambitions and a shared commitment for change, outcomes for children and young people in care have not sufficiently improved. There remains a significant gap between the quality of their lives and those of all children' (DfES 2007). This is undoubtedly true for London as well as for the rest of the country, despite the improvement in approaches described above.

Behaviour, school attendance, and exclusion from school are all huge issues for many London children, not just those in care. Where severely disruptive behaviour in schools is a result of mental health problems there are signs of an improving picture, with area inspections showing that there is better access to mental health services for many troubled young people; some schools now have primary mental health workers assigned to them, or there are arrangements for rapid access to professional help when they need it. School exclusions, particularly of BME pupils, are still too high in many authorities, although they have reduced in some areas. Schools and local authorities face some difficult dilemmas around exclusions. At the extreme end of the spectrum, violence, potential violence and knife or weapon possession demand a strong response. Pupils and their parents need to feel safe. On the other hand, children and young people involved in extreme incidents are often drawn from among the most disadvantaged and are the very young people who should be engaged through the Every Child Matters approach.

Some schools, together with their local authorities, are working effectively on this front. Multi-agency approaches, coupled with good behaviour management, are the essentials of effective approaches. In line with ECM principles of early intervention and prevention, authorities together with schools are developing targeted work with pupils at risk of exclusion, including restorative justice. Managed moves are working in some areas. There have been problems with the number of central government policy shifts with regard to exclusions, which often have a rapid impact on practice in schools and make it a difficult area of policy for local authorities to manage effectively.

Too many London children do not attend school regularly. A complex web of factors underpins attendance statistics and where authorities working with schools have analysed these carefully, they are able to improve the picture. This is often through working with other agencies, particularly the police or groups in the community. Consistent communication with parents has been shown to be a key element in improvement. For instance, several authorities with rapidly shifting demographics discovered that religious observance was impacting on attendance. They negotiated a maximum of three religious observance days with local faith leaders. Elsewhere, parents were alerted to lessons missed and their cost. Punitive approaches such as fixed penalty notices on parents have also been used n London.

Although schools are under pressure from both the government and local authorities to improve attendance, there are countervailing pressures in the system emanating from government policy. Children with poor attendance are often those least likely to achieve well and improve a school's league table standing. They may well be challenging to manage in school. Equally, they may be of uncertain status and therefore liable to move rapidly if they think that other government agencies such as the Home Office are looking for them. In theory, children such as these are key clients of Every Child Matters. In practice, they may well find themselves located on a fault line running between government policies.

An area of concern that is beginning to benefit from better communication and closer collaboration between agencies is youth offending. Indeed, multi-agency approaches, as advocated by ECM, were arguably piloted by youth offending teams (YOTs). There has been evidence of success in reducing both first time and repeat offending in areas where strong youth offending partnerships are active. These typically involve the police, community safety departments in local councils, youth services and the voluntary sector. Good youth holiday activity programmes have reduced offending in some areas and preventive approaches have been shown to reduce the numbers of first-time offenders steadily over time.

It is harder to evidence success at the sharp end of the offending spectrum. Gun and knife crime, often gang related, continues to take an inordinate toll on the lives of young black men in particular. This is an exceedingly difficult issue for schools, local authorities, the police, and their other partners. Though more effective and earlier approaches to meeting individual need may ultimately impact on the number of young people involved in a violent counter-culture, there is little evidence of impact at this stage.

Children's centres and extended schools are central to the development of Every Child Matters and have been key to developments in London. Children's centres provide early education and childcare, family support, employment advice, and health services, and aim to join up services to improve the life chances of young children. Originally targeting the most deprived areas, the government set a target in 2004 for a children's centre in every community. Much of the multi-agency work around early intervention is located in children's centres. The impact of this is beginning to register. Headteachers in one London borough report that extended parenting work programmes are already having an effect on children in the foundation stage. Elsewhere, formerly isolated parents have gained confidence from participating in children's centre programmes and now participate in their communities. Children's centre projects and programmes are major contributors to enhanced early years provision for some disadvantaged children.

Some authorities offer an outstanding range of health services through their children's centres. Having key health professionals on one site with other professionals makes it much easier for families and children to reach them. For instance, educational psychologists are able to work with parents locally and CAMHS has developed strong links with partners through work in the centres. Parents' feedback indicates that they feel they have better access to services and an increased sense of control. Some providers can now show that children in need are being identified at a much earlier stage as a result of work in children's centres. Other providers have successfully based work to reduce teenage conceptions and support teenage parents in children's centres.

With children's centres, as with much else associated with ECM, good partnership working is at the centre of progress. The OFSTED 2007 report on the inspection of children's services argued that 'strong partnerships are of pivotal importance – from strategic level to front-line working – in order to secure the necessary level of support and style of delivery that will have a positive impact on outcomes'(OFSTED 2007). In spite of the difficulties arising from reorganisations and financial deficits, partnerships with health in particular have borne fruit and underpin many of the improvements outlined above.

The development of extended services in schools was initiated in 2005, also as part of the Every Child Matters agenda. Government ambition is that by 2010 all schools will be offering extended services, including childcare, after school study support, leisure activities, business and enterprise activities, and parenting support, as discussed in the Essay 4 by Leaton Gray and Whitty in this book. Extended schools should be able to offer swift and easy referral to a wide range of specialist support services, and to offer wider community access to school facilities – including ICT, and sports and arts facilities. In 2007 OFSTED reported that 'full service extended schools were impacting positively on the attainment of their pupils – particularly those facing difficulties. They were also having a range of other impacts on outcomes for pupils, including engagement with learning, family stability and enhanced life chances' (OFSTED 2007). For vulnerable children in particular, the opportunity to access health, social care or youth service professional support through school improves the odds of good outcomes.

In London, progress on developing extended schools is good. Currently, 37 (32 per cent) of the 114 full service extended schools nationally are in London. Joint work between schools and health services on reducing obesity, promoting healthy eating and exercise is underway in several areas. In some areas good partnership working between the police, schools, and the wider community is helping to improve primary/secondary transition, to make for safer transport to and from school, and to manage drug and behaviour issues.

Other key parts of the ECM agenda are being introduced at varying rates and with varying degrees of success. London authorities are taking advantage of the move to children's services to think innovatively about a whole range of service issues. This is particularly the case with regard to aspects of their responsibilities where they know that outcomes have not been good in the past. Services for children with disabilities are a good example. Divided responsibilities, narrow and specialised roles, and poor communication between professionals in different sectors have often meant that these children have not had a good deal and that their parents have had a very hard time trying to persuade services to work together. A number of authorities are now setting up joint services for children and young people with disabilities. In one authority the disabled children's service has pooled resources from across the children's trust and offers an example of joint commissioning work leading to full integration.

## Some conclusions

The strong policy focus on London's children as a result of Every Child Matters has meant some progress and improvements. While the complex social issues and problems remain, the fact that they now have a high profile is a tribute to the way policy has developed in the last few years. There is no doubt that greater rigour is now being applied across the board to the planning, commissioning, delivery, and monitoring of services for children. The government and inspection agencies' focus on their ability to contribute to the five outcomes plays a large role in this. Similar pressure was brought to bear on schools rather earlier around the standards agenda with similar results. It is clear that greater rigour does lead to improvement. The issue of out-of-borough placements is a good example of an area where uncritical acceptance of historical practice has been replaced by detailed examination of policy and practice, leading to major change. The provision of services for children with disabilities is another.

Inspection and other evidence suggests that the new emphasis on listening to children and young people and acting on what they say is also beginning to contribute to services that are better fit for purpose. This aspect is still at an early stage of development but has significant potential for the future. Where universal services such as schools are concerned, it could be key to reducing disaffection and disengagement.

The ECM focus on disadvantaged groups, in particular looked after children, has opened up an area where scrutiny was long overdue. If unrelenting pressure from the centre continues to be exerted, there could be a major breakthrough in life chances for these and other neglected groups of children and young people.

However, there has to be a question about whether the ECM policy has got it right in relation to keeping the balance between universal, targeted, and highly targeted provision. While the policy was intended to be universal, the focus on targeted improvements in services for the vulnerable has, while seeing marked improvements in those services, perhaps meant a less strategic and holistic approach to a range of continuing intractable social issues.

New Labour governments since 1997 have had some considerable success at reducing poverty. Families with children in particular have seen gains through tax credits and child benefit which has had a marked impact on child poverty levels. Nevertheless child poverty remains a huge fact of life in London and is the single most significant factor impacting upon outcomes for children. For the poorest London boroughs and the schools with the highest numbers of children on free school meals (FSM), this is a sobering fact to face. Of course, as other essays in this book demonstrate, poor children in London can and do succeed dramatically in some places some of the time, but the effort required to make that happen is greater and the costs commensurate. On this, Every Child Matters has little to say that goes beyond exhortation.

Again, as discussed elsewhere in this book, there are marked differences in achievement between particular groups. The success that some authorities can evidence from developing and using targeted approaches specific to particular groups is far from universal. There are schools and authorities where such approaches have not yet been applied and where underachievement by settled diverse communities and the white working class has not been tackled in ways that work. Alongside that, there are the differing needs of new incoming groups. The London population is in constant flux and getting things right with personalised approaches for every child means developing a capacity to respond to changing need. It is not clear that ECM policy, with its broad focus on looked after children, children with disabilities, and underachieving groups, is sufficiently sophisticated to contribute to progress in the face of the complexities of London's shifting diversity.

In some of London's poor areas, particularly those where worklessness is the norm, aspirations are simply too low. This is a deep-rooted cultural issue requiring a sustained and unified approach across an area and there are few examples of well-developed strategies to tackle this. Many of the 'wicked issues' identified earlier in this essay are symptoms of this lack of aspiration. Teenage pregnancy, poor school attendance, and exclusion from school are all associated with low aspirations, as is failing to engage with education, training or employment post 16. Every Child Matters policy and practice is focused on response t4o individual need. Whether this focus can effect the necessary change in the wider cultural context that breeds low expectations is questionable.

There is also the vexed question of violent and gang related crime. This has a clear relationship to poverty and is located in a strong counter-culture. It is not surprising that the individually focused Every Child Matters policy offers no obvious short- or medium-term means to impact on this issue.

Finally, there is the question of context. Put starkly, London is a global city and national policy cannot control the globe. London housing markets reflect global developments. London's population shifts in response to world events. As people in the middle economic sector move out of London in search of affordable family housing, more poor people from diverse backgrounds move in. There is no stable state, and schools and other agencies remain fragile in consequence, endlessly engaged in the Sisyphean task of countering acute disadvantage and establishing stability and resilience as a basis on which individual children can start to build achievement.

In a city at the cutting edge of global change, ECM is necessary but not sufficient. It can strengthen the safety nets for those in danger of falling; it can identify potential problems early, move in and intervene in a way that counters disadvantage and secures better long-term prospects for the vulnerable;it can ensure that schools are not alone on the frontline in supporting vulnerable children. If it can secure the resources to work in a sustained way with those children in need who currently fall below the thresholds for intervention in many places, it could make a difference to their life chances. Its advocacy of involving children in shaping services could have a powerful impact. In schools for instance, if pupils are genuinely given the chance to help shape what and how they learn, there is real potential for re-engaging the disaffected and those who drop out.

But ECM has to operate in the wider cultural context. In London that context is complex, diverse, and fluid. Within it there are powerful competing subcultures. Whether it is black gangsta culture or fundamentalist religious ideologies, these counter-cultures are competing for the allegiance of London's children and young people.

That means not seeing ECM as a panacea but as part of the solution. It means sustaining the painstaking work of examining what is happening to individual children in schools and outside of schools, learning lessons from it and improving practice accordingly. It means continuing to improve schools and embed understanding of what works. Simultaneously it means ensuring an adequate understanding by teachers, social workers and other professionals of diverse cultures and behaviours, and how they impact on children and their learning.

It means all authorities and schools learning from successful practice in reducing underachievement by particular groups and putting the lessons into practice. It also means reaching out and working with communities and particular groups, engaging them through parent education or other means with the education of their children and raising their aspirations.

**References**

Department for Children, Schools and Families (2007) *Extended Schools: Building on Experience.* London: DCSF.

Department for Education and Skills (2003) *Every Child Matters.* London: The Stationery Office.

— (2007) *Care Matters: Time for Change*. London: The Stationery Office.

Department of Health (2004) *The National Service Framework for Children, Young People and Maternity Services.* London: DH.

Dobson, J., Henthorne,K., Lynas, Z. (2000) *Pupil Mobility in Schools – Final report.* London: UCL.

Greater London Authority (GLA) (2004a) *The State of London's Children Report*. London: GLA.

— (2004b) *Young Londoners' Survey*. London: GLA.

Government Office for London (2006) *Children in Care – The London picture*. London: GOL.

— ( 2007) *Where are we Now? Children's Services in London*. London: GOL.

Laming, Lord (2003) *The Victoria Climbié Inquiry Report*. London: The Stationery Office.

Learning and Skills Council (2007) *London Central Annual Plan*.

*London Bulletin* (2007) Issue 47. London: London Councils.

LSE (2007) *Population Mobility and Service Provision* London: LSE.

OFSTED (2006) *Improvements in London Schools 2000–2006*. London:OFSTED.

— ( 2007) *Narrowing the Gap: The inspection of children's services*. London: OFSTED.

Reed, J. and Robinson, P. (2005) 'From social mobility to equal life chances: maintaining the momentum'. In Pearce, N. and Paxton, W. (eds) *Social Justice: Building a fairer Britain*. London: Politico's.

Social Exclusion Unit (2003) *A Better Education for Children in Care*. London: Office of the Deputy Prime Minister.

The author has also made use of the Joint Area Reviews of Children's Services and Annual Performance Assessment letters to London boroughs issued by Ofsted.

# 6 The school workforce in London

Sara Bubb and Peter Earley

## Abstract

This essay focuses on the school workforce. It is about the people who work in London's 2,600 plus primary, secondary, and special schools. The workforce is crucial because it is the people in schools who make things happen; it is well known that staffing is not only the school's most expensive resource but also the most important resource. The need for a high-quality workforce and the importance of staff development and training cannot be underestimated. There is a growing recognition that the management and development of people – human resource management (HRM) and human resource development (HRD) – is more effective in enhancing the performance of organisations, including schools and colleges, than any other factor (Bubb and Earley 2007). This essay's main focus is on London's teachers – and particular attention is given at the end of the essay to an innovative scheme entitled the Chartered London Teacher (CLT) – but it is about other school workers too. The school workforce includes all those who work in schools, including teaching assistants, bursars, administrators, cleaners, playground assistants, and catering staff. After an introductory comment about working in London, this essay looks at some facts and figures about the school workforce before raising a number of key issues affecting London schools and all those who work in them. The essay concludes with some recommendations for policy makers. These centre on the school workforce – London's human resource – and its management (HRM) and development (HRD).

The scale of the educational challenge in London is unique within Europe. The city is dynamic and successful, both economically and culturally, and offers opportunities involving sports, culture, music, arts, museums, business, education, and government. However, it is a city of contrasts with extremes of wealth and deprivation – often in close geographical proximity. It has both higher than national average unemployment levels and, for those in work, higher overall earnings. People new to the country, such as economic migrants or those seeking asylum, tend to come to London. Twenty-eight per cent of pupils across London are known to be eligible for free school meals (FSM) (39 per cent in Inner, 20 per cent in Outer London). Half of pupils in Inner London speak English as a second language; there are over 300 first languages (DfES 2006).

Many schools are performing extremely well and add significant value, but there is a range of performance between schools and for groups of pupils (OFSTED 2006). Enabling every young person to achieve, no matter what their background, remains the number one challenge. The leadership and management of schools are important – which, as OFSTED notes, have improved more in London than elsewhere in the country (*ibid.*) – but London's teachers and support staff are vital in meeting this challenge.

The staffing of schools is a fundamental issue. It is often stated that the school's staff is its most important yet most expensive resource. How can children and young people learn without high-quality and committed staff? It is generally recognised that good staff make good schools, but schools too have a significant role in developing their workforce (Bubb and Earley 2007). In 2006, just over 1.2 million pupils attended schools in London (DfES 2007a). This was an increase of 14,000 pupils compared with 2002 and against the national trend. Approximately ten per cent of children across all key stages (126,000 in 2006) in London attend independent schools, which is well above the national average of seven per cent. With the independent sector competing for staff, how can the capital city attract even more teachers and support staff? So what do we know about the current school workforce in London?

## The school workforce in London: facts and figures

### *Teachers*

London has 63,600 (full-time equivalent) teachers, which is just over a sixth of all the (FTE) teachers in England (434,900). This represents an increase of 11 per cent since 1997 compared to only 8.1 per cent in England (DfES 2007a). London's teachers work in over 2,600 schools organised into 33 different local authorities without any overarching London body to unite them. The Inner London Education Authority (ILEA), abolished in 1990, had oversight of the Inner London boroughs.

Teacher recruitment, retention, mobility, experience, and quality present considerable challenges for London state schools. The DfES School Workforce Statistics (2006) show that teachers in London have less teaching experience than those in England as a whole: a fifth of Inner London teachers have less than three years' service and just over one-third (37 per cent) have less than six years' service (compared with 15 per cent and 29 per cent of teachers in England). Also, while only 3.8 per cent of 'teachers' in England and Wales are unqualified, in London 10.2 per cent are unqualified, and in some London boroughs the figure is over 17 per cent.

More London teachers than elsewhere are women under 40 (Hargreaves *et al.* 2007). Inner London has a young teaching workforce with nearly one-half of teachers under 40, compared to England as a whole (42 per cent). London schools have a higher teacher vacancy rate (1.2 per cent), exactly double that of the rest of the country (0.6 per cent). There are higher turnover and wastage rates for teachers in London (23 per cent and 12 per cent respectively) than England (19 per cent and 10 per cent). Nearly 40 per cent of teachers leaving schools in London are aged under 30 – much higher than the 25 per cent leaving nationally (DfES 2006). A significant number move into the burgeoning independent sector. Around two-thirds of the new independent schools in England opened since 2001 are in London (GLA 2005).

As might be expected given its composition, the percentage of teachers from black and minority ethnic groups (BME) is significantly greater in the London region (17.9 per cent) than the rest of England (5.4 per cent) and this percentage has increased from 17.4 per cent in 2006 (DfES 2007a). Data from a recent report on black teachers for the Mayor of London (2006) show that the highest percentages can be found in the boroughs of Hackney, Lambeth and Southwark (16–18 per cent), followed by Haringey and Brent (9 per cent). The highest proportions of teachers of black Caribbean origin are also in Hackney, Lambeth and Southwark (10 per cent), followed by Haringey and Brent (9 per cent). Lewisham schools have the highest proportion of teachers of black African origin (7 per cent). Westminster, Camden, Kensington and Chelsea, as well as the City of London, have a black teaching workforce of five per cent or less, yet each has a black pupil population of 20 per cent or more. However, despite the proportion of BME teachers working in London schools being more than three times the average for England, it still does not mirror the ethnic composition of the pupil population in our schools (see Essay 8 by McKenley).

London's schools also make considerable use of Overseas Trained Teachers (OTTs), although the exact number is not known. Regional statistics on initial teacher training from the (then) Teacher Training Agency (TTA 2004) show that in 2002–3 there were 471 trainees registered on the OTT programme in London. Over this period 93 achieved qualified teacher status (QTS) with the rest working towards the award. Two-thirds of the London OTTs were female and their average age was 33. However, it is not known how many OTTs are working in London's schools who are not registered for the award of QTS.

A survey of OTTs, commissioned by one of the teacher unions, found that most are located in Inner London schools (McNamara *et al.* 2004). Of the 277 schools involved in the research, 182 had employed 1,155 OTTs between September 2001 and March 2004. Three-quarters of the headteachers in the sample claimed they had recruited OTTs because no UK teachers were available at the time. The researchers also found that the majority of OTTs are female, under 30 years of age, primary trained, with about one-third having less than four years' teaching experience. Most came from the southern hemisphere: South Africa, Australia and New Zealand. Sixty per cent of the sample of OTTs had the status and salary of unqualified teachers.

Many OTTs are employed by agencies and engaged in supply teaching. Barlin and Hallgarten (2001) estimated that up to 4,000 supply teachers were deployed across London every day in 2000, although the exact proportion of such teachers who are OTTs is not known. Preston and Danby (2005) in their large-scale national survey of supply teachers found one-fifth were from overseas.

These statistics concerning overseas trained and supply teachers, along with the facts that about one in ten teachers in London is not qualified and that more than one in five pupils are taught by someone with less than three years' teaching experience, present their own challenges to London's state schools. The profile of teachers working in independent schools in London is not known.

Teach First, an innovative approach to training teachers for London secondary schools, was first set up in 2003. Teach First allows good graduates to work in challenging London schools for two years. It is specifically designed to attract people who would not otherwise have become teachers and there is a strong focus on recruiting teachers in subjects for which there is a shortage. Each year about 200 Teach First teachers experience a short training course after which they are allocated placements to teach in challenging schools in the Greater London area, where they teach a timetable equivalent to that of a newly qualified teacher (NQT). The scheme has been positively evaluated (Hutchings *et al.* 2005) and recently extended to Manchester (from September 2006) with expansion to other large English cities planned.

In part, Teach First has been a response to filling vacancies especially in subjects for which there is a shortage. This is a problem for London schools but vacancy rates have dropped from 3.5 per cent in 2001 to just one per cent in 2007. However, this is higher than the rest of England where it was one per cent in 2001 and is currently 0.5 per cent. The 2007 vacancy rates for the Inner and the Outer London weighting areas are 0.6 per cent and 0.2 per cent (nursery and primary), 0.9 per cent and 0.6

per cent (secondary), 2.7 per cent and 2.6 per cent (special) respectively (DfES 2007a).

Another group of London teachers that has grown in recent years is that of Advanced Skills Teachers (ASTs). There are 640 in post in London – 350 in secondary, 250 in primary and 40 in special schools (DfES 2007a). This represents a sixth of the national total of 4,045 ASTs. Launched in 1998, the Advanced Skills Teacher grade has introduced a new category of practitioner into maintained schools in England. All ASTs are assessed and judged to have satisfied a set of standards that describe an excellent classroom teacher. They are required to spend four days a week working in their own school and one day a week in other schools (outreach) to improve the practice of other teachers. Taylor and Jennings (2004) found that their potential was great but their actual impact was limited because of issues to do with deployment and support. The ASTs expressed 'at best a lukewarm level of satisfaction with the way in which their outreach work is managed'. This comment from an Inner London primary AST is not atypical:

> Since the day you awarded me AST status two and a half years ago, I have not been out anywhere to help anyone. The local authority has been awful at organising anything: it seems no one wants to take ownership of deploying ASTs. I am increasingly disenchanted.
>
> (Personal correspondence, 2007)

Whilst this is a national initiative, London also has its own CLT scheme (see later) and the London Commissioner's Teachers (DfES 2003). The latter consist of a small group of experienced ASTs who may be placed to work in London's most challenging schools.

### *Support staff*

The label 'support staff' includes all those people who undertake paid employment in schools, other than teachers and heads. Blatchford *et al.* (2006) have researched the impact of support staff and categorised them into seven groups:

1. TA equivalent (TA, learning support asssistant (SEN pupils), nursery nurse, therapist)
2. Pupil welfare (Connexions personal advisor, education welfare officer, home–school liaison officer, learning mentor, nurse and welfare assistant)
3. Technical and specialist staff (ICT network manager, ICT technician, librarian, science technician and technology technician)
4. Other pupil support (bilingual support officer, cover supervisor, escort, exam invigilator, language assistant, midday assistant and midday supervisor)
5. Facilities staff (cleaner, cook, and other catering staff)
6. Administrative staff (administrator/clerk, bursar, finance officer, office manager, secretary, attendance officer, data manager, examination officer, and PA to the headteacher)
7. Site staff (caretaker and premises manager).

Greater flexibility in school budgets and local management of schools (LMS) have meant the number and range of support staff working in schools have increased considerably over the last decade. The growth in the number of full-time equivalent support staff has outmatched the increase in teachers across the country. The total number of full-time equivalent support staff reached 305,500 in 2007: there were 162,900 teaching assistants; 65,900 administrative staff; 23,600 technicians; and 53,000 'other' support staff (DfES 2007a). Increases have occurred in both the number and type of responsibility and there is no reason to assume such growth in support staff will not equally be reflected in London's schools. For instance, 60 per cent of the workforce at Kemnal Manor, a specialist technology college for boys in Bromley, are support staff against a national average for secondary schools of approximately 24 per cent. This shift in staffing profile (including cover supervisors, lunch-time/break-time supervisors, lifestyle managers and administrative staff) has enabled teachers to focus more in the classroom on teaching and learning (www.tda.gov.uk/remodelling).

It is, however, interesting to consider the figures for Higher Level Teaching Assistants (HLTAs), a new form of support staff which has developed partly as a consequence of the government's remodelling agenda. The number of HLTAs in London is fewer than in other government regions but it is not clear why this is the case. Looked at as a proportion of the number of local authority pupils, the density is 0.67 in the capital, compared to 1.9 in the north east and 1.42 in the country as a whole (DfES 2007a). Teacher unions, possibly stronger in London than in other parts of the country, are largely against non-teachers covering for absent teachers, and this may offer a partial explanation for this relatively low uptake in HLTAs.

## School workforce issues

The above facts and figures, especially those concerning the greater use of overseas trained and supply teachers, the number of unqualified teachers, their limited experience and their teaching in non-specialist areas, present their own set of challenges to London schools. In this section we consider a number of workforce issues that apply particularly to London schools, including a) recruitment and retention, and b) the workplace, wellbeing and morale. We begin with an area that has always presented challenges for some London schools – obtaining staff and keeping them!

### *Recruitment and retention*

London suffers the most in terms of teacher shortages and although the number of vacant teacher posts has fallen recently there are about twice as many temporary posts in London than nationally. Even when vacancies are filled, OFSTED has found that staff are significantly less likely to be specialists in the subjects they teach in London than across the country (HMI 2003).

Teacher retention and turnover remain an issue for many London schools, especially those facing challenging circumstances or under notice to improve. Tim Brighouse vividly highlights the effects of variations in teacher turnover when he says:

> This can mean [that] a youngster, during the course of a five-year stay from Year 7 to Year 11 in an average sized challenging school, encountering ten times as many new teachers as more fortunate colleagues in schools further up the pecking order.
>
> (Bush 2005: vii)

Smithers and Robinson (2005: 5) state that the teaching profession is losing many of its members to 'unavoidable teacher loss due to retirement, change of profession, issues of salary, promotion and job security, etc', whilst the extent of teacher shortages in London means that some schools are 'losing 40 per cent of their teachers every year as more staff take early retirement. In one London primary school, the staff turnover was 200 per cent, meaning some teachers did not complete a year (2005: 5).

It is not uncommon in the most difficult-to-staff schools for school pupils to start the school year with one set of staff and end it with another. As Brighouse notes, 'while some of the senior teachers and those in the management team may stay for a while, the remainder of their teaching staff are often "here today and gone tomorrow"' (in Bush 2005: vii).

The earlier research of Hutchings (1999) and her colleagues (Hutchings *et al.* 1999) into teacher supply and retention in London found that the main reasons for teachers leaving their current posts or the teaching profession centred around three key factors: unruly pupil behaviour and ill-discipline; poor school leadership and management; and the demands of a heavy workload. Whilst efforts are being made to address the latter factors through, for example, the remodelling agenda and the leadership strategy of the London Challenge (Earley and Weindling *et al.* 2005), the issue of pupil behaviour remains. It should not, however, be seen only as a London issue: in a survey of over 800 teachers, 99 per cent have dealt with disruptive pupils in class, and over a third have faced physical aggression. These frequent disruptions in the classroom have made over half of the respondents think about leaving teaching and 54 per cent know someone who has left teaching as a result of pupil behaviour (ATL 2007). Schools with low attainment are often perceived to have behaviour challenges. Some teachers actively seek to work in these schools but many wish to avoid them.

The cost of housing continues to be a factor in the retention of teachers. Already by far the most expensive place to buy a house in Britain, between 2006 and 2007 house prices in London rose by another 16.3 per cent – the greatest leap in the UK. According to the Land Registry, an average home in the borough of Kensington and Chelsea cost £677,318 in 2006 – an increase of £95,000 on the previous year. In Hull, the average home costs £84,700 (Frankel 2007).

Attempts to help teachers afford to live in the capital have been successful but demand is high and further resources needed. The key worker living programme was introduced in 2004, and helped almost 5,000 teachers by giving interest-free loans of up to £100,000, although the more typical loan was £50,000. Between 2004–6, the scheme was allocated £725 million, much more than the £400 million ring-fenced for 2006–8. The Open Market HomeBuy scheme enables people to buy 75 per cent of a property, with an equity loan from the government and a lender covering the rest of the cost. The shared ownership schemes allow teachers to own a minimum 35 per cent share in a property while paying subsidised rent on the rest. On a salary of £29,000, a Hackney teacher was able to buy half of a new one-bedroom flat in Clacton for £105,000. She pays £330 a month in rent to the housing association and £500 a month in mortgage repayments (*ibid.*).

School leadership turnover is an issue too – the pool of potential leaders is diminished because many teachers do not stay in London in the long term. The Department for Children, Schools and Families

(DCSF) and National College for School Leadership (NCSL) are targeting London leaders through such schemes as Future Leaders, currently only found in London secondary schools. Teachers on this scheme are supported for two years; after spending a year in a residency school they are expected to secure a senior leader post in a 'complex urban school' and become a headteacher of such a school within four years (NCSL 2006).

Another issue concerning the leadership of London schools and which is related to staff recruitment and retention is the rapid promotion that individuals can achieve. Some teachers have been asked to take on major responsibilities at a very early stage in their careers: for example, a secondary teacher becoming head of a major department in only their second year and an NQT taking up responsibility for the co-ordination of staff development in their primary school. Is the increase in pay and status worth the stress and risk of burnout placed on individuals with such limited experience? The effects on London schools of such young inexperienced people taking on such key posts is not known, although OFSTED's report on London is very positive about recent improvements made both in terms of school performance and school leadership (OFSTED 2006).

## *Workplace, wellbeing and morale*

The workplace, staff wellbeing and morale are vital to retention. Cockburn and Haydn (2004) remind us of the 'soft' factors that can be influential in retaining people: 'friendly colleagues', 'pleasant surroundings', 'intellectual challenge', 'freedom', 'scope for creativity', and 'room for initiative'. A series of surveys of London teachers commissioned by the London Challenge suggests that teachers feel positive about their work and their workplace, with almost two-thirds recommending their school to their friends or their children (DfES 2004). However, the same research found that less than half of teachers reported that teacher morale was high. Factors influencing the choice of London school in which to work were varied but included good working conditions, travel to work distance, and being in a location that enables teachers to meet family (own children and schooling) responsibilities. Factors that may be important but are rarely noted include commuting and safety in travelling to/from school (the fear factor), the availability of parking and of course the Congestion Charge which cost £8 a day in 2007.

The study of the views of London teachers and students conducted by the National Foundation for Educational Research (NFER) for the London Challenge (Wilson *et al.* 2007) provides a very positive picture of London teachers' morale and motivation. However, on closer examination of their response rates it is not clear how many of their survey respondents were from challenging schools. Schools in challenging circumstances and under pressure to improve very often give the completion of questionnaires a low priority!

The Institute of Public Policy Research (IPPR) report for the (then) DfES (2005) – a small-scale qualitative study of teachers working in challenging schools in and outside of London – refers to 'push and pull' factors with regard to what motivates teachers to work in particular schools. These are summarised below:

- Good leadership and a strong, supportive senior leadership
- Support for learning and development, teaching assistants (TAs), learning mentors, and so on
- Effective systems for dealing with poor behaviour
- Support at the school level for teachers to learn how to deal with difficult behaviour
- Good atmosphere and supportive colleagues
- Opportunities for professional dialogue
- Teamworking and good departments
- Good working conditions, the physical state of the school, and resources (staff and equipment)
- Additional classroom support

- Class size
- Opportunities for professional development.

The IPPR study also pointed to the importance of good pay for motivation and morale, noting that teachers in London were least likely to feel positive about their pay and perceived increases in future salary and responsibility.

Pay and budgets are very important and people may require incentives to work in the most difficult schools. Working in challenging schools, of which London has many, is very demanding and requires stamina and resilience, more so than in other schools. The VITAE report found that teachers in challenging schools were more likely to experience greater challenges to their health, wellbeing, and thus resilience, than those who work in relatively more advantaged schools (Day *et al.* 2006). While commitment levels did not differ, the consequences for personal health certainly did: in more disadvantaged secondary schools, 63 per cent of teachers reported ill-health compared to 42 per cent in more advantaged areas (Stobart 2007).

Moynihan (2007) has argued the need for government deregulation of teacher salaries and a funding regime that is more closely targeted to the needs of the school. Such changes, he suggests, would give school leaders the flexibility they need to ensure that the most difficult schools to teach in had the most capable teachers and leaders. However, Bush (2005) is adamant that increasing pay would not resolve the problems associated with teaching in the most difficult schools, arguing that 'teachers' pay has risen significantly and schools already have the flexibility to use additional pay as a recruitment incentive' (2005: xiii). For her, teachers' terms and conditions are just as important as pay yet 'the demand for "accountability" puts teachers in more challenging schools under a difficult amount of pressure' (*ibid.*).

School staff want to feel valued and appreciate clear investments in training and development. However, the IPPR research found that teachers within London were less satisfied that their professional development and career progression needs were being met than were those teachers working in challenging schools outside of London. The Training and Development Agency (TDA) defines staff development as 'reflective activity designed to improve an individual's attributes, knowledge, understanding and skills. It supports individual needs and improves professional practice' (2007). But for us staff development is:

> an on-going process encompassing all formal and informal learning experiences that enable all staff in schools, individually and with others, to think about what they are doing, enhance their knowledge and skills and improve ways of working so that pupil learning and well-being is enhanced as a result. It should achieve a balance between individual, group, school and national needs; encourage a commitment to professional and personal growth; and increase resilience, self-confidence, job satisfaction and enthusiasm for working with children and colleagues.
>
> (Bubb and Earley 2007: 4)

It is about creating opportunities for adult learning – and not just teachers, which is why we prefer not to use the term 'professional' – ultimately for the purpose of enhancing the quality of education in the classroom.

Vivienne Porritt has been working as the Continuing Professional Development (CPD) consultant for London Challenge and helped school practitioners in London's local authorities to work together to develop *London's Learning*, a CD-ROM and web-based and community resource about staff learning at www.cpd.lgfl.net. The training and development cycle consists of six stages. The first two stages are the identification of needs and their analysis, taking into account what people already know and can do. The next challenge is to find the best way to meet needs: the range of activities is huge. The final stages in the cycle – monitoring and evaluating the impact of development and training – are neglected areas. Monitoring is concerned with checking progress, seeing that things are going according to plan and making alterations if necessary. Gauging the impact or evaluating its effectiveness on teaching and learning – the sixth and last stage in the staff development cycle – is more difficult but vital to staff in London schools.

The Chartered London Teacher (CLT) initiative provides a helpful framework for teachers' professional development.

## *Chartered London Teacher status*

Chartered London Teacher (CLT) status is a unique scheme which London Challenge set up in September 2004 to recognise and reward teachers' achievements and provide a framework for professional development. As well as having the prestige of being a CLT for life, when people obtain the award they get a one-off payment of £1,000 from the school budget and Fellowship of the College of Teachers, the body that manages the registration and award process.

Achieving CLT status takes at least two years after registration. People have to have taught in London for at least four years and be on the upper, advanced skills teacher or leadership pay scales by the time they get the award. They have to show how their knowledge, skills, and expertise have a positive impact on teaching and learning across the 12 CLT standards and complete a Professional Reflection. Diversity, communities, and cultures are important issues for urban teachers so, for instance, Standard 10 requires them to 'Build on, extend and apply knowledge of the range of communities, cultures and sub-cultures in London, to inform and promote individual pupils' learning' (DfES 2007b). The CLT Professional Reflection requires reflection on a specific activity or piece of work carried out or led by the teacher, one that makes a difference, in that it contributes to improved teaching and learning.

Because teachers work towards CLT as part of their day-to-day work and through their schools' performance management and professional development arrangements, the scheme has captured the interest of many. The numbers registered rose from 5,000 in July 2005 to 10,000 in February 2006 to 38,000 six weeks later, at the end of March 2006. By the end of July 2007, there were 38,800 people registered and 188 had gained the status. Thus, two out of three London teachers are registered for CLT: this is three-quarters of secondary, two-thirds of special school and one-half of primary teachers. Some boroughs have embraced CLT more than others. Four out of every five teachers are registered in Bromley, Harrow, Richmond and Kingston, but in Westminster and Waltham Forest the proportion is only one in three (Bubb and Porritt 2006).

The scheme has also the backing of unions, because as Mary Bousted says:

> ATL welcomes the Chartered London Teacher status, as we are in favour of any move which will assist the recruitment and retention of teachers in London. This will be especially important in the decade to come, as London will be one of the very few areas of the country to experience rising school rolls.
>
> (Bousted 2004)

The scheme has the potential to change the culture of teaching and raise the bar of professionalism. Working towards CLT status will help teachers to be more effective in two ways. First, the CLT standards require teachers to be highly effective in key areas that link to the government's priorities, such as cultural diversity, personalised learning, student voice, improving behaviour and the Every Child Matters agenda. Second, there will be a substantial pool of teachers with the status who can support the development of others, and so reduce variation in the quality of teaching and learning within and between schools in London.

CLT has the potential to be both a conduit and driver for knowledge transfer, particularly around the standards relating to diversity, communities and cultures. London teachers will have more incentive to work together on projects that impact on standards: learning from each other through observation and coaching as well as evaluating the impact of professional development. A virtual learning environment has been set up at www.lcll.org.uk to help. Although CLT is a status and not a qualification, working towards it will be an incentive for teachers to gain further qualifications. For instance, teachers whose PGCE carries M level credits will find that completing a Master's fits in well with CLT.

The unique feature of CLT is its potential to unify the profession in that it is for all sorts of London's teachers, so in many schools newly qualified, experienced teachers and headteachers are now working to achieve the same standards. CLT sits within the standards framework so it is a universal career development option for London. It is also a way of building a coherent approach to an individual teacher's professional development and needs to be integrated with a school's process of professional review. This will help teachers to develop and demonstrate the skills needed to meet the 12 CLT standards and is a powerful way to link career and professional development to professional review and school improvement.

In many London schools all the teachers are registered so the CLT standards and structure are becoming fundamental to professional development and collaboration, and aid the development of professional learning communities. CLT status not only offers opportunities for individual teachers but also schools and clusters of schools. Local authorities can be the umbrella that brings all the many organisations and networks together to create a shared picture of effective professional development that meets the needs of teachers in schools. London Challenge has set up a wide range of physical and virtual networks:

- CLT e-community
- Local authority CPD Advisers
- Primary and Secondary Training School networks
- A CPD partnership of strategic organisations such as the General Teaching Council, Training and Development Agency, Specialist Schools and Academies Trust, and the National Strategies
- London Science Challenge and London Maths Challenge
- Leading London's Learning, a pan-London CPD leaders group
- London Gifted and Talented networks
- AST network.

This infrastructure has been built over the last few years in London so that the many pieces of the CPD jigsaw become more joined up and, by working together, each can achieve more than the sum of the parts. However, building the infrastructure does not mean that exchange of practice and learning across London will happen. Indeed, there is anecdotal evidence that some schools are not providing sufficient encouragement to teachers who are keen to work towards achieving the status. There is much for these CPD networks to achieve to maximise the impact of professional development to bring about the changes inherent in the current landscape and to achieve further improvement (Bubb and Porritt 2006).

The scheme is well placed to take forward the notion of New Professionalism. It will be a missed opportunity if London schools do not take full advantage of CLT and the other initiatives noted above. The new performance management guidelines and professional standards for different stages of a teacher's career should be levers for – and be driven by – CLT. Key messages can be given about the importance of linking professional development with performance management, self-evaluation and school improvement. The judgements of headteachers and performance reviewers will need to be robust as well as transparent, and the moderation of CLT standards will drive more discussion about the quality of teaching within and across schools.

The chance to achieve CLT status will hopefully encourage teachers to start their careers in London state schools (the percentage starting in London of all newly trained teachers dropped from 18.3 per cent in 1998–9 to 13.6 per cent in 2002–3 [Bubb and Porritt 2006]). It should also encourage the one in ten teachers in London who is not qualified to gain qualified teacher status, and so improve the quality of teaching in subjects for which there is a shortage. The opportunity of CLT status will be an incentive to stay in London state schools because achieving it takes from around two to six years and carries with it a one-off payment of £1,000. But most of all, CLT status needs to be something worth working towards and achieving, something that recognises the achievement of teachers succeeding against the odds and raises esteem. Building and maintaining the prestige of CLT will be vital over the next few years.

## Conclusion and recommendations

> The most important factor in raising levels of attainment in schools facing challenging circumstances is a high quality, stable workforce, backed up by good leaders.
>
> (DfES 2005: 8)

This essay has argued the need for a high-quality workforce and has stressed the importance of effective staff development and training. As the above quote states, there is a need for good leadership and management of the workforce (HRM), which includes a concern for their training and development (HRD). This is more effective in enhancing the performance of schools and colleges than any other factor (Bubb and Earley 2007).

Members of the school workforce in London, especially those working in our most challenging schools, should be given the highest respect and rewarded accordingly. There is a need to revisit and reappraise existing policies aimed at recruiting and retaining high-quality staff in London's schools. There needs to be greater recognition of the fact that a school is only as good as the quality of its workforce – but especially its teachers. London has often been seen as the best place to work and some teachers make a positive decision to work in challenging inner-city schools. For the benefit of London's children we need to ensure, however, that teaching in London remains an attractive and appealing option for our most able staff.

This essay has examined a number of key issues affecting London schools and those who work in them. We conclude with a set of recommendations for policy makers that follow from the main themes outlined in this essay. These recommendations centre on the school workforce – London's human resource – and its management (HRM) and development (HRD).

In terms of HRM we recommend that first of all there should be a funding regime that is more closely targeted to the needs of the school. Additionally, complex urban schools and those facing challenging circumstances should have a greater flexibility in controlling budgets to enable higher pay for staff. Increased levels of subsidised housing and public transport should result in increased teacher retention in the capital, which is one of key London issues.

Further recognition of the 'push and pull' factors in staff recruitment and retention needs to focus on issues around the quality of school leadership and management, student behaviour and staff well-being (stress, workload, resilience). Factors leading to low staff morale and job satisfaction, such as lack of support and recognition or inadequate resources, need addressing. With regard to schools in challenging circumstances and under 'notice to improve', there needs to be more recognition of the fact that individuals' performance is under much greater scrutiny.

Our recommendations for HRD focus on ensuring that the range of training and development on offer meets the needs of all members of the school workforce and inclusion of all staff within performance management systems and individualised CPD. Support networks, both formal and informal, should be developed (e.g. time to work with colleagues, specific support for dealing with behaviour issues).

With regard to specific groups of staff, Advanced Skills Teachers should be deployed more strategically and have access to better support and professional development to maximise their effectiveness. Co-ordination at local authority level needs to be improved, but a London-wide system of sharing information and for deploying ASTs across boroughs would be beneficial at many levels. Overseas trained teachers should be encouraged to gain QTS as soon as possible and have access to professional development based on an accurate analysis of their strengths and needs. Other members of the school community should be able to benefit from their strengths, experiences, and knowledge. The potential value of achieving CLT status should be promoted and, having registered their teachers, schools should be encouraged to help their staff achieve it.

Finally, all schools in London should be encouraged to take part in initial teacher training in recognition of the benefits it gives.

**References**

Association of Teachers and Lecturers (2007) 'Bad behaviour by pupils is rampant and teachers are voting with their feet – ATL survey'. Press release, April 2007 (see ATL website).

Barlin, D. and Hallgarten, J. (2001) *Supply Teachers: Symptom of the problems or part of the solution?* London: Institute of Public Policy Research.

Blatchford, P., Bassett, P., Brown, P., Martin, C., Russell, A., Webster, R. and Haywood, N. (2006) *The Deployment and Impact of Support Staff in Schools,* RR776. London: DfES.

Bousted, M. (2004) Comment on E-politix *Forum Brief: Teachers' Pay.* <http://www.epolitix.com/EN/ForumBriefs/200403/365b0d76–3993–4565-a97e-0ef61d0c388b.htm>

Bubb, S. and Earley, P. (2007) *Leading and Managing Continuing Professional Development: Developing people, developing schools* (2nd edn). London: Sage.

Bubb, S. and Porritt, V. (2006) 'Recognising and nurturing urban teachers: Chartered London Teacher status'. Paper presented at BELMAS Conference, Aston, 6–8 October.

Bush, A. (2005) *Choice and Equity in Teacher Supply.* London: Institute of Public Policy Research.

Cockburn, A. and Haydn, T. (2004) *Recruiting and Retaining Teachers: Understanding why teachers teach.* London: RoutledgeFalmer.

Day, C., Stobart, G., Sammons, P., Kington, A., Gu, Q. and Mujtaba, T. (2006) *Variations in Teachers' Work, Lives and Effectiveness.* RR 743. London: DfES.

Department for Education and Skills (DfES) (2003) *The London Challenge: Transforming London secondary schools.* London: DfES.

— (2004) *London Challenge: Survey of pupils and teachers.* Research Report 643. London: DfES.

— (2005) *Why Here? Report Of The Qualitative Work with Teachers Working in Schools Above and Below Floor Targets.* Research Report 666. London: DfES and IPPR.

— (2006) *School Workforce in England.* London: DfES.

— (2007a) *School Workforce in England.* London: DfES.

— (2007b) *Chartered London Teacher Guidance.* London: DfES.

Earley, P. and Weindling, D. with Bubb, S., Coleman, M., Crawford, M., Evans, J., Pocklington, K. and Woodroffe, L. (2005) *An Evaluation of the Leadership Strategy of the London Challenge*. London: Institute of Education.

Frankel, H. (2007) 'Far from home'. *Times Educational Supplement*, 4 May.

Greater London Authority (GLA) (2005) *Statistics of Schools in London: Key facts 2001–2005.* London: GLA.

Hargreaves, L., Cunningham, M., Hansen, A., McIntyre D., Oliver, C., and Pell, T. (2007) *The Status of Teachers and the Teaching Profession: views from inside and outside the profession*. Research Report 831A. London: DfES.

Her Majesty's Inspectorate (HMI) (2003) *Schools' Use of Temporary Teachers.* London: Government Printing Office.

Hutchings, M. (1999) *Teacher Supply and Retention in London 1998–1999.* London: Teacher Training Agency, University of North London.

Hutchings, M., Maylor, U., Mendick, H., Menter, I.and Smart, S. (2005) *An Evaluation of Innovative Approaches to Teacher Training on the Teach First Programme.* London: IPSE.

Hutchings, M., Menter, I., Ross, A. and Thomson, D. (1999) *Teacher Supply and Retention Project.* London: Institute for Policy Studies in Education, University of North London.

McNamara, O., Lewis, S. and Howson, J. (2004) *The Recruitment of OTTs.* Birmingham: NASUWT.

Mayor of London (2006) *Black Teachers in London.* London: GLA.

Moynihan, D. (2007) 'Headteachers can and do make a difference'. In O'Shaughnessy, J. (ed.) *The Leadership Effect.* London: Policy Exchange.

National College for School Leadership (NCSL) (2006) *Future Leaders*, www.ncsl.org.uk.

OFSTED (2006) *Improvements in London schools 2000–06*, www.ofsted.gov.uk.

Preston, C. and Danby, M. (2005) *Who are the Supply Teachers?* London: MirandaNet & Select Education.

Smithers, A. and Robinson, P. (2005) *Teacher Turnover, Wastage and Movements Between Schools.* London: DfES.

Stobart, G. (2007) *Teachers' Work, Lives and Effectiveness over Time – the VITAE project.* INSI Research Matters No. 30. London: Institute of Education.

Taylor, C. and Jennings, S. (2004) *The Work of Advanced Skills Teachers.* Reading: CfBT.

Teacher Training Agency (2004) *Regional Report – ITT in London.* (Available on website).

Training and Development Agency for Schools (2007) *Continuing Professional Development: A strategy for teachers.* London: TDA.

Wilson, S., Benton, T., Scott, E. and Kendall, L. (2007) *London Challenge: Survey of pupils and teachers 2006.* RR 823. London: DfES.

# 7 Reconfiguring urban leadership: some lessons from London

Hilary Emery and Kathryn Riley

## Introduction

Cities today are linked by global trends: the information and communications revolution; population movements (tourists, migrants, immigrants, refugees); global disasters, as well as worldwide sporting events. This essay draws on London and sets out to contribute to the wider educational debate about urban education in three ways:

- First, by describing the context for school leadership in London, illustrating the challenges and opportunities of this cosmopolitan city.
- Second, by analysing and drawing lessons from the impact of a range of London-based leadership strategies designed to develop the capacity of London's school leaders.
- Finally, by highlighting the qualities of urban leaders, illustrating the tasks and broader community challenges of urban leadership.

City schools have always faced challenges. Over recent years, however, the demands, pressures and expectations on the leaders of our city schools have increased exponentially. With these mounting challenges, a growing international concern has emerged about standards in urban schools, the attainment of disadvantaged young people, and the achievement gaps in school systems.[1] Reviewing the UK evidence, David Bell[2] concluded that, despite improvements, there was an urgent need 'to close the gap in achievement' between youngsters in the most deprived areas and other young people (Bell 2003).[3] Leadership has come to be viewed as an important vehicle for closing that gap.[4]

## Leading in London

### *The challenges and opportunities of the city*

London is a city with a rich historical legacy, unparalleled resources and contrasts. There are extremes of wealth and poverty, often in close geographical proximity (Lupton and Sullivan, Essay 1). It is a fast moving, ethnically diverse city, embracing 33 boroughs, each with its own features, distinctive but overlapping communities, and separate political administrations.[5] Geography and history combine to shape the context for leadership in London. Impoverished downtown areas can become gentrified in relatively short periods of time, as new populations move in and out. At the turn of the twentieth century, London's East End locals clashed with Irish and Jewish immigrants to find work in the docks. At the beginning of the twenty-first century, London's docks have declined and the Thames is for tourist launches rather than cargo boats to distant lands. London's East End is now home to many Bengali people, and other immigrants from across the globe, as well as predominantly white working class communities who have lived there for many generations.[6]

Hounslow,[7] for example, is in close proximity to Heathrow Airport, and this has a significant impact on the flow of populations and communities. One in eight pupils in one Hounslow secondary school visited as part of a review of the leadership of London schools is a refugee or an asylum seeker (Riley and West-Burnham 2004). Many Hounslow families are closely tied to the airport by employment, and children expect transience as parents return to their country of origin, or relatives are granted or denied residence. Planes flying low overhead are a constant reminder of movement and travel, uncertainty and opportunity.

The way in which school leaders respond to the local context, and to the needs and aspirations of communities is, in its turn, governed by underlying values and beliefs, the nature of society, or what young people can achieve. Undoubtedly, leadership is a profoundly value-laden activity (Begley and Johansson 2003; Furman 2003; Burns 1978; Riley *et al.* 2004; West-Burnham 2002). In the next section of the essay, we explore the challenges and opportunities of leadership in London and how these values play out.

## *The challenges and opportunities of leadership*

The cultural and community diversity of many London schools is often a source of great strength. Three out of four secondary school students in London's 13 Inner London boroughs are classified as of minority ethnic origin.[8] Schools reap the benefits of the multiplicity in our societies: the creativity, energy, resilience and exuberance of the children; and the rich cultural understanding and experiences of their parents. School leaders enjoy the buzz of London and relish the vibrancy of the city and the availability of museums, theatres, and concert halls, all of which enable teachers to show their pupils 'the very best there is'.[9] Being a London school leader can be 'addictive'. The rewards are significant:

> When you support families, and the kids do well, then you know you have been more influential than you would be elsewhere. I have been a secondary head for 13 years, but I am still caught up with the excitement of London. There is so much you can do educationally.
>
> (Riley and West-Burnham 2004: 11)

Equally too, the challenges are considerable: poverty and mental health problems, community tensions in some parts of London, which can generate gang culture, drugs, street crime, violence, and dysfunctional families. There are specific locality-based challenges, including what headteachers have described as 'a white underclass' of girls and boys with very low expectations, high levels of disaffection from society and 'a dismissive attitude towards learning' which makes it difficult for schools 'to maintain a culture of learning' (Riley and West-Burnham 2004: 12). Grace (2006) draws attention to the race, class, and gender contradictions of urban education. He points to the challenges that schools face in striving to encourage working-class girls to realise their potential; in persuading working-class boys that, with the changes in the labour market – particularly the decline of the UK's manufacturing base – employers require a more skilled workforce; and in tackling the underachievement of black Caribbean pupils, particularly boys.[10]

Complex social factors can lead to disciplinary problems and racism. There are issues of Islamophobia and tensions between established immigrant community groups and more recently arrived communities that are heightened by international terrorism, including the 2005 London bombings. Headteachers may find themselves centre stage, struggling to reconcile different faiths and beliefs. In the following extract, a headteacher involved in an urban leadership project covering a number of UK cities describes her sense of being caught between different cultural expectations and generational demands:[11]

> Even when you think you've got absolutely everything sorted, you're faced with a petition, people coming to your door, outside the school leafleting about you. And it just happens so quickly, and out of the blue. We do make allowances for Muslim dress, it's been happening for years, why now? And it's to do with Fundamentalist issues outside the school and whispers ...
>
> There is also the dilemma of respecting the community and understanding that you have to support your students ... So on the one hand you've got to respect their culture, on the other hand I've got to support my (students) and what's best for them as individuals. And that's really hard sometimes. There's nobody to give you advice. You just have to go with your conscience.
>
> (Riley *et al.*, 2004)

The sense of isolation described in this extract is not unusual. Many leaders of London's most challenging schools operate as the interface between those sections of the community that feel disempowered and a range of public institutions (see Louis 2003 for a comparable US analysis). One headteacher captured the London experience in the following terms:

> We are asked to go with families to the Housing Office, or to get them registered with a GP (General Practitioner). Where people feel disempowered, they go for help to the most available people in authority, and that means us. Because we smile at them at the beginning of the day, they hope that we can help with all their wider problems.
>
> (Riley and West-Burnham 2004: 15)

In some parts of London, there is high pupil mobility which can challenge teachers' skills and energy. Staff morale can be fragile and a key challenge for urban leaders is to manage the emotions and reactions of their staff.[12] A transient pupil population is frequently matched by a transient teacher population. London's teaching force is younger than the national average, with a drift away from London schools as teachers reach their late 30s (GTC 2006). But mobility also has its compensations. London's teaching force is a rich international mixture, and while the youngsters who arrive from war-torn countries can be demanding of time, many of these displaced young people are highly motivated to succeed.

Nevertheless, instability is a central element of what makes London unique in the British educational system. The diversity of pupils and communities, and most importantly, the pace at which they change, is more marked that in any other British city. Leading in London can come to feel akin to being in charge of the repainting of the Forth Bridge in Scotland: a relentless endeavour in which nothing ever appears to be fully sorted. Unsurprisingly, London headteachers see themselves as expert jugglers, keeping ahead of the next crisis, having to make quick decisions and 'spinning plates all the time to keep them in the air'. The personal toll can be high, not only in terms of hours worked but also in terms of families and relationships:

> My life-work balance is horrendous. I am a single mother with a 15-year-old daughter. My social life is sparse, my house is falling down. Our recent bid for {Specialist} College status wiped out 18 months of my life, every week-end, every half-term. I often wake at four in the morning, rehearsing what I will have to do the next day.
>
> (Riley and West-Burnham 2004: 17)

And yet, as another headteacher concluded:

> It's the best job in the world. We are talking about the challenges, but it gives us great pleasure to be able to manage them. (*Ibid*: 14).

## Change strategies for London

Over the last decade there have been a number of policy initiatives that have had an impact on the leadership of London's schools. Most have been national developments targeted at areas of significant deprivation and underperformance, in London and elsewhere. These have included community-focused initiatives (e.g. Neighbourhood Renewal), as well as specific education initiatives: for example, Excellence in Cities (EiC), and Education Action Zones (EAZ).[13] Evaluating the management and impact of EiC and EAZs, the Office for Standards in Education (OFSTED) identified the centrality of leadership to improvement; if schools were to make the optimum use of the funding, then effective leadership was needed to 'create a climate and structure' conducive to change (OFSTED 2004: 70).

Nevertheless, despite these interventions, a political concern that standards in London were not improving fast enough remained and in 2003, a specific London programme – the London Challenge – was introduced (see Essay 3, Brighouse). A key component of the London Challenge was its emphasis on leadership and management.[14] The DfES established a London Leadership Strategy and located it within the

National College for School Leadership (NCSL) and the London Leadership Centre at the Institute of Education, University of London, became a partner institution (DfES 2003).[15]

### *The leadership agenda*

Underpinning the London Challenge was a strong commitment to leadership development through the designated London Leadership Strategy. London headteachers were drafted in to develop this and to lead aspects of its implementation. Successful headteachers were encouraged to analyse their own needs, innovate, and experiment, and draw on the strands and resources of the Challenge. There was a strong emphasis on collaboration among schools, and a raft of leadership development opportunities were put in place for staff at various stages of their careers. A range of organisations were commissioned to undertake leadership development.[16]

'Investing in Diversity' has been one such innovative programmes, designed to increase the confidence and competence of middle and senior leaders from black and minority ethnic backgrounds, i.e. black and global majority leaders.[17] By 2007, more than 600 school leaders had been through the programme. Investing in Diversity has a strong moral and ethical foundation and encourages participants to locate themselves as black and global majority school leaders, as opposed to leaders who happen to be black (Riley and Campbell-Stephens 2007). It is making a significant impact on the goal of appointing school leaders who reflect London's racial and ethnic diversity. As many as a third of each cohort gained promotion by the end of their one-year course (Earley *et al.* 2005).

The London Challenge team also promoted the development of a model for urban leadership based around nine characteristics of urban leaders (NCSL 2005). Assessment centres were used to enable participants to gauge their progress and development needs. However, a review of the model found that, while commendable in principle, it was not well suited to reconciling assessment and development. The centres identified potential and could help in selection and recruitment, but did not support leadership development (Matthews *et al.* 2006).[18]

## *Fresh challenges*

The demands on leaders of schools in London did not stand still while the London Challenge was being developed. Other national strategies developed by successive Labour governments came on stream. Of particular relevance to leadership and policy development in urban education were the School Workforce Agreement; the development of extended schools; and the spread of academies.

Responding to rising concerns about teacher workloads, the government introduced the School Workforce Agreement.[19] The Agreement (set up within the framework of a social partnership of employers, unions, and government) provided all teachers with ten per cent planning, preparation, and assessment time and introduced dedicated headship, leadership, and management time for school leaders.[20]

A National Remodelling Team (NRT) was established within the NCSL to lead the change management and remodelling process that schools were encouraged to adopt. The remodelling process introduced a new dimension into school leadership with the establishment of change teams involving a broad range of staff, to lead the implementation of the agreement. While some headteachers and school leadership teams enthusiastically embraced this approach, others simply implemented the agreement without changing structures or ways of working.

OFSTED's evaluation of the implementation of the Agreement concluded that senior managers had not benefited from remodelling to the same extent as other staff, and that 'the demands of managing an increasingly diverse workforce increased their workload, especially that of deputy headteachers' (OFSTED 2005: para 8).

Secondary schools did not embrace remodelling to the same degree as primary schools, and those in London were the slowest to change (OME 2006). As the London Challenge and other initiatives had provided London schools with significantly higher budgets than primary schools elsewhere, the financial imperatives to change were not as great. Thus an unintended consequence of one policy of support (the London Challenge) was to inhibit the implementation of another policy (the Workforce Agreement). Nevertheless, many schools in London, as elsewhere, have remodelled in ways that have implications for leadership, as well as for children and young people. For example, staff at Carlton Nursery School in Brent, London commented:

> Our eventual goal is real distributed leadership, as we move away from the old hierarchical structure, though we believe that no one should have to work beyond what they are paid to do. You have to remember that the bottom line for many nursery schools is that the majority of staff are not teachers which means that you have to be more inclusive to make it work. Remodelling for us is about social capital and social justice.
>
> (TDA 2007: website)

A second ongoing policy challenge has been the implementation of extended schools, a key strand in the Every Child Matters agenda of whole system reform of children's services.[21] The aim has been to put the child at the centre of services, by connecting schools more closely to other services, such as health, social care, and the police.[22] Schools are required to provide a core offer of swift and easy access to appropriate support services, parenting support, a varied menu of activities across the year and, in primary schools, access to childcare. The government target is that by 2008, half of primaries and a third of secondary schools will provide access to extended services, and that by 2010 all schools will provide access.

As with the Workforce Agreement, the leadership and management challenges of extended services have been considerable, requiring high levels of commitment from school leaders to translate 'the principles of extended services into good practice in their setting' (OFSTED 2006a: 9 para 16).

For many schools, the development of extended services (along with other government initiatives such as Excellence in Cities and Education

Action Zones) have been the impetus to develop new models of leadership, including system leadership where a headteacher may lead a number of schools or a range of services in the local area.

A 2007 report on school leadership undertaken for the DfES by PriceWaterhouseCoopers described a range of emerging leadership models in response to the new challenges that schools were facing. These included greater involvement of non-teaching staff in school leadership, flatter management structures, collaborative models of working such as federations, and various models of system leadership (PWC 2007). The report's controversial proposal to open headship to people without a teaching background, such as School Business Managers, has been contested by headteacher unions (NAHT 2007). The report concluded that school leaders and headteachers were perceived to be doing a good job compared to leadership groups in other sectors.

The third national policy which has had an impact on London schools has been the high-profile academies policy. Academies, initially called city academies, were introduced as a radical new approach to improving struggling, low performing inner-city schools. The policy has involved public or private sponsors and a significant injection of capital funding by the Department for Children, Schools and Families (DCSF) – until June 2007 the Department for Education and Skills (DfES) – for new build or refurbishment of schools (DfES 2007a). Academies stand outside the funding and governance arrangements that cover other state schools and are expected to innovate in leadership and management and to create new opportunities in deprived communities. The academies policy has been highly contested in London and elsewhere, as it has the potential to be divisive (although has become less so, as the policy has developed).

To date, evidence of the impact of academies is variable. Nevertheless, the policy has significant implications for education leadership in urban areas.[23] While the leadership models emerging in academies are similar to those observed in other schools, a significant difference is the strengthened role and influence of the governing body. Academy sponsors select the majority of governors and the governing body is relatively small, with governors expected to take on more 'responsibilities for ethos, strategic direction and leadership' (DfES 2007b: 17). This signals what may emerge as an area of significant leadership development in all schools, as governors take on new responsibilities for the wider school workforce, children's services and, potentially, the leadership of a number of schools in a local area through federations and the new Trust school proposals.[24]

## Reconfiguring urban leadership

In this section of the essay we reflect on some of the lessons from the range of leadership initiatives discussed, and go on to explore what it means to be an urban leader in London, or in other challenging contexts. The broad lessons offered reinforce central messages from the literature on change management, including the importance of connecting improvement efforts to the needs and priorities of practitioners and school leaders (Darling-Hammond 1997; Tyack and Cuban 1995; Sarason 1990). They also highlight the importance of rejecting 'all purpose' reform solutions which, as Cuban argues, 'treat all schools the same while neglecting the vital linkages between cities, their schools and the country's economic and social well-being' (Cuban 2003: 2). On the basis of the London experience, we would also agree with Cuban's conclusion, that successful reforms need to be less prescriptive and more locality based (*ibid.*), and add to this that urban settings require a distributed leadership with context-specific solutions which are non-prescriptive and locally responsive (Harris 2003; Keys *et al* 2003; MacBeath *et al.* 2007).

Our reflections are organised under four themes:

- The London story
- Leadership lessons from London
- Reconfiguring urban leadership: tasks, qualities and vision
- Reconfiguring urban leadership: relationships, connections and communities.

## *The London story*

The London story is one of considerable success (see Essay 3, Tim Brighouse). Despite the increased complexity and the growing demands made on schools in recent years, London's schools have demonstrated significant improvements in pupil achievement and attainment. National inspection evidence confirms this pattern. Leadership, management, and the quality of teaching have improved significantly, with the percentage of secondary schools judged good or better for leadership and management reaching 73 per cent in London, compared with a national average of 58 per cent (HMI 2006).

Given the raft of initiatives that have been directed towards London schools (of which the London Challenge was only one, albeit a very significant one), it is impossible to ascribe these improvements directly to one initiative, or to identify a direct association between changes in school leadership and improvements in outcomes. Nevertheless, a number of suppositions can be made about its impact.

A national evaluation team led by Pam Sammons and Peter Matthews focused on elements of the Leadership Strategy, including the provision of consultant leaders to work with the leaders of schools in challenging circumstances in London.[25] The team concluded that there was an association between the degree of engagement in the Leadership Strategy's programmes and 'both enhanced leadership effectiveness and differential improvement of results' (Matthews *et al.* 2006: 6).[26] The Consultant Leaders programme was deemed to have been particularly effective.[27]

Some 30 Consultant Leaders, serving headteachers, were appointed. They took a dual role with colleagues in challenging contexts: *consultancy* (mentoring, coaching, and facilitating) and *brokerage* (providing access to a range of courses, resources, and expertise). Their impact was at three levels: primarily, with the headteacher at a personal level ('building morale and confidence to lead change,' which was deemed to be a particularly effective strategy); secondly, through direct involvement with the senior leadership team;

and finally, through working with middle leaders. Matthews *et al.* concluded that:

> Particularly in highly challenging schools or those undergoing reorganisation, the friendship, professional and moral support of a linked Consultant Leader is claimed to have made the critical difference between sinking and swimming for a headteacher facing unduly difficult issues. More generally, Consultant Leaders help the head to focus on key issues amid a welter of demands, expectations and interventions. They undoubtedly provide a sounding board, but help the headteacher to filter, choose, decide and implement policies.
>
> (2006: 21)

Consultant Leaders achieved this through 'humility'; winning the trust of headteachers; through 'patience, courtesy and empathy'; and by demonstrating a commitment to teaching and learning 'to increase opportunities and raise achievements of students' (*ibid*. 25; 12).[28]

Nevertheless, there was evidence that some headteachers felt overwhelmed by the challenges they faced, and had been unable to select from, and use strategically, the opportunities available through the London Challenge. There was also evidence that the quality of engagement with, and support for schools by, local authorities was variable. The London Challenge advisers appeared to have had 'the best picture (of schools) and local authorities [and], with some very supportive exceptions, the worst' (*ibid.* 2006).

## *Leadership lessons from London*

The London Challenge's focus on leadership, and what is needed to support and sustain it, is a critical element in any policy strategy designed to make significant headway in challenging urban contexts. Leadership is put to the test not only by the pace of social transformation but also by local challenges (political, cultural, or religious) and global events. School leaders have to make speedy responses to highly charged events and find solutions which go beyond the pragmatic and require tolerance, sensitivity, and emotional intelligence. Schools on the various points of the 'front line' in the most challenging of contexts, face the toughest and the most acute dilemmas, including having to meet the needs of disaffected students and their families (Riley and Rustique-Forrester 2002).

The London Challenge has done much to support and develop leadership capacity in London, and there are a number of lesson to be learned, both in terms of the strength of its approach, and its limitations.

- **Lesson I – Establish the vision and set the climate and expectations:** A clear vision and positive climate is an essential feature of success. The Commissioner for London Schools, Professor Tim Brighouse, took a strong personal lead in promoting the London Challenge and encouraging innovation. His very personal style and commitment generated enthusiasm and promoted innovation during his visits to London's secondary schools. He articulated a clear vision of what London could offer its young people, and the ways in which school leaders and school staff could make a difference. London's first Minister for Schools, Stephen Twigg, had a high level of engagement in the Challenge and was a strong advocate.

- **Lesson II – Focus on collaboration and capacity building**: There was a strong emphasis in the London Challenge on collaboration, and the initiative was less prescriptive than other national initiatives. As a result, London's school leaders welcomed the investment and the opportunities. The involvement of London leaders in developing the policy design, and in supporting implementation, created a more inclusive approach which, in its turn, has served to strengthen leadership capacity. That increased capacity includes a cohort of black and global majority school leaders who can be expected to take up leadership positions in future years. Other initiatives are also coming into play to help 'grow' the next generation of urban leaders.[29]

- **Lesson III – Get personal:** Leading a challenging urban school is a demanding and very personal task. It is dependent on relationships and beliefs, as well as skills. Providing headteachers of the 'Keys to Success' schools with a London Challenge Adviser and with a Consultant Leader whose role it has been to understand the complexity of the challenges, and to provide support in a critical but non-punitive way, has been an important and highly successful tactic.

- **Lesson IV – Make it sustainable and maintain the vision:** The challenges for London schools will continue and, inevitably, new ones will emerge. Issues of faith, culture, and beliefs will continue to have an impact across London. The London Challenge promoted a London-wide vision for education which needs to be continued, if the successes are to be sustained in the long term. System capacity remains an issue in London. How the 'Londonness' of education is brokered in a highly fragmented system, and a vision for London as a multicultural, multi-faith city is brought together, remains to be seen.

- **Lesson V – Recognise the strengths of the capacity building model:** There has been a twin track approach to improvement in London and to supporting struggling urban schools. On the one hand, there has been a strong capacity building and developmental model to change (encapsulated with considerable success in the 'Keys to Success' schools). On the other hand, the national academies policy[30] has taken some London schools out of the local governance framework. If whole system change is to take place, a greater integration of the two approaches is needed, and strategies developed to reduce discontent and disconnections.

## Reconfiguring urban leadership: tasks, qualities, and vision

Research studies throughout the 1990s demonstrated the significance of school leadership in achieving school improvement. It is only recently, however, that there has been a particular focus on the role of leadership in schools in disadvantaged areas. In their review of the literature on leadership in urban and challenging settings, Keys *et al.* (2003) were unable to find any clear evidence about whether the leadership styles or strategies of urban headteachers were different from those of other successful headteachers. Nevertheless, they concluded that research pointed towards the importance of being able to prioritise and set direction, motivate and build capacity. Successful urban leadership requires a distributed leadership with context-specific solutions which are non-prescriptive and locally responsive (Harris 2003).

Riley argues there is something distinctive about urban school leadership (Riley 2004; Riley forthcoming 2007a; Riley 2007b).[31] This is about pace, complexity and the day-to-day challenges in community contexts that are demanding and volatile. Drawing on research (Harris 2003; Riley *et al.* 2004; Riley and West-Burnham 2004; West-Burnham 2002), the National College for School Leadership endorsed this analysis about difference, suggesting that:

> Although the challenges in urban schools are of the same kind as in other schools, their intensity, volatility, frequency and variety create a distinct leadership challenge.
>
> (NCSL 2005: 6)

Undoubtedly, school leaders have to maintain their own view of what is right and fair in the face of challenges and threats from different – and sometimes diametrically opposed – viewpoints of children, parents, and communities, who come from an enormous range of religious, ethnic, political, social, cultural, and economic backgrounds. The distinctiveness of urban leadership in challenging contexts (be it London, Belfast, Liverpool – or Chicago, New York, or Toronto) is about depth and complexity: the *daily* repetition of incidents and situations which require reserves of tolerance, compassion, authority, patience, and resilience (Riley forthcoming 2007a). As well as developing their own resilience, urban leaders need to build the resilience and commitment of their staff – qualities essential to good classroom practice (Day *et al.* 2006) – and to children and communities.

The intensity of the challenges is made more acute in London by the inherent instability, in terms of both pupil and staff turnover. It is the pace and consistency of change (as well as the diversity of pupils and communities) which probably makes parts of London unique in the British educational system.

What then are the qualities which urban school leaders need? And what are the important tasks? Tim Brighouse has emphasised the importance of energy, enthusiasm and hope, drawing attention to the impact that these can have on school climate:

> To be a leader in most urban schools – especially those serving youngsters from families facing socio-economic challenge – requires character and a range of qualities including indomitable will and a passion for success that brooks no denial. ... It's true to say that what leaders do, the time they spend on task and especially how they do it, has a huge influence on the climate and culture of the school.
>
> (NCSL 2005: 1)

Kathryn Riley argues that, while there is not one set of unique characteristics which distinguish urban schools leaders from their colleagues elsewhere, there are a number of unifying elements (Riley forthcoming 2007a, forthcoming 2008). These include: motivation to make a meaningful difference to the lives of children and young people; a deep and profound commitment to their own learning and that of others; a strong sense of professional identity, which may lead them to challenge conventional wisdoms; and energy and creativity, which will enable them to maintain the momentum and seek creative solutions to complex problems. In work carried out for the Esmée Fairbairn Foundation, Riley emphasises the importance of developing a sense of wholeness which enables urban leaders to acknowledge the challenges *and* the joys of leadership: the children themselves, their liveliness, and exuberance; the support of staff and senior teams, the pleasure in seeing a child or a member of staff enlivened by experiencing learning in new ways.

> Achieving this sense of wholeness enables school leaders to reconcile, what on the face of it, may seem to be the irreconcilable, and to strike a balance between the unremitting demands of the job and a sense of personal well-being. It is this balance and focus which will contribute to rich educational gains for students, staff and communities – and enable school leaders not only survive the job, but to grow and thrive.
>
> (Riley forthcoming 2007a: 17)

These findings about intensity and complexity are echoed in the work of other researchers in the field. Alma Harris and Christopher Chapman observe that school leaders in challenging urban contexts are constantly managing problems associated with the school's context; are people-centred; and combine a strong moral purpose with a readiness to collaborate with their colleagues (Harris and Chapman 2003). Tim Brighouse identifies six tasks of leadership: creating energy; building capacity; meeting and minimising crises; extending the vision; securing the environment; and seeking and charting improvement (Brighouse 2003). Although, in his view, all of these leadership tasks have to be pursued simultaneously, 'securing the environment' (creating a 'wow' factor) requires the most intensive investment, and can only be achieved by engaging staff and students in shaping what the new environment is to be. Nevertheless, it is the key ingredient which will create the 'tipping point'[32] leading to success.

> Both the staff room needs an uplift and the teachers themselves need the tools and respect to do their jobs ... And of course both sufficient pupils and enough staff need to be involved in the discussions about the changed environment ... When things are really dysfunctional the majority (albeit a silent one) don't want the dysfunctionality to continue. So enlisting everyone's views on how it can change is vital and releases and creates energy. In any organisation – particularly those who are on the wrong side of the 'chaos/complexity versus creative (incipiently)/coherence' divide – very small things can be the 'tipping point' to creating success.
>
> (*ibid.*: 5)

In striving for this 'tipping point,' vision is critical, and story telling becomes an important way of sharing and extending the vision – not only within the school but also with the community.

## Reconfiguring urban leadership: relationships, connections and communities

It is probably true to say that school leaders have always had to create the story of what their school is about. However, the new dynamic is that our urban schools serve children and young people from very diverse cultures and communities. This means that schools have to understand the community contexts (which can change very quickly) and work with communities to create some shared beliefs about what can be achieved (Riley *et al.* 2004; Riley and Stoll 2005). To do this, urban school leaders need to understand the ways in which communities can and do change, and develop strategies which will create a closer *alignment* between schools and communities. This alignment must be based on stronger community networks and links, and engage in a very different dialogue and debate with communities which goes beyond reaching out to help the community and is about learning from, and making better use of, existing resources in the community.

Riley and Seashore (2005) explored this issue in a review of school and community leadership, challenging the assumption that all multi-ethnic cities have low social capital and arguing that, communities – including poor communities – are full of untapped resources which go beyond cohesive social relationships that provide caring support for children (see for example, Bauch 2001). Although achieving cohesiveness in challenging urban settings is extremely difficult, if communities have untapped resources, school leaders need to find out where and what they are, and encourage relationships that will enable schools to gain access to them. While there are data to suggest that a mixture of democratic involvement and networking can contribute to school improvement (Leistyna 2002), there is also evidence that cities with similar demographics vary significantly in their civic capacity to support schools and to connect to communities (Stone 2001).

Riley and Seashore acknowledge, however, that school leaders cannot do everything:

> If they currently teach, manage school finances, coordinate professional development, and work with new governing boards, they are already pressed. Working to engage disparate community groups that may have resources to buttress the school's goals is very time consuming and may have little short-term payoff. The notion that school leaders have community responsibilities that go beyond educating students is so new that current school leaders have few role models or honed skills to help them begin these tasks.
>
> (2005: 23)

This new and expanded focus on communities raises important issues about the ways in which urban leaders carry out their role. It places greater weight on the importance of distributed leadership and more collaborative system-wide forms of leadership.[33] As schools take on an expanded role, headteachers need to develop 'school-based teams of educators'; become more 'adroit at selecting meaningful professional development activities'; and more skilled at creating 'the workplace conditions to implement these new practices' (Barnett 2001: 4).[34]

In the context of challenging urban environments, Riley offers a model for leadership that is based on building mutuality and trust between schools and communities. The model is a collaborative one, which has a strong ethical and moral foundation, linked to social justice and to broader concerns about environmental sustainability. It is a very locality-based model, deriving from the community context, and is dependent for its success on building on, and connecting to, local networks. The specific elements of the model include:

- Understanding the local context and discovering the community
- Knowing the challenges and celebrating the opportunities
- Redefining the notion of community by connecting a school's internal professional community to the local community/ies
- Developing self-knowledge and building emotional resilience
- Fostering mutuality and trust
- Creating a shared belief in possibilities.

(Riley forthcoming 2007a: 18–19)

## Final reflections

Many city school leaders choose to work in challenging circumstances, driven by a keenness to improve the lives of children and young people, and by a strong sense of moral purpose. They often experience the ambivalence of leadership: problems and opportunities, frustration and fulfilment. While many of the leadership dilemmas are constant over time – as are the impulses which have taken people into that role – so great is the nature of social transformation, and so different are the demands on young people today, that many of the conditions and demands of leadership are new and untested (Riley 2004; Riley and MacBeath 2002).

The lessons from London reinforce the message that leadership is far more than a role-based function assigned to one individual. It is, as Riley and Seashore have argued, an organic activity that extends beyond the school's immediate community and is a 'network of relationships between peoples, structures and cultures' (Riley and Seashore 2000: 214). This notion of networks, connections, and a more shared responsibility for the educational needs of young people in a locality is at the heart of the growing interest in system leadership. David Hopkins (2007) defines this as a form of leadership in which school leaders are willing to take on a broader, system-wide role that embraces the successes and attainments of students across the locality.

The London experience has shown that many school leaders are willing and capable of taking on this role, and that solutions to some of the 'problems' of urban leadership may lie with those most directly and intimately involved with them on a daily basis – the school leaders, themselves. Providing school leaders with resources and development opportunities to work together across London is leading to a reconstruction and redefinition of leadership. It is also leading to a recognition that the challenges of London, and the educational challenges for children and young people across London schools, cannot be solved by individuals but is a collaborative enterprise. Whether and how this will continue to happen in London remains to be seen.

**Notes**

1 Evidence from the US points to a pattern of educational underachievement and disadvantage in urban areas. See, for example, Munich and Testani 2003.

2 At the time Her Majesty's Chief Inspector of Schools.

3 In the US, this policy concern has been reflected in the 2001 legislation *No Child Left Behind* which focuses on the performance of schools and school districts.

4 See Ainscow and West, for example, who argue that urban school leaders have a key role to play in improving urban schools, by setting a framework which encourages 'interdependent, collaborative relationships' (Ainscow and West 2006: 135).

5 In 1990, the central educational administration for London, which covered the 13 Inner London boroughs (the Inner London Education Authority), was disbanded by a government led by Margaret Thatcher. Today, there is an umbrella authority for London (the Greater London Authority) with limited powers.

6 In the 1950s Michael Young and Peter Willmott documented the impact of major changes in East London's Bethnal Green (Willmott and Young 1957).

7 Hounslow is in West London.

8 The comparable figure for Outer London is 47.1 per cent, and for all secondary schools in England 16.8 per cent (HMI 2006).

9 Comments from a headteacher interviewed as part of a review of leadership in London (Riley and West-Burnham 2004).

10 See Essay 8, Jan McKenley, for a discussion of these issues.

11 The project, 'Leadership on the Front-line' is an ongoing research and development activity led by Professor Kathryn Riley which brings together schools leaders across the UK to develop greater understanding about the community context and challenges of urban leadership, and to develop a common language to discuss the complexities of context (Riley *et al.* 2004; Riley forthcoming 2007a; Riley 2007b; Riley forthcoming 2008).

12 This point is supported by findings from a major review of school leadership, the authors of which point out that 'the working conditions in which teachers find themselves have a significant influence on their emotions ... These emotions, in turn, shape their classroom practices and influence what pupils learn' (Leithwood *et al.* 2006: 108).

13 Funding for these initiatives has typically been for three to five years.

14 See Essay 3 for a fuller discussion of the London Challenge.

15 The Centre (which later became the London Centre for Leadership in Learning) worked closely with DfES and NCSL to foster a range of professional development activities, particularly those focused around leadership. It took a lead role in creating the framework for the Chartered London Teachers, initiated research and linked programmes to sustain leadership development and offered forward thinking about emerging education and children's services policy issues in London, such as the impact of the Every Child Matters agenda which is discussed in Essay 5.

16 There were other developments funded by the London Challenge which, whilst not directly focused on leadership development, drew on the knowledge and skills of serving headteachers, increasing their capacity to take a lead in key areas of policy and practice such as *Re-engaging Disaffected Students in Learning* (Riley *et al.* 2006a & b).

17 The programme, led by Rosemary Campbell-Stephens, was developed at the Institute of Education's London Centre for Leadership in Learning, building on an earlier project, SHINE, funded by the Esmée Fairburn Foundation. It is organised over a 12-month period as a residential weekend with linked twilight sessions.

18 The National College for School Leadership ended the funding of the assessment centres in late 2005.

19 The agreement was implemented in three phases between 2003 and 2005 with 99 per cent of schools compliant.

20 Nationally, the agreement has led to a substantial increase in the number of support staff working in schools including higher level teaching assistants (HLTAs) and cover supervisors.

21 See Essay 5 for a broader discussion of Every Child Matters.

22 The legislative framework for Every Child Matters was established through the 2004 Children Act.

23 In 2007 there were 23 academies in London as listed in the DfES database and of these, significant numbers were due to open during the 2006/07 academic year (DfES 2007a).

24 The publication in May 2007 of new school governance regulations, which include the responsibility of governors to take account of parents' views and to set up parents' councils, lends weight to this as a potential avenue for new leadership development (DfES 2007b).

25 The costs of consultant leaders accounted for about 22 per cent of the funding of the initiative (Earley and Weindling 2006).

26 These findings reinforce the messages from earlier evaluative data on the London Challenge about the link between engagement in activities and impact (Earley *et al*. 2005).

27 The general trend of rising standards in London schools was marked in the 'Keys to Success' schools, particularly those to which Consultant Leaders had been attached.

28 George Berwick, one of the leading Consultant Leaders, described the role as being about enhancing leadership capacity which, over time, should lead to school improvement (Earley and Weindling 2006:.42).

29 For example, based on greater understanding about urban leadership, the Institute of Education's Centre for Leadership in Learning is running a range of activities focused on developing the urban leaders of the future. This draws on the project Leadership on the Front-line (see Note 11).

30 London's only elected body for London, led by Mayor Ken Livingston, has a limited remit for education.

31 This is based on work carried out with urban leaders across the UK, but particularly in London.

32 This concept is based on Gladwell 2002.

33 In a review of schools sustaining school improvement in disadvantaged communities, the editors noted that 'in all eleven schools it appears that autocratic models of decision-making are avoided, and leadership responsibilities are shared wherever possible' (National Commission on Education 1996: 340).

34 The OFSTED review of the extended schools concluded that 'Effective leaders

and managers coordinated and facilitated the planned delivery of services and enabled others to move the provision forward' (OFSTED 2006a: 10, para 20).

**References**


Ainscow, M. and West, M. ( 2006*) Improving Urban Schools: Leadership and collaboration.* London: Open University.

Barnett, B. (2001) *The Changing External Policy Context and the Role of the School Principal.* Nottingham: National College for School Leaders.

Bauch, P. (2001) 'School-community partnerships in rural schools: Renewal and a sense of place'. *Peabody Journal of Education, 76*(2): 204–221.

Begley, P.T. and Johansson, O. (2003) *The Ethical Dimensions of School Leadership*. Netherlands: Kluwer.

Bell, D. (2003) 'Access and achievement in urban education: Ten years on'. London: Speech to the Fabian Society.

Brighouse, T. (2003) 'Leading successfully in difficult circumstances.*'* Lecture presented to Sheffield Hallam University, 22 January.

Burns, M. J. (1978) *Leadership.* New York: Harper and Row.

Cuban, L. (2003) *Oversold andUunderused: Computers in the Classroom.* Cambridge, Mass: Harvard University Press.

Darling-Hammond, L. (1997) *The Right to Learn.* San Francisco: Jossey-Bass.

Day, C., Stobart, G., Sammons, P. and Kington, A. (2006) 'Variations in the work and lives of teachers: Relative and relational effectiveness'. *Teachers and Teaching: Theory and Practice*, 123(2): 169–192.

Department for Education and Skills (DfES) (2003*) Statistics of Education: Schools in England*. London: Department for Education and Skills.

— (2005) *London Challenge: From Good to Outstanding*. London: Department for Education and Skills.

— (2007a) *What are Academies?* London: Department for Education and Skills, The Standards Site. <www.standards.dfes.gov.uk/academies/what_are_academies/?version=1>

— (2007b) *New School Governance Regulations*. http://www.governornet.co.uk/publishArticle.cfm?topicAreaId=1&contentId=1342&pageStart=1&sortOrder=c.publishDAte

Earley, P. and Weindling, D. (2006) 'Consultant Leadership a new role for head teachers?'. *School Leadership and Management* 26(1): 37–53.

Earley, P., Weindling, D. and Crawford, M. (2005) *Evaluation of the Leadership Strategy of the London Challenge.* London: Institute of Education.

Furman, G. (2003) 'UCEA Presidential Address'. *UCEA Review,* Winter, XLV(1).

General Teaching Council (GTC) (2006) *Annual Digest of Statistics, Registered Teacher Profiles, 2005–6.* London: General Teaching Council, June.

Gladwell, M. (2002) *The Tipping Point.* USA: Little, Brown & Co.

Grace, G. (2006) 'Urban education: confronting the contradictions: an analysis with special reference to London'. *London Review of Education*, 4(2): 115–131.

Harris, A. (2003) 'Effective leadership in schools facing challenging contexts'. *School Leadership and Management*, 22(1): 15–26.

Harris, A. and Chapman, C. (2003) *Effective Leadership in Schools Facing Challenging Circumstances,* Final Report. Nottingham: NCSL.

Her Majesty's Inspectorate (HMI) (2006) *Improvements in London Schools* 2000–*2006.* London: Office for Standards in Education (062509). <www.ofsted.gov.uk>

Hopkins, D. (2007) *Every School a Great School*. Maidenhead: Open University Press.

Keys, W., Sharp, C., Greene, K. and Grayson, H. (2003*) Successful Leadership of Schools in Urban and Challenging Contexts*. Nottingham: National College for School Leadership.

Leistyna, P. (2002)'Extending the possibilities of multicultural community partnerships in urban public schools'. *Urban Review,* 34(1): 1–23.

Leithwood, K., Day, C., Sammons, P., Harris, A., and Hopkins, D. (2006) *Successful School Leadership: What it is and how it influences pupil learning.* Nottingham: National College for School Leadership, NCSL Research Report RR 800.

Louis, K. S. (2003) 'Democratic values, democratic schools: Reflections in an international context'. In J. MacBeath and L. Moos (eds), *Democratic Learning: The challenges to school effectiveness*. London: Routledge Kegan Paul.

MacBeath, J., Gray, J., Cullen, J., Frost, D., Steward, S. and Swafield, S. (2007) *Schools on the Edge*. London: Chapman Sage.

Matthews, P., Sammons, P., Gu, Q., Day, C. and Smith, P. (June 2006) *Supporting Leadership and Securing Quality: An evaluation of the impact of aspects of the London Leadership Strategy*. Nottingham: National College for School Leaders.

Munich, J.R. and Testani, R.E. (2003) *The Price of Leaving No Child Behind: The financial impact of high standards on urban school districts.* Georgia, GA: Sutherland Asbill and Brennan LLP.

NAHT (2007) Website: National Association of Headteachers <www.naht.org.uk>

National Commission on Education (1996) *Success against the Odds.* London: Routledge.

NCSL (2005) *A Model of School Leadership in Challenging Urban Environments.* Nottingham: National College for School Leadership.

OFSTED (2004) *Excellence in Cities. The primary extension – real stories.* London: Office for Standards in Education, December.

— (2005) *Remodelling the School Workforce.* London: Office for Standards in Education, December.

— (2006a) *Extended Services in Schools and Children's Centres.* London: Office for Standards in Education.

— (2006b) Inspection of Massbourne Community Academy. London: Office for Standards in Education. <www.ofsted.gov.uk> (Ref: 134693).

OME (2006) 'Professional roles and responsibilities of different professional groups'. *A study by Incomes Data Services for the Office of Manpower Economics.* London OME.

PriceWaterhouseCoopers (PWC) (2007) *Independent Study into School Leadership.* London: Department for Education and Skills.

Riley, K.A. (2004) 'Schooling the citizens of tomorrow: The challenges for teaching and learning across the global North/South divide'. *Journal of Educational Change,* 5(3): 389–415. Netherlands: Kluwer.

Riley, K.A. (forthcoming, 2007a) 'Improving City Schools: Who and what makes the difference?'. In C. Sugrue (ed.), *New Directions for Educational Change: International perspectives.* London: Routledge.

Riley, K.A. (2007b) *Surviving and Thriving as an Urban Leader: Reflective and analytical tools for leaders of our city schools.* London: Esmée Fairbairn Foundation and the London Centre for Leadership in Learning, Institute of Education.

Riley, K.A. (forthcoming, 2008) 'Leadership and urban education'. In B. McGaw, E. Baker and P. P. Peterson (eds) *International Encyclopaedia of Education* (3rd edn). Oxford: Elsevier.

Riley, K.A., with Ellis, S., Hallmond, S., Johnson, J., Seddon, J., Smith, K., Tarrant, J. and Weinstock, W. (2006b) *When You Feel Good You Learn Well: Lessons from the Project: Re-engaging disaffected students in learning.* London: London Challenge Design Collaborative, published by Thomas Tallis School.

Riley, K. A., Ellis, S., Weinstock, W., Tarrant, J. and Hallmond, S.(2006a) 'Re-engaging disaffected students in learning, insights for policy and practice'. *Improving Schools* 9(1): 7–17.

Riley, K.A. and Campbell-Stephens, R. (2007) *Formative Feedback, Investing in Diversity.* London: London Centre for Leadership in Learning, Institute of Education.

Riley, K.A., Hesketh, T., Rafferty, S., Young, J., Taylor-Moore, P. Beecham, Y. and Morris, S. (2004) *Urban Pioneers – Leading the Way Ahead: FirstlLessons from the project leadership on the front-line*. London: Institute of Education, Issues in Practice Series.

Riley, K.A. and MacBeath, J. (2002) 'Leadership in diverse contexts and cultures'. In K. Leithwood, P. Hallinger, G.C. Furman, P. Gronn, J. MacBeath and K. Riley (eds). *Second International Handbook of Educational Leadership and Administration.* Dordrecht: Kluwer.

Riley, K.A. and Rustique-Forrester, E. (2002) *Working with Disaffected Children: Why students lose interest in school and what can be done about it.* London: Chapman/Sage.

Riley, K.A. and Seashore, K.L. (2000) *Leadership for Change and School Reform.* London: Routledge Falmer.

Riley, K.A. Seashore, K.L. (2005) *Exploring New Forms of Community Leadership: Linking schools and communities to improve educational opportunities for young people*. Nottingham: National College for School Leadership.

Riley, K.A. and Stoll, L. (2005) *Leading Communities: Purposes, paradoxes and possibilities.* Professorial Lecture. London: Institute of Education, 1–34.

Riley, K.A. and West-Burnham, J. (2004) *Educational Leadership in London.* Nottingham: National College for School Leadership.

Sarason, S. (1990) *The Predictable Failure of Educational Reform.* San Francisco and Oxford: Jossey-Bass.

Stone, C. (2001) 'Civic capacity and urban education'. *Urban Affairs Review, 36*(5): 595–619.

TDA (2007). Website Workforce remodelling case studies <http://www.tda.gov.uk/remodelling/nationalagreement/resources/casestudies/remodelling/whitefield.aspx>

Tyack, D. and Cuban, L. (1995) *Tinkering Toward Utopia: A century of public school reform.* Cambridge, Mass: Harvard University Press.

West-Burnham, J. (2002) Invited Lecture, New Heads Conference. Nottingham: National College for School Leadership.

Willmott, P. and Young, M. (1957) *Family and Kinship in East London.* London: Penguin Books.

# 8 Ethnic diversity in London schools

Jan McKenley

> 'I love dis great polluted place
> Where pop stars come to live their dreams
> Here ravers come for drum and bass
> And politicians plan their schemes
> The music of the world is here
> Dis city can play any song
> They came to here from everywhere
> Tis they that made this city strong....'
>
> (From 'The London Breed' by Benjamin Zephaniah, 2001)

## Introduction

London is quintessentially defined by its ethnic diversity, not only in comparison with the rest of the United Kingdom but also arguably among other world cities. It is therefore the defining ground for cultural and ethnic diversity, and equality issues in urban education in this country. The purpose of this essay is to explore elements of the historic interplay between immigration, race, and urban education policies as they have impacted on education in London.

As Lupton and Sullivan note in Essay 1, in 2007 Greater London has more than 50 communities of 10,000 or more. All but one of the top 25 local authorities in the Office for National Statistics' league table of ethnic diversity is a London borough. Based on 2001 census data, London has a total population of just over 7 million; minority ethnic communities comprise one-third. Nearly three-quarters of England's total black African population live in London, as do six out of ten black Caribbean, half the Bangladeshi population, one in four Indians, a third each of England's white Irish, dual heritage and Chinese populations, and one in five Pakistanis.

Cultural diversity has not always been welcomed by the white host population and is reflected in the patterns of 'white flight' from Inner London boroughs; there are still nine Outer London boroughs, which are considered less than 'highly diverse'.[1] London's school population, however, is more ethnically diverse than the population as a whole, with the highest percentage of pupils with English as an additional language (EAL) in the country.

**Table 8.1** Ethnic group of London pupils 2005

| | **Inner London** | | **Outer London** | | **Greater London** | |
|---|---|---|---|---|---|---|
| | Primary | Secondary | Primary | Secondary | Primary | Secondary |
| White British | 24% | 26% | 50% | 53% | 41% | 45% |
| White other | 11% | 10% | 8% | 8% | 9% | 8% |
| Indian | 3% | 3% | 7% | 9% | 6% | 7% |
| Pakistani | 3% | 3% | 4% | 4% | 4% | 4% |
| Bangladeshi | 11% | 11% | 1% | 1% | 5% | 4% |
| Black Caribbean | 11% | 12% | 5% | 5% | 7% | 7% |
| Black African | 17% | 16% | 9% | 7% | 12% | 10% |
| Chinese | 1% | 1% | 1% | 1% | 1% | 1% |
| Other and mixed | 19% | 18% | 15% | 13% | 17% | 15% |

*(Source: DfES 2006)*

## The interplay of immigration and urban education policy

The presence of minority ethnic communities in Britain prior to the twenty-first century was comprehensively researched by Peter Fryer in his seminal book *Staying Power: The history of black people in Britain* (1984). But although there were black communities in London as early as the Elizabethan period, their impact on education was a late twentieth century phenomenon. In looking at the interplay between immigration and urban education policy, I draw on the empirical research on the post-war history of London schools, conducted between 1997 and 2001 (McKenley 2005).

Commonwealth citizens from the Caribbean, Africa, and the Indian sub-continent were recruited to assist in the rebuilding of London's infrastructure and the welfare state in the aftermath of the Second World War. They formed sizeable populations in Haringey, Brent, Ealing, and the boroughs of the former Inner London Education Authority (ILEA) in the post-war period. These boroughs also received numbers of economic migrants and asylum seekers from Turkey, Cyprus, and Vietnam in the 1970s and other strife or war torn areas like Somalia, Ethiopia, Kosovo, and Bosnia in the latter decades of the twentieth century.

Britain's East African Asian communities settled here following their forced expulsion from first Kenya in 1967 and then Uganda in 1971.

Britons of Chinese heritage were not officially counted as a separate category until the 1991 census, which numbered the community as 156,938, although there has been Chinese settlement in East London since the nineteenth century.

**Table 8.2** Largest ethnic groups in London by census category

| | |
|---|---:|
| White British | 4,287,861 |
| White other | 594,854 |
| Asian: Indian | 436,993 |
| Black African | 378,933 |
| Black Caribbean | 343,567 |
| Mixed (all) | 226,111 |
| White: Irish | 220,488 |
| Asian: Bangladeshi | 153,893 |
| Asian: Pakistani | 142,749 |
| Asian: Other Asian | 133,058 |
| Chinese: Other Ethnic Groups | 113,058 |
| Chinese: Chinese | 80,201 |
| Black or Black British: Other Black | 60,349 |
| **TOTAL** | **7,172,091** |

*(Source: www.statistics.gov.uk, table KS006)*

More recently there have been refugees from Afghanistan, Iraq, and Zimbabwe to add to the increasingly significant numbers of economic migrants and their families from Eastern Europe, now reflected as 'white minorities' in the annual schools census.

## The impact of immigration on schools

Historically there was little response by central government in the early days of visible minority ethnic settlement in Britain in the 1950s. Local education authorities (LEAs) were left completely unsupported to handle the unexpected, and consequently unplanned for, number of West Indian and Asian pupils who came to join or were born to Commonwealth migrants (Bhatnager 1970). As Nandy wryly observes:

> Through the 1950s Britain acquired a coloured population in, so to speak, a fit of absence of mind. Since the process of immigration was not planned, it was on the whole no one's responsibility in particular to anticipate and to provide for the foreseeable consequences of the process.
>
> (Nandy 1971: 7)

Hawkes also notes:

> Apart from occasional bursts of publicity in a few areas it was a local, semi-secret affair, a worry to sub-committees, the object of a few items in the local or educational press, and principally, one extra problem for already hard-pressed teachers.
>
> (Hawkes 1966: 1)

The first formal item of governmental policy from the Department of Education and Science on the placement of immigrant children was not issued until 1965, Circular No. 7/65. The Education of Immigrants (DES 1965) instructed local authorities to avoid the over-concentration of immigrant children in one institution by a policy of dispersal by 'bussing' – providing transport to ensure that the numbers of immigrants were distributed across a range of schools and so did not rise above one-third of the total school population in any school. In practice this meant educating a significant number of immigrant pupils outside their local area.

Few authorities, including the 13 Inner London boroughs administered by the Inner London Education Authority (ILEA), adopted this approach, although certainly in the early 1960s there was some political support in Outer London for the policy of dispersal. Indeed, Education Survey 13, 'The Education of Immigrants' by HM Inspectorate states that the policy of dispersal identified in Circular 7/65 emerged as a result of a 'potentially serious situation' (DES 1971b: 16) in Southall, West London in 1963. After a meeting with white parents, who were protesting about the adverse impact of large numbers of Indian children on the education of white children in certain local primary schools, the then Minister of Education, Sir Edward Boyle, agreed that a limit of 30 per cent was advisable.

Nevertheless, the ILEA was not alone in rejecting this advice, which was judged to have been ill conceived, particularly with regard to primary age pupils (Maclure 1970). Statistics compiled in February 1969 for the Parliamentary Select Committee on Race Relations and Immigration (House of Commons 1969) suggested that only a quarter of the authorities that had more that two per cent of immigrants on the school roll complied with the instruction. Townsend (1971) notes that the dispersal strategy did not tend to apply to West Indian pupils but to pupils who could not speak English.

## Post-war developments in London

London's leadership in education was critical during the post-war period. What is often omitted from accounts of 'race' and the education of immigrant children in the post-war period is their location within a wider social and educational debate on the merits and demerits of comprehensive secondary education, which was at its most intense after the Second World War. The 1944 Education Act laid down no rules governing the pattern of provision to be made for secondary education. However, the Ministry of Education in the late 1940s was insistent that comprehensive schools must be large schools of at least 1,600 pupils to be able to serve the ability profile of 'grammar, technical and modern' in a similar ratio as they existed at that time. This required a minimum of ten forms of entry divided typically into two grammar streams (for those who had passed the selective 11 plus exam), two technical streams (for those opting for a more vocational training) and six or seven modern streams for those wanting a general education.

The rhetoric of meritocracy and entitlement, which inspired the debate on comprehensive schooling, was lost in the lived experiences of many immigrant pupils and their families. Interviews with fathers of pupils of black Caribbean heritage reveal their perspective on the comprehensive schools they joined in the post-war period. Colin, one of the fathers in the study (McKenley 2005) recalls his secondary school:

> Top stream – two black kids – expected to take O levels; second stream expected to do mostly O levels, some CSEs; third stream – each stream had six classes, expected to do half and half – was 60% black and the bottom stream had only one white kid. You could tell what stream you was in by the colour of the class and the work they were doing.
>
> (McKenley 2005: 58)

These were the schools that many of today's parents and grandparents of black and minority ethnic pupils and students attended on arrival in the late 1950s and 1960s. Despite the radical rhetoric of meritocracy and equality, pupils from the Caribbean and Asia found themselves in the lower and remedial streams of the comprehensive schools, with serious consequences. As Errol, another black father in the study bitterly summarises:

> The history of education is a history of failure in my family. When I look round at all my brothers and their families, my cousins, my nephews and nieces, I am the only one who succeeded educationally.
>
> (*op cit*: 160)

In short, while national and local government were taken up with discussions and disagreements about how schools should be organised and how many of them were necessary to meet the post-war boom, many of the intergenerational seeds of underachievement and disaffection were sown. Much of the intergenerational sense of injustice, felt particularly by the black Caribbean community at the structural and institutional racism, stems from those early experiences of education and exclusion in London secondary schools. For many immigrant and white working class families, London's saving grace was, as described by Fullick in Essay 11, its further, adult, and community education provision, which provided a comprehensive programme of daytime and evening 'night school' courses.

While government policies on the education of immigrants were largely non-interventionist for much of the post-war period 'special' provision was made to meet the increasing numbers of pupils with English as an additional language through Section 11 of the Local Government Act (1966). As Mehmedbegovic describes in Essay 9, this has been used to fund a variety of pedagogical and organisational responses to particular minority ethnic groups. Interestingly, Section 11 was funded and administered through the Home Office, not through education, until it was replaced by the Ethnic Minority Achievement Grant of the 1990s.

## Differential attainment – historical perspectives

> Extra resources should be applied where required, but no attempts made to turn 'geese' into 'swans'. It is cruel to try and make a non-academic into an academic whether at a middle class fee paying school or a down town comprehensive or primary. 'Geese' are more use anyway to those who have eyes to see, in their own habitat just as beautiful.
>
> (Memorandum from the Chair of Haringey Community Relations Council to the Parliamentary Select Committee on Race Relations and Immigration, 1973)

The Race Relations Act 1968 heralded the formation of the Commission for Racial Equality and signalled a more active shift in educational policy towards minority ethnic groups in general, and West Indian pupils in particular. These developments were chronicled in the deliberations of what was to be the highly influential Parliamentary Select Committee on Race Relations and Immigration, whose concerns about the educational achievement of immigrant children were considered in detail. Established in 1968, not only did the Committee receive a wide range of submissions and personal testimonies, but they also commissioned and published a series of reports from 1969 onwards (for example, Townsend 1971), which reveal the government's laissez-faire approach to the education of immigrant pupils. In his evidence to the Select Committee on Race Relations and Immigration on 14 May 1969 Sir Herbert Andrew, Permanent Under-Secretary of State for Education, replied thus to a question about the absence of leadership by the department:

> I do not think we are in a position as a Department to give leadership except that we might encourage sensible and rational and humane tolerant attitudes within educational institutions. I think the Department is not so much leading as in part following.

The education of immigrants was the subject of various Department of Education reports (1965, 1971a, 1971b, 1972). However, it was not until 1981 that the interim findings of the first significant Committee (chaired by Sir Anthony Rampton) on educational achievement were published under the title: *West Indian children in Our Schools*. The committee's final report *Education for All* was published in 1985 after the Committee was reconstituted controversially by the new Conservative administration and placed under the chairmanship of Lord Swann. Testimonies by Inner and Outer London school staff and submissions to the Committee paint a vivid picture of the challenges London schools faced in seeking to meet the needs of minority ethnic pupils and their families.

Not everyone saw the arrival of immigrants as negative or problematic. In his personal evidence to the Select Committee on Race Relations and Immigration on 1 April 1969, the headteacher of Clissold Park

School (then a 1,000 pupil mixed Hackney secondary school with an immigrant intake of some 60 per cent) said:

> May I add something which is not always realised: one great benefit which large numbers of immigrant children bring to a school such as mine is that almost every single one wants to stay on at school after the statutory leaving age. They create in the school the tradition of staying on and by doing so they draw up with them into this the white boys and girls from the area who otherwise would have gone as soon as the law allowed. So quite an extraordinary percentage of all nationalities do stay on beyond the leaving age – 90 per cent in my own school, which, in an area like this, is remarkable.
>
> (House of Commons 1969: Vol 1–2)

Clearly however, other teachers shared the colour prejudice endemic in the wider indigenous community at that time. A decade later, the Rampton Committee (House of Commons 1981) would devote a section of its report on the impact of teacher-racism on the education of West Indian children, largely because of its frequent citation by West Indian pupils and their parents as a significant factor. Such views were not helped by the disproportionate numbers of black pupils placed in special schools that had been the focus of a widespread campaign by black organisations at least ten years earlier.

Anxieties about the over-referral of West Indian children to special schools had been expressed by members of the North London West Indian Association as early as 1965 (Taylor 1981). Bernard Coard's (1971) highly influential pamphlet *How the West Indian Child is Made Educationally Sub-normal in The British School System*, published in 1971, is the most cited critique of this outcome of educational policy on immigrant pupils and was based on his analysis of the 1967 ILEA Language Survey.[2] For example, the ILEA Report of 1967–8 on Norwood Girls School in Lambeth included a table of the proportion of immigrants in other local secondary schools, based on the 'Form 7 immigrant return' for 18 January 1968. Norwood is recorded as having 21.5 per cent; Tulse Hill Boys 20.2 per cent, but the highest return was for Parkside, the local special school, with 55 per cent.

## Commitment to race equality in education – the Inner London Education Authority's (ILEA) response

The 'social and political maelstrom' of the 1970s had given way to worldwide economic recession signalled by the decline in the manufacturing industry, the backbone of British industry. This change created tensions between the indigenous and immigrant population as unemployment soared. Conscious of this and of the need to secure the best possible schooling for all future citizens, the ILEA responded to the growing diversity of its schools by setting up the Centre for Urban Educational Studies in 1970. Its early remit was to develop methods and materials for English language teaching as well as establishing a training programme for teachers.

As we have just noted, mass unemployment in the mid-1970s, particularly youth unemployment, became a reality for the first time since the economic depression of the 1930s. This proved a difficult period for young people generally, but particularly for those young men from traditionally working class areas, where the adverse consequences of this structural unemployment were manifest. In London and other urban areas, black youth unemployment was disproportionately high and contributed to the vulnerability of young black Caribbean males, typified in the disproportionate numbers of black men 'stopped and searched on suspicion' and prosecuted under what became known as the 'SUS' laws.[3] There were widespread community campaigns against the racism of the police and the continuing growth of nationalist right-wing fascist and anti-immigrant groups such as the British National Party and the National Front.

It was no surprise when the turbulent 1970s culminated first with the election of the Conservative leader, Margaret Thatcher, as Prime Minister in 1979 and then the following year with a series of riots, rebellions, and uprisings in those areas of English cities where black Caribbean communities had settled. Major disturbances began in the St Paul's area of Bristol in 1980, followed by unrest in Toxteth, Liverpool; Handsworth, Birmingham; Brixton, South London and Tottenham, North London.

These are just a sample of the challenges the Inner London Education Authority faced in delivering its commitment to *Equality for All*:

> It is for the Authority to provide an effective comprehensive education service capable of responding to the requirements of all groups and individuals and providing appropriate opportunities for all. The Authority serves a city where the presence of people of diverse cultures and patterns of belief, behaviour and language is of great importance. All have the right to co-exist as equals and in so doing they will be dependent, as people in any cohesive society must be, on mutual respect and support. Their future will do much to determine the future of the city and the quality of life within it.
>
> (House of Commons, 1969)

In July 1981 the Schools Sub-Committee of the ILEA agreed that, within the Authority, there should be a thorough examination of achievement in schools. In her foreword to *A Policy for Equality: 'Race' and anti-racist statement and guidelines* (1983), Frances Morrell, Leader of the ILEA, stressed the focus on the levels of achievement of pupils from different social classes, from different ethnic backgrounds, and from both sexes. Echoing the Race Relations Amendment Act some 20 years later, a clear set of policies and procedures were outlined.

Many of the Authority's schools followed this lead and set up working parties to look at their practice through the lens of race equality and diversity in the curriculum. It was not uncommon for schools to close for an afternoon to debate major educational policy initiatives and to design their response.

The ILEA equalities policies were launched at a series of high-profile conferences starting at the Royal Festival Hall in October 1981. An Equal Opportunities Unit was established at County Hall. The message was put forward to everyone through three one-day conferences involving teachers, officers, parents, governors, and community groups. Ethnic monitoring was established in the teeth of opposition and sabotage from some trades unions, but the authority persisted with the setting up of a multi-ethnic Inspectorate and later teams to support the work in schools.

**Table 8.3** Major reports, in chronological order

Coard, B. (1971) *How the West Indian Child is Made Educationally Subnormal in the British School System*. London: New Beacon Books.

House of Commons (1969) *Select Committee on Race Relations and Immigration: The problems of coloured school leavers Vols 1–2 Report, Proceedings and minutes of evidence session 1968–9* London: HMSO.

House of Commons (1972) *First Special Report from the Select Committee on Race Relations and Immigration: Statistics of immigrant school pupils session 1971–2*. London: HMSO.

House of Commons (1973) *Select Committee on Race Relations and Immigration: Fifth enquiry on education session 1972–3 Vols 1–3 Report, Evidence and appendices*. London: HMSO.

House of Commons (1981) *Interim Report of the Committee of Inquiry into the Education of Children from Ethnic Minority Groups: West Indian Children in our schools*. London: HMSO Cmnd 8273 Chairman: Mr Anthony Rampton.

House of Commons (1985) *The Report of the Committee of Inquiry into the Education of Children from Ethnic Minority Groups: Education for all*. London: HMSO Cmnd 9453 Chairman: Lord Swann.

The manifesto pledges of the Conservative Party to privatise the cornerstones of the welfare state placed it on a collision course with London governance. After long campaigns, both the Greater London Council and the Inner London Education Authority were eventually abolished by the Conservative administration in part because of their commitment to radical change in the face of government intransigence or indifference. But they also became vulnerable to charges that they were not providing value for money. Despite considerable investment in schools and support, educational underachievement was endemic in some schools and boroughs, particularly among black and white working class communities.

Reform of teachers' pay and conditions was clearly signalled in the Conservative manifesto for the second term of the Thatcher government.

Increased cultural and ethnic diversity of schools in the 1980s was part of a range of challenges that schooling in London was facing at that time. Education in Inner London was detrimentally affected during the campaign to abolish the ILEA. It was a time of turbulence in the Outer London boroughs also, with a series of acrimonious disputes between teachers and their employers, which led to the withdrawal of goodwill by members of the main teaching unions. Inevitably there was an adverse impact on large numbers of London school children and among the most vulnerable were the pupils from minority ethnic communities.

**Table 8.4** Key educational reforms enacted by the Conservative government from 1979 to 1992

**THE LEGISLATION**

1980: The Education Act allows parents to express a preference for the school of their choice, and established the Assisted Places Scheme. Parents are given increased representation on governing bodies, and the right to information concerning the curriculum and organisation of the school.

1981: The parents of children with special educational needs (SEN) are given the right to participate in the assessment of those needs, and in an annual review of the statement of special educational needs.

1986: The Education Act (N0.2) describes parents' responsibilities within school governing bodies, and institutes an annual school governors' report to parents at an obligatory meeting.

1988: The Education Reform Act, through establishing open enrolment, strengthens parents' rights to choose their children's schools, and to appeal should a school refuse to admit their child. Schools are required to give parents more information concerning a child's programme of work, and his or her progress within it. Parents are given the right to vote their school out of local authority control.

1989: The Children Act gives priority to the welfare of children, and outlines parents' rights and responsibilities.

1991: The Parent's Charter. Parents to be given information on their child's progress, to find out how the school is being run and to compare all local schools.

1992: Parents are to be consulted before schools are inspected by the Office for Standards in Education (OFSTED).

*(Source: OECD 1997)*

Education reform was all-encompassing, with parental choice at its core. The publication of the Education Reform Bill in 1986 and its enactment in 1988 led to the introduction of local financial management for schools, the deregulation of admissions criteria and the creation of new kinds of schools. Schools were allowed to 'opt out' of local authority control and become grant maintained (GM) schools. The Act allowed city technology colleges (CTCs) to be established, which were independent of the local authority and sponsored by businesses. Provision for assisted places was made to provide financial assistance to the parents of able pupils who had successfully secured a scholarship place at an independent school.

The Education Reform Act was followed swiftly by the introduction of a National Curriculum with national public examinations at the end of each of its Key Stages at age seven (Key Stage 1(KS1)); 11 (Key Stage 2 (KS2)), 14 (Key Stage 3 (KS3)) and 16 (Key Stage 4 (KS4)). Lastly, the introduction of the Charter Initiative across all major public services was manifest in education with the publication of the Parents' Charter by the Department of Education and Science. Of particular relevance to London schools was the requirement for all schools to publish their end of Key Stage test results annually and report these to parents; and regular inspection on a four-yearly (now six) cycle of all maintained education institutions by the newly established OFSTED.

Despite some misgivings about OFSTED and debates about its impact on the education system in England, the Parents' Charter was welcomed by black and minority ethnic parents because of its emphasis on transparent procedures and public reporting of an individual school's standards and academic performance.

## Post-ILEA: the Inner London context after 1990

Following the abolition of the ILEA in 1989, Inner London education was reorganised into 13 education authorities (including the Corporation of London). Once it became clear that the break up of the ILEA was inevitable, some boroughs welcomed the opportunity to plan and experiment. For example, both the Liberal Democrat local administrations in Tower Hamlets and Islington introduced radical neighbourhood planning and renewal strategies, in which local schools were central. Councillors in Wandsworth and Westminster saw themselves as standard bearers for the new Conservative education policies and published plans for specialist 'magnet' schools, and for new teachers' pay and conditions arrangements. Local authority school support services were reorganised into self-financing business units. Others found the transition very difficult, for example, Hackney and Lambeth. Michael Barber (1992), who was chair of Hackney's Education Committee and involved in the widespread consultation about the new Hackney education authority, was disturbed to discover most clearly in Hackney but in other boroughs too,

> that among many black and ethnic minority parents, there was perception that the ILEA had failed. Given the levels of achievement, particularly among Afro-Caribbean students, such fears could not be dismissed ... the main accusation black parents made was that teachers did not have sufficiently high expectations.
>
> (Barber 1992: 10)

Furthermore traditional admissions criteria and local agreements were challenged by the Greenwich judgement of 1989, which established that LEA maintained schools could not give priority to children simply because they lived in the authority's administrative area; parents could only express a preference but could not be guaranteed the place of their choice.[4] Admissions has continued to be of particular concern to black and minority ethnic communities who feel that access to particular schools is often more difficult for them than for other groups.

After 1992 the requirement to publish exam results and the outcomes of OFSTED inspections revealed numbers of inner-city schools 'failing to provide an acceptable standard of education'. While the minority ethnic communities welcomed this they were soon rightly incensed to discover that their children were disproportionately represented both in those schools perceived to be underperforming and requiring 'special measures' and in those forced to close. At first the DfES did not publish school results broken down by ethnic groups, leaving individual LEAs to collect and publish such data as they saw fit. However, the election of a new Labour government in 1997 put an end to this national indifference; results were analysed by gender and ethnicity. Schools and LEAs were encouraged to take up the challenge of narrowing the achievement gaps between the highest and lowest attaining pupils through a national strategy to raise standards in literacy and numeracy, particularly among under-achieving groups.

## Twenty-first century challenges

Since 2000, Diane Abbot MP has hosted the 'Education and the Black Child in London' conference. Sponsored now by the Mayor's office and the London Development Agency, it draws hundreds of parents, teachers, advocates, and government ministers and acts as an annual reminder about black African and Caribbean achievement. The educational attainment of London's minority ethnic communities has not been the same across all groups, although all pupils enter schools at much the same levels of achievement.

Pupils of Indian and Chinese origin consistently achieve test scores above the national averages, while pupils of Gypsy/Traveller, Bangladeshi, Pakistani, Turkish, and Caribbean heritage achieve well below the national average. Although the pattern of achievement had improved by 2006, the gap between the highest and lowest performers had not narrowed. London schools have improved their performance but the London Challenge – to reduce educational inequality in London – remains relevant.

A report by the Prime Minister's Strategy Unit, Ethnic Minorities and the Labour Market (2003) identified African, Caribbean, Bangladeshi and Pakistani groups as having the lowest educational and occupational status. This, together with the numbers of black and Asian boys who are excluded from school and are in disproportionate numbers in the prison system, poses a major crisis for these sections of London's multi-ethnic community as well as the education system.

As Tim Brighouse describes in Essay 3, the London Challenge was created to produce a sea change in performance among London's secondary schools. Since its creation there has been much activity among various London agencies with regard to the performance of children from minority ethnic communities.

**Table 8.5** Major reports

'Class Acts – Diversity and opportunity in London' (2003). Report by the Council members of the Association of Local Government.

Department for Education and Skills (DfES) 2003 *Aiming High.*

Gillborn, D. and Gipps, C. (1996) *Recent Research on the Achievements of Ethnic Minority Pupils.* London: OFSTED Publications.

Gillborn, D. and Mirza, H. (2000) *Education Inequality: Mapping race, class and gender: a synthesis of research evidence.* London: OFSTED Publications.

MacPherson, W. (1999) *The Stephen Lawrence Inquiry: Report of an inquiry* London: HMSO.

*Rampton Revisited: The educational experiences of black boys in London schools* (2004). London: London Development Agency.

Education inequality has been the subject of many reports since the Labour government came to power in 1997. Influential research on the underachievement of minority ethnic pupils was commissioned from London's Institute of Education, including two key reports for OFSTED: *Recent Research on the Achievement of Ethnic Minority Pupils* (1996) and *Education Inequality: Mapping race, class and gender: a synthesis of research evidence* (2000).

Strategies to raise the achievement of minority ethnic pupils are now more differentiated under the overall policy umbrella of 'Aiming High' (DfES 2003). These strategies have benefited from academic research, much of it from London-based HE institutions, which have made a significant contribution to creating more evidence-based policy initiatives through the DfES (Aiming High) and the National KS3 and KS4 strategies. Academic experts and others are now regularly called to provide expert witness to policy reviews on black exclusions, to chair School Improvement Boards, and as members of the London Mayor's Commission on Education and the Black Child, which published *Rampton Revisited* in 2004. These evidence-informed policy reviews have been key in shifting the focus from 'underachievement and the endless cataloguing of failure' to one of 'achievement and strategies to disseminate success', said to characterise the shift from twentieth to early twenty-first-century discourse on 'race' and education. Two good practice reports on the achievement of black Caribbean pupils in primary and secondary schools produced by HMI for OFSTED in 2002 also signalled the change: unusually, the featured London schools received much positive media attention.

This shift has been evident since 2003 in government strategies to increase the achievement of minority ethnic groups. The DfES funded a national study on raising the achievement of black Caribbean pupils, involving 30 secondary schools in the main urban conurbations, 20 of which were London schools. The study was evaluated by the Institute of Education, University of London, in collaboration with the University of Bristol (DfES 2006). London schools have been at the forefront of strategies to raise the attainment of other minority ethnic groups as part of the government's Minority Ethnic Achievement Project, which focuses on underachieving bilingual learners. London Challenge secondary schools were involved in a small-scale KS3 strategy pilot project on raising the achievement of black Caribbean boys sponsored by the London Challenge. A similar pilot to address the underachievement of white working class pupils was also funded, and involved East London authorities.

As described by Emery and Riley in Essay 6 training the next cadre of minority ethnic school leaders has been a key preoccupation of the London Challenge and the 'Investing In Diversity' programmes; initial as well as post-qualification teacher education at London's Institute of Education is showing signs of making a significant impact on the drive to make the London education workforce, including the leadership of that workforce, more representative of the communities it serves.

## New responses – new challenges

A key feature of these new programmes is the active engagement with minority ethnic parents in support and steering groups. The projects are challenging schools to listen and learn from the minority ethnic parents, and to build on the capacity and desire for a more equitable partnership in the education of their children. These forms of collaboration characterise the way forward for a new discourse on community leadership in education, that will build on London's radical roots, the energy of its communities, and the energies of its schools.

London has always been the centre of community activism and many of the policy initiatives undertaken to build race equality and social cohesion are the result of sustained pressure from groups as diverse as the All London Teachers against Racism and Fascism, the Black Parents Movement, the Muslim Council of Great Britain, and local Community Relations Councils. London is the home of national demonstrations and lobbies of parliaments, race riots, and rebellions. Its schools have not been immune from these influences. Pupils and parents of immigrant heritage, as well as staff, have high expectations about institutional commitments to equality and social justice.

In 1969, members of the NUT made the following submission to the House of Commons Select Committee, stating:

> There is a row of teachers here and not one of us has been trained to look after immigrants. We just got ourselves involved in it. It is a climate of opinion among the whole public; of which the teachers ought to be leaders that makes people get themselves involved in things.
>
> (House of Commons, 1969)

The same comments about the significance of schools and teachers' leadership are true today. That is why the London Challenge is such a compelling idea to many in the London school workforce. Responding to incidents such as the bombs on London Transport in July 2005, is part of the fabric of life for the London school workforce. The rhetoric of community cohesion, equality of opportunity, and social justice is enacted or undermined in London schools.

Achievement in London schools is on a rising trend but for some minority ethnic groups there is only muted optimism. For others, even this sense of optimism is under severe strain. Professor Gus John rightly talks of an education project that has become contaminated by the death of aspiration and self-belief, and

> characterised by an implosion within our communities to the extent that the mainstream schooling agenda is a massive irrelevance for many Black students, boys and girls, who are dealing with issues in their homes and communities that make what goes on in the average classroom sound like a catechism class.
>
> (Cited in Richardson 2005: 101)

Exclusion rates continue to be a national scandal. Nationally, 30,000 pupils of black Caribbean heritage were given fixed term exclusions in 2006 and over 1,000 were permanently excluded. This represents the official tip of an iceberg of educational failure through forcible and often involuntary disengagement. The link between exclusion as a systemic problem in London schools and the increasing numbers of black young men in the prison system is known and as yet unaddressed. There is no London curriculum and there should be one, as the government's recent report on citizenship acknowledges.

Coping with changing identities, diversity, and mobility is a taken-for-granted skill of London teachers, but it has to be acquired. It may not be implicit, but it is fundamental to the success of the capital's schools. Knowing more about the intergenerational experiences of education and the achievement cultures of the families that schools serve is growing in importance. The remodelling of school workforces, combined with the Every Child Matters agenda, has led to a new diversity of skills, experience, and awareness required by school staff teams. Schools and local authorities are becoming bolder and more creative in their deployment of staff and warming to their commissioning role in responding to the changing needs of pupils and their families.

The pace of change continues to accelerate. The colours in the mosaic are changing: in 2007 the fastest growing minority ethnic groups in London are no longer of Asian and Caribbean heritage; white Europeans and African people form the majority of the new arrivals in schools. Doreen Lawrence, mother of the murdered black teenager Stephen Lawrence, believes the answer for many communities is that:

> We as black people have it within ourselves to demand more and insist we get it, because for too long we have overlooked our worth. We need to think about our contribution to the economic wealth of this country and what our votes mean at election time.
>
> (Cited in Richardson 2005: 10)

London is the economic engine of the country but it is also the place to which others look to understand how to manage cultural diversity and mobility in educational settings. *Britishness* has been proposed as a unifying national concept by the Prime Minister, Gordon Brown, but it has yet to capture the public imagination nationally and is a highly contestable concept – being a Londoner is not.

Harold Clunn described London in 1932 as a place that 'has outgrown the population and dimensions of a capital and has become a nation of itself, busier and more populous than many sovereign states that fill a considerable space on the map of Europe' (Clunn 1932: 7 cited in Block 2006: 212).

Yesterday's challenge for London is tomorrow's challenge for Britain.

## Notes

1 Defined by the Office for National Statistics as a less than 50 per cent chance that two people chosen at random will belong to the same ethnic group.
2 The ILEA Language Survey showed that although immigrant pupils numbered 15 per cent of the total numbers of pupils in ILEA schools, they comprised 28.4 per cent of children in ESN schools; of those, three-quarters were of West Indian origin.
3 See the poems in 'Dread Beat and Blood' by Linton Kwesi Johnson, 1975.
4 One consequence is that at the time of writing, there are 217 admissions authorities in London, although proposals to address the situation are being discussed by a pan-London body of education officers and civil servants (Summer 2004).

## References

Barber, M. (ed.) (1992) *Education in the Capital.* London: Cassell.

Bhatnager, J. (1970) *Immigrants at School.* London: Cornmarket Press.

Block, D. (2006) *Multilingual Identities in a Global City: London stories.* London: Palgrave Macmillan.

Brighouse, T. (2002) 'Comprehensive schools then, now and in the future – is it time to draw a line and the sand and create a new ideal?'. The Caroline Benn, Brian Simon Memorial Lecture, 28 September.

Cabinet Office (2003) *Ethnic Minorities and the Labour Market Final Report,* March 2003. London: The Cabinet Office.

Coard, B. (1971) *How the West Indian Child is Made Educationally Sub-normal in the British School System.* London: New Beacon Books.

Coleman, J. *et al.* (1969) *Equality of Educational Opportunity.* Cambridge, Mass: Harvard University Press.

Department of Education and Science (DES) (1965) Circular No. 7/65 *The Education of Immigrants.* London: HMSO.

— (1971a) *Potential and Progress in a Second Culture. A survey of the assessment of pupils from overseas.* Education Survey 10. London: HMSO.

— (1971b) *The Education of Immigrants.* Education Survey 13. London: HMSO.

— (1972) *The Continuing Needs of Immigrants.* Education Survey 14. London: HMSO.

— (1981) Circular 1/81 Education 1980: *Admission to Schools.* London: HMSO.

— (1991) *The Parents' Charter: You and your child's education.* London: HMSO.

— (1992) *Choice and Diversity: A new framework for schools.* London: HMSO.

Department for Education and Skills (DfES 0183/2003) *Aiming High: Raising the achievement of minority ethnic pupils.* London: HMSO.

—(2006a) *Ethnicity and Education: The evidence on minority ethnic pupils aged 5–16*, DfES Research Topic Papers.

— (2006b) *Evaluation of Aiming High: African Caribbean achievement.* DfES Research Report RR801.

Gillborn, D. and Gipps, C. (1996) *Recent Research on the Achievements of Ethnic Minority Pupils.* London: OFSTED Publications.

Gillborn, D. and Mirza, H. (2000) *Education Inequality: Mapping race, class and gender: a synthesis of research evidence.* London: OFSTED Publications.

Hargreaves, David H. (2003) 'Leadership for transformation with the London Challenge'. The Annual Lecture of the London Leadership Centre, 19 May 2003.

Hawkes, N. (1966) *Immigrant Children In British Schools.* London: Institute of Race Relations and Pall Mall Press.

House of Commons (1969) *Select Committee on Race Relations and Immigration: The problems of coloured school leavers. Vols 1–2 Report, Proceedings and Minutes of Evidence. Session 1968–9.* London: HMSO.

— (1972) *First Special Report from the Select Committee on Race Relations and Immigration: Statistics of immigrant school pupils. Session 1971–2.* London: HMSO.

— (1973) *Select Committee on Race Relations and Immigration: Fifth enquiry on education. Session 1972–3 Vols 1–3 Report, Evidence and Appendices.* London: HMSO.

— (1981) *Interim Report of the Committee of Inquiry into the Education of Children from Ethnic Minority Groups: West Indian children in our schools.* London: HMSO Cmnd 8273 Chairman: Mr Anthony Rampton.

— (1985) *The Report of the Committee of Inquiry into the Education of Children from Ethnic Minority Groups: Education for all.* London: HMSO Cmnd 9453 Chairman: Lord Swann.

ILEA (1983) *A Policy for Equality: 'Race', equality and anti-racist guidelines.* London: ILEA.

Layton-Henry, Z. (1992) *The Politics of Immigration: Immigration, 'race' and 'race' relations in post-war Britain.* Oxford: Blackwell.

LDA (2004) *Rampton Revisited: The educational experiences of black boys in London schools.* London: the Education Committee of the London Development Agency.

Little, A. (1975) 'Achievement of ethnic minority children in London schools'. In G.K. Verma and C. Bagley (eds) *Race and Education Across Cultures.* London: Heinemann.

London Transport Museum (1994) *'Sun a-shine, Rain a-fall' London Transport's West Indian Workforce.* London: LT Museum.

McKenley, J. (2001) 'The way we were: conspiracies of silence in the wake of the Empire Windrush'. *Race Ethnicity and Education*, 4: 309–328.

McKenley, J. (2005) *Seven Black Men: An ecological study of education and parenting.* Bristol: Aduma Books.

McKenley, J., Power, C., Demie, F. and Ishani, L. (2003) *Raising the Achievement of Black Caribbean Pupils: Good practice in Lambeth schools.* Lambeth: LEA.

Maclure, S. (1970) *One Hundred Years of London Education 1870–1970.* London: Allen Lane Penguin Books.

Manzoor, S. (2004) 'A cross to bear'. *The Guardian*, 10 June.

Nandy, D. (1971) Foreword in J. McNeal and M. Rogers, *The Multi-Racial School: A professional perspective.* Harmondsworth, Middlesex: Penguin Books.

OECD (1997) *Parents as Partners in Schooling.* Paris: Organisation for Economic Co-operation and Development.

OFSTED (2002) *Achievement of Black Caribbean Pupils: Good practice in secondary schools.* London: OFSTED Publications HMI 448.

Richardson, B. (ed.) (2005) *Tell it Like it is: How our schools fail black children.* London and Stoke-on-Trent: Bookmarks Publications and Trentham Books.

Rubinstein, D. and Simon, B. (1969) *The Evolution of the Comprehensive School 1926–1966.* London: Routledge & Kegan Paul.

Smith, D.J. and Tomlinson, S. (1989) *The School Effect: A study of multi-racial comprehensives.* London: Policy Studies Institute.

Taylor, M. (1981) *Caught Between: A review of research into the education of pupils of West Indian origin.* Windsor: NFER–Nelson.

Townsend, H.E.R. (1971) *Immigrant Pupils in England: The LEA response.* Windsor: NFER.

Zepheniah, B. (2001) *Too Black, Too Strong.* Highgreen, Northumberland: Bloodaxe Books.

# 9 'Miss, who needs the languages of immigrants?' London's multilingual schools

Dina Mehmedbegović

## Introduction

One of the most complex, unique and fascinating aspects of London is its linguistic landscape. Its streets are rich with evidence that London is inhabited by people who speak and read many languages. Multilingual cacophony fills the air in all public places. Newsagents throughout London display an impressive range of publications in a variety of scripts used by European and world languages. Business signs, service information, and adverts presented bilingually are a regular feature of the London scene. Some parts of London even have bilingual street signs: in Chinatown they are in English and Chinese; in Tower Hamlets in English and Bengali; St Mary's Hospital in Paddington has all its signs in English and Arabic, while in South Kensington the strong presence of the French-speaking community is evident through its buildings, including the French Cultural Centre, Lyceum, and a number of French primary schools.

This essay explores London's linguistic wealth and the way education policies and practices have impacted on this wealth and on its many multilingual pupils. The essay makes recommendations for a more inclusive model of engaging with multilingualism in London schools than the one that currently prevails. This model, which is based on the author's own research and experience in London schools, wider academic research, case studies of good practice, and relevant pedagogical theories, has as its basis the desire to create more opportunities for London's multilingual learners in order to unlock more of their linguistic potential for their benefit and for that of London.

## The linguistic wealth of London

A recent report by the Greater London Authority (GLA) estimated that one-fifth of adults in London have a first language other than English (GLA 2006). The report suggested that this figure should be treated as an underestimate. It is based on a sample of 11,000 Londoners contributing to the Labour Force Survey (LFS). Given that the LFS only surveys people in work, it cannot be regarded as fully representative. Also, this figure is not inclusive of adults who identify English as their first language, but regularly use another language at home and in the community. An example would be second or third generation Asian immigrants. Local authority data from across London shows that the number of multilingual children in London schools is one-third of the school population; the London Challenge figure for the multilingual students in Inner London secondary schools of 52 per cent (Chartered London Teachers' Conference presentation 2007) would also suggest that the estimates for adults should be higher.

At the time of writing, the Department for Education and Skills (DfES) school population data does not yet provide sufficient detail to help with the accuracy of these figures. It is based on a 'yes' or 'no' survey with regard to pupils being exposed to a language or languages other than English in their homes or communities. The most detailed insight into the number, variety, and distribution of languages used by London pupils remains that provided by the Multilingual Capital Study (Baker and Eversley 2000). According to this study, which is in need of updating, the number of home languages recorded by London schools is 360. With the introduction of the new DfES guidance on collection and recording of data on pupils' languages (DfES 2006a) it is expected that more authorities will collect individual languages data from January 2007. However, collection of languages data remains voluntary for schools and local authorities. Therefore, complete data returns are not guaranteed even under the new guidance, especially during the initial period.

Certain local authorities such as City of Westminster have been consistently collecting this type of data for a number of years. Westminster, at the heart of Inner London, is in many ways representative of London language trends. It shows some of the most prominent features of multilingualism in London: an extraordinary linguistic variety, very random distribution, and consistent increases in the number of speakers and languages. Westminster Language and Ethnic Minority Service records 143 languages used by Westminster pupils (Westminster EMA Annual Conference 2006). In terms of the distribution of languages, the figures vary from15.6 per cent Arabic speakers being the largest group of pupils with English as an additional language (EAL), followed by Bengali speakers at 9.7 per cent, to the groups like Tigrinya, Twi-Fante/Akan, Gujarati and Chinese speakers who are the smallest groups represented; they each make only 0.4 per cent of the total school population (City of Westminster Data Department 2007) In the recent past there have even been completely isolated cases recorded, such as one Maori speaker (City of Westminster Data Department 2003). In terms of the increase, in the last five years overall, recorded numbers of bilingual pupils have gone up by more than ten per cent. Currently, the percentage of bilingual pupils in Westminster primary schools is 69.4 per cent and in secondaries 59.3 per cent. The joint percentage for primary and secondary sector is 65,2 per cent (*ibid.* 2007: 9–10). In terms of the uniqueness of London's position in the UK, at national level the same period has seen an increase of just over two per cent. Currently, primary schools in England have 12.5 per cent bilingual pupils, while in secondaries this number decreases to 9.5 per cent (DfES 2006b).

## Multilingual school children

Pupils who have English as an additional language (EAL) will vary greatly in terms of the linguistic competencies in their two languages, in some cases more than two languages. At present there is no one recognised definition of bilingualism. In the literature, there is a whole spectrum of definitions. At the maximal end of the spectrum, bilingualism is defined as 'the native-like control of two or more languages' (Bloomfield 1933), while at the minimalist end even the knowledge of a few phrases in another language will count as bilingualism (Diebold 1964). The definition used in London and nationally for the purposes of collecting data and allocating Ethnic Minority Achievement Grant (EMAG)[1] is as follows:

> Bilingual is the term currently used to refer to pupils who live in two languages, who have access to, or need to use two or more languages at home and at school. It is not to mean that they are competent and literate in both languages.
>
> (City of Westminster 2002)

By placing the emphasis on 'living in two languages', this definition allows for the inclusion of a variety of profiles of bilingual pupils. These different profiles can be divided into three main categories:

### *(1) Bilinguals born and educated in Britain*

Britain experienced waves of immigrants from new Commonwealth countries in the 1960s. As a result there are presently many well-established communities of, for example, Indians, Bangladeshis, and Pakistanis in the UK. Certain local authorities have prevailing numbers of pupils from these backgrounds occupying particular geographical locations. In Tower Hamlets, Bengali speakers make up almost one-third of the whole population, while schools in the same local authority have an even higher ratio of Bengali pupils (DfES 2006b). Children from these backgrounds are in most cases fluent speakers of their first languages, which they use in their family and community contexts on an everyday basis, but for many of them their literacy development and formal learning happens in English only. Some of these children attend religious Islamic schools where they develop reading skills in Arabic, but only specifically for the study of the Qur'an. In the case of Bengali Sylheti speakers, Sylheti is not a written language, therefore their first language skills often do not include literacy in standard Bengali.

Baker elaborates on some wider social issues that are relevant to these groups. He uses the term originally coined by Ogbu in 1987, in the context of the United States. Ogbu terms minorities whose origins are rooted in slavery, conquest, and colonisation, 'castelike' or involuntary minorities. 'Castelike' minorities:

> fill the least well paid jobs, are often given poor quality education, and are regarded as inferior by the dominant majority who sometimes negatively label them as 'culturally deprived', with 'limited English proficiency' with 'low innate intelligence' or pejoratively as 'bilinguals'.... Such a group experience disproportionate failure at school.
>
> (Quoted in Baker 1996: 362)

At the turn of the century Gillborn and Mirza identified at national level the biggest gap in the achievement of pupils between white British and Pakistani and Bangladeshi children with EAL (Gillborn and Mirza 2001). The DfES report *Ethnicity and Education* (2005) provides further evidence that this continues to be the case nationally. In London the picture is more complex. Looking at the average London figures no obvious EAL group of pupils is at the low achieving end. (Some of the black Caribbean pupils, whose performance is below average, classify as EAL, if they have French Creole as their home language, but this is a minority.) In fact Bangladeshi and Pakistani students in London achieve better than white British, on average. Once these figures are broken down there is a 20 per cent variance not only between different local authorities, but even within the same families of schools, meaning schools matched on a number of variables (London Challenge 2006: 23–25).

Current data for the City of Westminster identifies its substantial Bangladeshi school population as one of the underachieving groups. The attainment gender breakdown for this group shows the peculiarity of lower attainment by girls than boys (City of Westminster Data Department 2007). Westminster teachers who have discussed with the local authority targeted support for Bangladeshi girls have identified conflicting messages received in the community and at school with regard to women's role in the family and wider society as a factor impacting on low expectations and lack of motivation (City of Westminster Secondary EMA report December 2006, unpublished). In terms of second language acquisition (English acquisition), it is puzzling that substantial groups of EAL children born and educated here often seem to plateau, having well-developed Basic Interpersonal Communication Skills (BICS) and not very well-developed Cognitive Academic Language Proficiency (CALP).[2] Frequently, children who are BICS proficient go unnoticed in the classroom in terms of needing further support. They are confident and fluent speakers of English, but they find academic writing very difficult, which is the main obstacle to their achievement within the education system (Cummins 1991; 2001).

### *(2) Recent immigrant bilinguals*

This particular group covers many varieties of language skills. Most of these children will be new to English, unless they are coming from countries that are ex-British colonies where English is still widely used in education. In some cases these children have studied English as a foreign language in their countries of origin.

The skills that these bilinguals have in their first languages can vary. Some have well-developed literacy skills in their first languages and (depending on their age) a sound knowledge of grammar. This especially applies to children arriving from Eastern European countries. At the other end, there are children who have no literacy skills in any language and who are new to schooling. These are children coming from countries like Somalia, which has not had compulsory education for over ten years, due to political conflict. Somali children therefore tend to arrive with only oral experience and skill in their first language and no experience of formal schooling. In the period 2000–4, Inner London schools had been experiencing a big influx of 'new to schooling' children. The Westminster New to Schooling Working Party identified around 170 such children in Westminster schools across Key Stages 2–5 (KS2–KS5). The majority of these were Kurdish and Somali (Westminster EMAS Annual Conference 2004).

According to Cummins (1991), it takes up to two years for children to develop BICS, but it can take a further five years to develop CALP. Some children from different European linguistic backgrounds are greatly helped by the fact that Greek and Latin origins run through most scientific and academic vocabulary in the European languages. This is a significant additional point in terms of the transfer of skills between their first and second language. In some cases, this means that EAL beginners from this particular group find it easier to engage with an academic text or task than with language interaction within the BICS domain. The BICS domain in English is etymologically largely Anglo-Saxon based and therefore has fewer similarities with the European languages from other groups.[3] The second language acquisition and its dependence on the proficiency of the first language is complex and Cummins' model with regard to specific groups of EAL learners has to be applied with flexibility.

There is also a distinction to be made between the acquisition of 'primitive and complex aspects of speech' (Vygotsky 1962). Primitive aspects are the ones that every child acquires spontaneously in their native language through everyday activities. The way in which this language is acquired means that children will conjugate and decline correctly, but without any awareness of doing so. On the contrary, learning a foreign or second language requires a high level of conscious language use from the beginning. According to Vygotsky, 'with a foreign language, the higher forms develop before spontaneous fluent speech ... The child's strong points in a foreign language are his weak points in his native language, and vice versa' (1962: 109). In practice, this is often manifested in requests by this group of children to be explicitly taught grammar.

*(3) Settled immigrant bilinguals*

Settled immigrant bilinguals, meaning those who have been here for several years, have acquired Basic Interpersonal Skills in English and they are at different stages of developing their Cognitive Academic Proficiency Skills. In comparison to minority groups that have been in the host country already for several generations, they often have the advantage in the sense that even though they are struggling with establishing themselves in a new environment, they have not yet internalised the power structures of the host society:

> Immigrant minorities tend to lack power, status and will often be low down on the occupational ladder. However, they do not necessarily perceive themselves in the same way as their dominant hosts. Such immigrant minorities may still suffer racial discrimination and hostility, yet are less intimidated and paralysed by dominating majorities compared with 'castelike' minorities.
>
> (Baker 1996: 362)

Supporting research evidence for this theory is provided in a study carried out by Corson in Australia. This study looked at the achievement of settled bilingual immigrants from Italy, Portugal, and Macedonia in comparison to their peers, who were native English speakers. Children from both groups were from similar socio-economically underprivileged backgrounds and of similar abilities. The findings of the study showed that EAL children outperformed native speakers in all language tests used and in school examinations (Corson 1992).

For children, parents, and communities of all three groups the issues of first or home language maintenance are challenging. Supporting children in developing as *additive bilinguals,* meaning bilinguals who gain linguistically and cognitively by acquiring another language while maintaining and developing the use of their first language, has many obstacles. The most detrimental is the low status of many first languages (languages that are not categorised and taught as Modern Foreign Languages in the National Curriculum), which often leads to the loss of first language. This phenomenon is termed *subtractive bilingualism.*

## Policy, practice and training

The extraordinary linguistic variety that it so much a feature of London classrooms has long represented an enormous policy and organisational challenge to the capital. London schools operate within the DfES current recommended model of practice which is based on the principles of inclusion and full access to the curriculum. These principles underpin the widespread practice of the provision of in-class support to EAL pupils. Although the conceptualisation of this practice is pedagogically and socially sound, it presents a range of issues, which are discussed below.

The first White Paper of the New Labour government (Excellence in Schools, 1997) acknowledged the existing inequalities in experience and achievement of minority ethnic pupils, including EAL children. Two years later, a review was undertaken of the only piece of legislation which had been addressing the additional needs of minority ethnic children for 33 years (Section 11 of the Education Act from 1966). Over time Section 11 had been used to fund very different pedagogical and organisational models such as physical dispersal of EAL children in the 1960s known as 'bussing', and the establishment of separate language centres in the 1970s (Clegg 1996). The review in 1999 led to its re-branding and restructuring. It became the Ethnic Minority and Travellers Achievement Grant (EMTAG). In the year 2000 Travellers were given a separate grant, and its current title is EMAG (Ethnic Minority Achievement Grant). The grant that had been supervised and distributed by the Home Office was finally placed under the more appropriate supervision and administration of the DfES in 1999.

Currently, 85 per cent of EMAG funding is devolved to schools according to a formula. Ethnic grouping data and EAL data collection are requirements. Collected data are used for needs analysis and grant distribution. Schools have the autonomy to decide whether they employ qualified EAL teachers, bilingual assistants or home–school liaison workers. They also decide whether to buy back into the Local Authority Ethnic Minority and EAL advisory and support service.

One of the key issues with this grant has been its short funding cycle. A three-year funding cycle has prevailed until recently, which has led to frequent restructuring and uncertainty about the long-term future of the work and is regarded by many as having seriously damaged the quality of provision in this field. Many teachers have left EMAG work because of the lack of career path and high job insecurity. To recruit new teachers in this field has become increasingly hard (OFSTED 2001). This lack of long-term financial commitment at government level makes it very difficult to have a long-term strategy at the local authority and school level and has been a main point of criticism from OFSTED.

OFSTED recommended long-term funding as the key to establishing consistent provision and tackling the problem with staffing. They also recommended the development of a national strategy and recognised training for specialist teachers (OFSTED 2001: 40–1).

The government acted upon the 2001 recommendations. The funding cycle was increased to five years; a primary EAL pilot that was initially implemented in 21 London schools is now being rolled out nationally and there is a pilot being developed for secondary schools as well. Two secondary programmes focus on more advanced bilingual students (meaning those born here or having had seven or more years of education in the UK). These programmes focus on developing speaking, writing, and thinking skills at a more academic level; and in 2006 an EAL New Arrivals Excellence Programme was announced as a response to managing increased migration from European countries.

This two-year programme will be initially developed in London schools (www.standards.dfes.gov.uk/naep).

However, there still remain serious immediate concerns with EMAG policy. The main one is that the future of EMAG funding after March 2008 is again uncertain. From evidence provided by the National Association for Language Development in the Curriculum (NALDIC), devolving most of the grant to schools has resulted in a decrease of specialist staff in schools, replacing qualified with unqualified staff, increase in short-term contracts and 'a wide interpretation of the kinds of expenditure which relate directly to raising the achievement of ethnic minority learners' (NALDIC 2006). Additionally, many schools and local authorities are not satisfied with the current formula. The main criticism is that it does not accurately capture the variety and complexity of the needs of EAL students (IPPR 2005).

One common feature, which is very easy to identify in all the different models of implementation of Section 11 and EMAG, be it a withdrawal or mainstreaming model, is that the focus of additional language teaching has been about remedying deficiency. There is an array of deficiency-based terminology still present in schools, in referring to speakers of other languages going through the natural process of acquiring English as their additional language. Descriptions such as 'children with problems or difficulties in English', 'children with no language', 'severe EAL', 'children with bilingual problems' are not uncommon. This type of terminology indicates that the underlying perception of the specific needs of bilingual children has been less about supporting them to develop as bilinguals and to draw on the wealth of their language experience in their mother tongue and in English, and more about concentrating on what these children do not have – competency in English, making that the starting and the central point of their educational experience. From a pedagogical point of view this militates against setting a context in which children can succeed. At the same time it has to be acknowledged that London teachers work with best intentions for their pupils and there are many excellent projects supporting multilingualism currently running in London schools.[4]

While in the field of education practice on the whole there is a common understanding that successful learning always starts from drawing on previous experience, contextualising new knowledge, and building on existing skills, much current practice means that EAL learners often find it difficult to benefit from any of these basic principals in relation to their first or other languages. Only a small minority of EAL learners in London learning their second or additional language and learning all other subjects in that second language will have their teachers acknowledge and make links with their skills and knowledge in these other languages. While recognising the progressive nature of much work developed in London, the majority of practice makes no links between the languages that bilingual children bring with them and the language they are acquiring (based on lesson observations, focus discussion groups, and interviews with bilingual students in Inner London schools, in the period 1997–2007).

Examples of the inclusion of first languages in the curriculum can be found in many Redbridge schools. Newbury Park Primary School won the European Languages Award in 2005 for using 40 languages spoken by its pupils in the curriculum (CILT website). Valentine's High School in the same authority has over 70 per cent of EAL students located in one of the most deprived areas of London. This school has turned around patterns of minority ethnic underachievement that have been a feature of the national scene for decades. The attitude of the headteacher at the time to first languages was: 'There is no inclusive curriculum if you don't include first languages' (a London headteacher, in Mehmedbegović 2004).

Much work with multilingual learners in schools appears to be operating from the basis of cognitive theories of bilingualism which developed at the end of the nineteenth and the beginning of the twentieth centuries. Approaching language competencies and skills separately in two different languages is based on the Model of Separate Underlying Proficiency (Cummins 1980). This Model is often represented by two separate balloons in one's head representing his/her two languages. There is no bridge or link between them. They exist separately. It has to be acknowledged that this is not because the majority of teachers are familiar with this or any other model of cognitive theory of bilingualism. (Again, no criticism is intended to individual teachers. The system simply does not provide sufficient training on bilingualism.) It can be argued that the reason that most practitioners 'act out' the Model of Separate Underlying Proficiency is first of all because it comes naturally to monolinguals to engage with one language only; and then there are many other factors such as the challenge of supporting a child in using or maintaining a language that teachers themselves do not speak, the dominance of the National Curriculum, and the prevalence of parents who want their children only to speak English.

Newly Qualified Teachers (NQTs) who go to work in London schools arrive having had very little input, often one lecture, on working with EAL learners (based on the author's experience of providing training and support to NQTs in Westminster schools, 2001–2007). Considering the fact that during their teaching career in London they are not likely to teach one lesson without having EAL children in their class, this is a seriously insufficient preparation for the reality of London schools. This issue has been raised by NQTs themselves with the Teaching Training Agency (TTA) (TTA NQTs survey 2003). The Teaching Development Agency (TDA), successor to the TTA, has responded to these concerns by supporting the development of the Multiverse Website for NQTs, which provides examples of good practice and relevant research findings. Individual Post Graduate Certificate in Education (PGCE) providers in London, such as the Institute of Education (IOE), currently provide two whole days of EAL training for PGCE students in Modern Foreign Languages (MFL) and are looking to develop an EAL module for PGCE MFL students.

However, according to a recent report, current training and support still do not appropriately equip teachers: 'Many class and subject teachers are struggling to offer the kind of language conscious pedagogy necessary to enable EAL learners to engage with the language and content of the curriculum' (NALDIC 2006a).

Currently there is an increased recognition that teachers in the capital need a distinct set of skills and professional knowledge in order to engage with 'complex issues of diversity and pupil learning found in London schools' (DfES 2004). As part of the London Challenge, the Chartered London Teacher standard (CLT) initiative, launched by the DfES in September 2004, puts a significant emphasis on the knowledge of the range of communities, cultures, and subcultures in London and developing inclusive practices (DfES 2004). However, there is a strong focus on culture in CLT, which has the danger of creating a culture–language dichotomy. Many London practitioners are already advanced in terms of accommodating multiculturalism as one of the defining elements of citizenship, education, and everyday life, whilst multilingualism mainly manifests itself as part of a school's data. Often, the fact that a school lists 40 languages spoken by 30 per cent of its pupils will not be visible in the classrooms, notebooks or schemes of work. It is a missed opportunity therefore that the CLT status scheme does not specifically mention linguistic diversity. The importance of multiculturalism to excellent teacher practice in London is recognised, but the recognition of excellent teacher practice in relation to multilingualism is left more open. Also, it is not ideal that EAL learners are mentioned under the point that refers to 'reducing individual barriers to learning' and that in the same sentence with SEN pupils (DfES 2004). Referring to bilingualism as 'a barrier to learning' undermines a natural process of new language acquisition and can perpetuate attitudes to bilingualism as a problem rather than as a resource.

For practitioners at the senior level and headteachers, the situation is somewhat similar. There is no compulsory EAL module in the National Professional Qualification for Headship (NPQH) training. Even though there is a compulsory module on racial and cultural diversity, again it cannot be taken for granted that multilingualism will be sufficiently covered under these two headings. The data and evidence collected in a study of four London headteachers provides an insight into the absence of professional development that specifically addresses multilingualism (Mehmedbegović 2004). Securing sufficient input on multilingualism for future headteachers currently going through training and for existing heads through professional development is of vital importance in a system where headteachers have almost unlimited autonomy to decide how to utilise funds allocated to schools for bilingual children. London schools cannot afford a leadership vacuum in this area, as without good leadership existing pockets of good practice in using first languages in the curriculum and supporting children to develop bilingually can easily be lost. This is a serious issue for the leadership of schools in London, which need heads who will champion good practice that enhances English acquisition and multilingualism.

In terms of the development of EAL practitioners, it has taken several decades to achieve an appropriate offer of nationally recognised accredited courses. The OFSTED report *Managing Support for the Attainment of Pupils from Minority Ethnic Groups* (OFSTED 2001), recognised that lack of standardised qualifications is one of the key difficulties in recruiting specialists in this field. Therefore many schools employ non-specialist staff or divide the time allocation among mainstream staff. In addition there is a growing concern with the fact that the EAL community of teachers is increasingly becoming an ageing professional community, because younger colleagues are not choosing to specialise in this field, which is regarded as offering unstable employment, an uncertain future, and with limited career opportunities (NALDIC 2007).

Since the publishing of the OFSTED report in 2001 the DfES has promoted a nationally recognised course in Ethnic Minority Achievement (EMA). The Institute of Education and University of Birmingham have both been supported by the DfES to run EMA courses. The course at the IOE has attracted much interest amongst London EAL practitioners who welcome the opportunity to have a longer term professional development leading to a recognised qualification and the possibility of continuing their studies at the Master's level (MA). However, many interested teachers do not get the opportunity to enrol on the course mainly for two reasons – the cost of the course, and the time off work they need to attend lectures.

## Creating favourable conditions for multilingual pupils in London

The title quote for this essay: 'Miss, who needs the languages of immigrants? You need to be good at English, very good at English' was the reply of a 14-year-old student in a London school, when asked if the fact that she was fluent in Kurdish and Arabic was going to help her pursue a desired career in tourism (Mehmedbegović 2004). Since it is very unlikely that this student had arrived from Iraq with the view that Arabic is not needed or useful, it makes one question what factors in her new environment make this student, within only 11 months of living in London, see the languages she brings as redundant.

This section will explore a range of issues and attitudes to multilingualism that impact on both children and adults, and the processes of language maintenance and language loss in the multilingual communities. It will also review the implications of these issues for developing an education policy for London that values and celebrates the multilingual wealth of the city.

### *Valuing bilingualism and minority languages*

Britain, in comparison to some other European countries, for example the Scandinavian countries, Belgium and Switzerland, does not have a culture that supports or values bilingualism in individuals or communities. Even Britain's native bilingual communities, such as Welsh speakers, have gone through a whole history of language rights denial. It was only in 1993 that the Welsh Language Act was passed, which for the first time since Welsh was banned in Wales in the sixteenth century, guaranteed a 'basis of equality' between English and Welsh. (An earlier Act of this nature was passed in 1967 but it was much more limited in scope.)

In London many immigrant communities maintain their languages through obtaining funding for mother tongue education. In general, mother tongue schools are largely unrecognised by the mainstream system and the work done by children in these schools receives very little recognition outside their communities. Research conducted with Bosnian parents living on the outskirts of London confirmed that even the recent experience of individual communities is that of an education system that still takes no interest in supporting first language maintenance (Mehmedbegović 2003). But there are signs that this attitude of official non-intervention in community language maintenance, which has prevailed since the Swann Report (DES 1985), is changing. Funding has been made available for a Mother Tongue Resource Unit based in London, which supports around 2,000 supplementary schools and the current Parliamentary Under Secretary of State for Schools, Lord Adonis, has recognised and praised the role of supplementary mother tongue schools (www.dfes.gov.uk/speeches/2006/).

The Nuffield Inquiry that researched the UK's capability in languages identified the fact that there is a lack of routes to qualified teacher status and into mainstream teaching for community language teachers as a 'policy failure, inappropriate in a democratic society and costly in social terms'. The members of the Inquiry perceived this situation as resulting in the perpetuation of 'under-class of language teachers and by extension of languages' (The Nuffield Foundation 2000: 37).

There is no doubt that at a time of teacher shortage community schools could become an important recruitment pool for trainee mainstream teachers. There are 2,000 registered supplementary schools, the majority of which are based in London. These schools probably have at least 4,000 languages teachers who are native speakers of an impressive number of languages. It is likely that many of these teachers would welcome the opportunity to teach in mainstream schools and gain qualified teacher status. Recruiting these teachers could ease the workforce issue that is going to arise from the implementation of the National Languages Strategy in the primary sector (Hansard 2002). In this way there could be a considerable investment in developing the skills and qualifications of London's multilingual minority ethnic groups. The expected benefits would be that London would have a teaching force that is more representative of the communities it serves, and it would earn the city a proud place on the European and global scene in terms of the range of languages it offers and perhaps even the possibility of 'exporting' interpreters and linguists in the future.

The Qualification and Curriculum Authority (QCA) published a report in 2006 on *Community Languages in Secondary Schools*. It provides case studies of schools in four cities, including London, that have different levels and types of provision for teaching community languages. As the main point for the success of these initiatives the QCA researchers identified full support of senior management in creating an environment where teachers and students have positive attitudes to linguistic diversity. They acknowledge that bilingual students often need encouragement to study their mother tongue, because they and their parents may lack awareness of the benefits first language maintenance brings, or may perceive European languages as having more status in the school system (QCA 2006: 2).

In fact, many secondary schools in London enter students for GCSE exams in first languages. Schools are keen to facilitate this, partly because it can serve to improve their performance in the league tables. Since only a small number of London schools offer GCSE courses in the first languages of many of these students, support is provided outside of the system through mother-tongue schools. In addition, there are signs that schools are using the autonomy and flexibility they have to shape their curriculum to offer languages such as Chinese, where economic imperatives provide a good rationale for making radical curriculum decisions. And in this context it is welcome that, following the Nuffield Report, Goldsmiths College in London introduced in 2002 a PGCE in community languages.

### *Modern foreign languages and minority languages in the National Curriculum*

MFL were for the first time introduced as a compulsory part of education in 1989 (*Orders for Modern Languages*, DES 1989), which brought Britain more into line with European standards. Apart from introducing modern languages as compulsory it also classified languages into two categories. The first category listed the languages of the European Community; category two listed a mixture of international and languages spoken by minority ethnic groups in Britain (community languages – Arabic, Bengali, Chinese, Gujerati, Hebrew, Hindi, Punjabi, Russian, Turkish, and Urdu). Schools were obliged to offer one of the languages from the first category, while other languages were optional. Children who wanted to study more than one language had to do so outside the National Curriculum. No flexibility was given to schools to make choices that would reflect the linguistic heritage of their students. This policy was short lived and after only 14 years it was abandoned. Foreign languages have not been a compulsory subject beyond KS3 since 2003.

This decision, which was criticised by many as reinforcing the dominant monolingual culture in England, came at the same time as the rest of Europe was subscribing to 'the Mother Tongue plus two languages' European language policy (Council of Europe 2003). According to the Dearing Report, which evaluated the position of MFL in the education context, the number of students taking GCSE in languages has fallen from 80 per cent (while it was mandatory) to 51 per cent. In some schools where languages have fallen to a very low level a realistic expectation is that it will take up to three years to improve practice and increase the number of students obtaining GCSEs. Aside from numbers, studying MFL has become another aspect of the social divide. Pupils with free school meal (FSM) entitlement are significantly less likely to gain a language GCSE (DfES 2006c: 3–4; 23).

The impact of England's monolingual culture on the economy and on society was well documented in the Nuffield Inquiry Report, which revealed that 20 per cent of potential orders were lost due to a lack of skills in languages. A one per cent increase in export is worth two billion pounds to the UK economy. In terms of specific industries, tourism relies on nearly 20 million customers a year from non-English speaking countries having sufficient proficiency in English, while key staff at a London airport were found to be not only unable to respond to a request in another language, but unable to distinguish if the request was in French or Spanish (The Nuffield Foundation 2000: 23)!

The fact that England, unlike any other European country, has categorised languages into MFL, with high status and educational value, and world languages/minority languages/community languages, with low value, has been one of the main obstacles to remedying the underutilisation of the existing linguistic skills. It is increasingly obvious that abandoning this division on MFL and other currently spoken languages makes sound economic and social sense and would be a significant step towards having an equal opportunity system applied to languages. That does not mean that some languages will not be seen in a particular timeframe or setting as more favourable. This is not the issue. The issue is the institutionalised hierarchy of languages, which needs to be removed.

Another significant development is the National Language Strategy in the primary sector (DfES 2002). This opens up the possibility of having languages available in primary schools and this time schools can decide which language they will offer. All languages are seen as equally appropriate for achieving the language learning aims of the strategy. Giving a language the status of a mainstream subject taught within the National Curriculum will positively impact on the status of that language in the wider society. Therefore, communities that use that language will be more motivated in terms of language maintenance.

A welcome pointer to the future is that with the change of leadership in the government in June 2007 it has been proposed that schools should be given more flexibility to shape their curriculum and will be encouraged to offer languages perceived to be of economic importance to Britain, such as Mandarin and Urdu (www.dfes.gov.uk/pns).

### *Valuing English*

There are 700 million speakers of English today; 300 million speak it as their first language, 300 million as their second language and 100 million as a foreign language. It is used in 60 out of 150 countries as the official or semi-official language (figures as given in May 2001). English dominates science, the internet, air traffic, pop culture, and the film industry (May 2001). Therefore, it is difficult to argue against the view that many monolingual English speakers perceive themselves as well-equipped linguistically for the modern world, with no need to invest time in learning another language. Often this attitude reflects onto speakers of other languages. Research that was focused on the attitudes of Bosnian parents found that five out of ten parents considered English more important than Bosnian. In some cases this was expressed in a very strong manner: 'You are nobody if you don't speak English'. None perceived their language more important than English (Mehmedbegović 2003). Considering the fact that the respondents had spent only 12 years in this country, and that 12 years ago Bosnian was the only language used and needed by these people, the transformation of their value system, especially bearing in mind that they arrived as adults, is significant. Bourdieu (1991) terms this process *misrecognition*, which refers to the acceptance of the greater value of the dominant language as natural, without recognising it as a social and political construct. The end result of this process is *symbolic violence*, with which minority groups often comply and in a way even support, due to the misrecognition that their linguistic capital is of a lesser value, and that it is natural to lose it and replace it with the one that has more value, in this case English.

Trevor McDonald, patron of the National Centre for Languages (CILT) and a chairman of the Nuffield Inquiry, has raised the issue of 'our haste to ensure they [multilingual school children] acquire good English', which frequently results in missing the opportunities to ensure they maintain and develop skills in their other languages too. He calls for a culture shift from 'English only' to 'English plus' that brings a range of educational benefits, enhanced communication skills, and an openness to different cultural perspectives (CILT 2006: 2). It only needs to be added that shifting to 'English plus' thinking is as relevant to English native speakers and monolinguals as it is to multilingual children.

## A future model for London multilingual schools

This section will set out principles that should underpin practice that has the potential to move London schools that are multilingual in their intake towards becoming schools that are multilingual in their ethos and classroom practice. These principles are: making bilingualism an integral part of teaching and learning; encouraging biliteracy; advancing a multilingual ethos into a plurilingual ethos and ensuring relevance to monolinguals.

### *Recognising bilingualism in mainstream schooling and making bilingualism an integral part of teaching and learning*

A bilingual child brings to school a resource for her/himself, an additional dimension to linguistic and cognitive functioning that the use of two languages creates, and also a resource for everybody else in the classroom. At the moment, these resources that bilingual children bring to schools resemble the emperor's new clothes narrative. The majority of teachers 'do not see them' (minority languages) as something that can be used for any proper, curriculum related learning; headteachers and local authorities 'do not see them' because they are not going to help reach their targets; the government 'does not see them' because they are not on the agenda; parents 'do not see them' because of the pressure to acquire good English, and lastly children 'do not see them' because they are not important in school. The only difference between the invisible resources of bilingual children and the invisible emperor's new clothes is that the emperor had nothing on, while everybody pretended that he was draped in the finest robes. In the case of bilingual children, educators and policy makers have pupils coming to schools with treasure boxes full of linguistic resources and yet the children are made to feel their treasure is valueless, in fact, a burden. Eventually, many children abandon their linguistic treasures, not even noticing they are being 'robbed'.

Failure to recognise bilingual children as resources in schools was also criticised by the Nuffield Inquiry. According to their report, bilingual children are still seen in schools 'rather as a problem than a resource', while on the whole 'multilingual talents of UK citizens are underrecognised, under-used and all too often viewed with suspicion'. The report points to a lack of corelation between demand and supply in language acquisition and utilisation. Bilingual children in the UK speak languages that are of great importance in international and economic affairs of the country, yet the existing skills in these languages go unrecognised, are under-deployed or dismissed as a problem (The Nuffield Foundation 2000: 36).

A London headteacher stated: 'Educators focus on teaching and learning – bilingualism doesn't come into play. I don't think people think about it' (Mehmedbegović 2004). In the most simple terms the first principle of good practice would be the exact opposite to this statement: there is no teaching and learning for bilingual children (or adults) where bilingualism *doesn't come into play* or to use a more appropriate phrase, where bilingualism is not an integral part of it.

There is considerable empirical evidence to support this principle in the field of neuropsychology. Researchers have been working on identifying the differences between monolinguals and bilinguals in terms of left and right brain hemisphere use. The outcomes have resulted in the agreement among most researchers that the brain functioning of bilinguals differs from the brain functioning of monolinguals. However, there are disagreements on how they differ. The empirical evidence covers differences in a variety of variables, such as visual presentation and processing, audio processing, cortical activity of each hemisphere, levels of the right hemisphere engagement, levels of lateralisation, and heterogeneity in the hemispheric organisation (Hammers and Blanc 1989: 42). The main point of this empirical evidence is that the bilingual brain operates, processes, and therefore learns, differently from the monolingual one.

Obviously the crucial question is: how do London schools, some of which have 40 or more languages represented, implement this principle? First of all, bilingual children and their parents need to be given a clear, affirmative, consistent message by the school and their teachers in terms of a healthy bilingual linguistic diet. It should be a part of the Healthy School Initiative. As well as using every opportunity to say: 'It's good for you to eat fruit and vegetables every day'; it should also be said: 'It's good for you to speak, read and write in other languages'. This basic principle became clear while doing a focus discussion with a group of Bangladeshi boys in Pimlico School. One boy identified bilingualism as the reason for their underachievement, while another student stated: 'I don't think having two languages is a problem. I read in a scientific journal that it develops your brain' (Hanoman and Mehmedbegović 2004: 14). Schools should not have 14-year-old students left to their own initiative to look for answers as to whether bilingualism is good for them or not. Students (and parents) should be explicitly told.

While some teachers believe that bilingual children are only interested in learning and achievement in English, and in the author's experience some bilingual children are initially surprised when given a task in their first language and then embarrassed and unwilling to do it, in most cases this is a temporary phase. Where home languages are a part of teaching and learning throughout schooling, starting with early years, with the aim of supporting bilingual children in developing their full potential and positive attitudes towards this specific intellectual potential that they have, the impact of it will be evident in improved results across the curriculum as a whole.[5]

## *Encouraging biliteracy*

Many bilingual children currently in schooling have not developed and are not developing literacy in their home languages. In some cases there are valid reasons, e.g. that some of them speak a language which is not written (Sylheti). In most cases children will only develop full literacy skills in their home language if they attend a mother tongue school. The attendance at mother-tongue schools varies from community to community, and is also different for the same community in different settings. For children that attend mother tongue schools there is excellent support if their mainstream teachers are aware of it, and these children are given recognition for their efforts and the extra time that they spend in school. Also biliteracy can be supported within mainstream schooling by giving children opportunities to produce their written work bilingually. Charmian Kenner has documented a number of successful ways of developing biliteracy in London schools (Kenner 2000; 2004; Kenner *et al.* 2007). Strategies promoted by Kenner are based on giving bilingual children and parents the lead and the expert role in the classroom, while teachers join in as learners. These strategies also impact on developing the ethos of collaborative learning, where children experience the shift in power and authority from teachers to pupils or parents.[6]

According to Cummins, encouraging biliteracy enables bilingual children to benefit in the following ways:

> 1) the application of the same cognitive and linguistic abilities and skills to literacy development in both languages; 2) transfer of general concepts and knowledge of the world across languages ...; and 3) to the extent that the languages are related, transfer of specific linguistic features and skills across languages.
>
> (Cummins 2001: 191)

Children will neither fully benefit from these advantages, nor from higher utilisation of the overall potential that bilingualism offers, if they do not develop biliteracy. However, biliteracy will not develop just by being immersed in a particular language community. It cannot be assumed that these types of transfer described above will occur automatically. Cummins advocates 'giving this process a helping hand' by providing opportunities for children to read and write and to acquire academic registers in both languages. Also, explicit teaching focused on contrasting and comparing the two languages gives children the tools to become conscious users of their two languages, which leads to a greater metalinguistic awareness. It is important to emphasise that teachers can facilitate this process without being speakers of particular languages.[7]

### *Advancing a multilingual ethos into a plurilingual ethos*

The basic line of the multilingual ethos is opposite to the attitude that multilingualism is a private matter of the ethnic minority communities. Multilingualism should be seen as fundamental to the fabric of this society in the same way that different cultures and religions are. The principle of providing basic knowledge on the diversity of faiths and their differences could also be applied to languages. For example, language awareness units with information on languages spoken in Britain, their origins, scripts, differences, and similarities could easily be made part of the citizenship scheme or National Literacy Strategy. Within the National Secondary Strategy there is already an element that can be further developed. The English strand of the strategy recommends that all students, native speakers and EAL, carry out investigations and projects around different languages in etymology and morphology and make parallels between different languages (DfES 2000).

In fact, the European Council has advanced the development of a pedagogical approach to this issue and it would be beneficial if practitioners were to engage with its recommendations on a wider scale. One of the propositions of the European Council is that every pupil should have a Language Portfolio in which to enter anything significant in the experience of or engagement with other languages and cultures. This means that even if a pupil cannot use a language in conventional ways, it is still valuable to recognise that he/she has, for example, done a project on it and has certain theoretical knowledge about it. Or if a pupil has spent a certain period of time exposed to it, within family, community or while abroad; participated in an oral discussion involving several languages; or analysed a linguistic feature in one language in relation to another language and similar examples (Tosi and Leung 1999).

The central point of the approach of the European Council is that education should see developing communication skills as its aim, where communication is seen to encompass the standard state language, home languages, European languages, and other world languages. Very importantly, 'attitude formation, language and cultural awareness are the priorities' in this process that develops 'individual's understanding of the physical and social environment and ability to function effectively in the local, national and international environment' (Tosi and Leung 1999: 17).

As one of the most diverse cities in the world, London could take the lead in following the European thinking that has shifted towards developing the concept of *plurilingualism.* The main distinction between multilingualism and plurilingualism is that a multilingual approach is about having many different languages co-exist within individuals or society with the ultimate aim of achieving the competency of 'the native speaker'. A plurilingual approach, on the contrary, places the emphasis on the process of learning the language of home, society, and other peoples; developing communicative competencies as a lifelong activity; and in different situations flexibly calling upon different parts of this competence in order to achieve effective communication. At the same time plurilingualism recognises an all-encompassing communication competence that is made up of the different languages that one person has been exposed to and a partial nature of the knowledge anyone can have of one language, be it their mother tongue or not. Therefore plurilingualism removes the ideal of the native speaker as the ultimate achievement and replaces it with the aim of an effective pluralistic communicator who draws on a varied repertoire of linguistic and cultural knowledge in a flexible, creative, and individual way (Council of Europe 2001: 4–5; 169).

### *Ensuring relevance to monolinguals*

One aspect that is often lacking in a model of good practice for bilingual pupils is the principle of making it relevant to monolinguals. The fact that London is so highly multicultural and multilingual makes it, if not essential, then at least justifiable, that every pupil and citizen engages with it. In the past, the Inner London Education Authority

(ILEA) had as one of its policy statements that 'all children should have the opportunity to learn how other languages work and be encouraged to take an interest in and be informed about the languages spoken by their peers and neighbours' (ILEA 1982). Currently, the National Secondary Strategy is promoting engagement with other language systems on the premise that one has a greater understanding of the functioning of his/her own language system and metalanguage when there is a point of comparison. The linguistic potential of London is a significant resource. Conditions need to be provided for future generations to develop attitudes that will enable them to make this potential beneficial to the city as a whole.

Today nobody is truly monolingual. We are all exposed to different languages in education; on holidays; through film, media, music; we use computer languages; we are exposed to signs and print in different languages on an everyday basis, and so on. Any monolingual pupil in a London school would find many experiences and elements they could write in their language portfolio. The job that needs to be done is that of starting to recognise the contribution, in some cases a modest contribution, and in others, significant, that all these other languages and types of communication make to monolinguals' communication skills and knowledge.

## In conclusion

London has been described as 'a mini-version of the world, most ethnically diverse and cosmopolitan city in the world, where the globe is on the doorstep – Planet London' (*Time Out* May 2006). London thrives on its diversity. It is an essential component of its character and appeal. The way London has embraced its cultural diversity inspires the thought that it cannot be too long before London also wakes up to the potential of its linguistic wealth.

## Notes

1. Government funding given to schools and local authorities for addressing the needs of EAL and ethnic minority students.

2. BICS are the language skills that develop in everyday communication supported by face-to face-interaction; non-verbal cues; motivation and need to communicate, and the fact that they are always context embedded. CALP, on the other hand, is the area of context reduced language proficiency and includes the use of subject-specific vocabulary, and register and deployment of higher order language skills, such as analysis, synthesis, critical literacy, creative expression (Cummins 1979).

3. For a detailed discussion on Anglo-Saxon and Greek–Latin etymological division of the English language, see Cummins 2001.

4. The 2001 OFSTED Report and 2006 QCA Report listed below contain examples of good practice.

5. Cummins refers to around 160 studies conducted in the last 40 years in different countries, all of which provide evidence that bilingualism has positive effects on overall cognitive development and academic achievement (Cummins 2001).

6. Newbury Park School in Redbridge has been awarded European Language Award 2005 for developing a toolkit that can be used by all teachers in school to promote and teach the basics of the 46 languages spoken by their pupils. The toolkit is available from the school's website and they welcome visitors.

7. Teachers are often concerned about being able to work with languages they do not understand. CILT newsletter regularly publishes case studies of schools that successfully remove such barriers.

## Bibliography

Baker, C. (1996) *Foundations of Bilingualism and Bilingual Education.* Clevedon: Multilingual Matters.

Baker, P. and Eversley, J. (eds) (2000) *Multilingual Capital.* London: Battlebridge Publications.

Bloomfield, L. (1933) *Language.* New York: Holt, Rinehart and Winston.

Bourdieu, P. (1991) *Language and Symbolic Power.* Cambridge: Polity Press.

CILT (2006) *Positively Plurilingual.* London: CILT.

CILT website <www.cilt.org.uk>

City of Westminster (2002) *Language and Basic Skills Service Handbook.* London: City of Westminster LEA.

City of Westminster Data Department (2003) *Key Statistics.* London: City of Westminster LA.

— (2007) *Key Statistics.* London:City of Westminster LA.

City of Westminster Language and EMA Service (2006) Secondary EMA Report, City of Westminster LA, unpublished.

Clegg, J. (ed.) (1996) *Mainstreaming EAL*. Clevedon: Multilingual Matters.

Corson, D. (1992) 'Bilingual education policy and social justice'. *Journal of Education Policy*, 7(1): 45–69.

Council of Europe (2001) *Common European Framework of Reference for Languages: Learning, teaching, assessment.* Cambridge: Cambridge University Press.

— (2003) *Action Plan for Language Learning and Language Diversity.* Brussels: Council of Europe Policy Documents.

Cummins, J. (1976) 'The influence of bilingualism on cognitive growth: a synthesis of research findings and explanatory hypotheses'. *Working Papers on Bilingualism*, 9: 1–43.

— (1979) 'Cognitive/academic language proficiency, linguistic interdependence, the optimum age question and some other matters'. *Working Papers on Bilingualism*, 19: 121–9.

— (1980) 'Psychological assessment of immigrant children: logic or intuition'. *Journal of Multilingual and Multicultural Development*, 1: 97–111.

— (1981) *Bilingualism and Minority Language Children.* Ontario: Ontario Institute for Studies in Education.

— (1991) 'Interdependence of first and second language proficiency in bilingual children'. In Bialystok, E. (ed.) *Language Processing in Bilingual Children*. Cambridge: Cambridge University Press, pp. 70–89.

— (2001) *Language, Power and Pedagogy.* Clevedon: Multilingual Matters.

— (2007) *Evidence-based Literacy Strategies: Bilingualism as a resource within the Classroom.* Conference Presentation, Metropolitan University, London, March 2007.

Department of Education and Science (DES) (1989) *Order for Modern Languages.*

Department for Education and Skills (DfES) (2000) *National Secondary Literacy and Numeracy Strategy.*

— (2002) *National Languages Strategy.*

— (2004) *Charted London Teacher Standard*.

— (2005) *Ethnicity and Education*, Report.

— (2006a) *Guidance on Collection and Recording of Data on Pupils Languages.*

— (2006b) *Statistical Survey.*

— (2006c) *Languages Review.*

<www.dfes.gov.uk/naep>

<www.dfes.gov.uk/pns>

<www.dfes.gov.uk/speeches>

Diebold, A.R. (1964) in Baker, C. (1996) *Foundations of Bilingual Education and Bilingualism*. Clevedon: Multilingual Matters.

Education Act, Section 11 (1966).

Excellence in Schools (1997) White Paper.

Gillborn, D. and Mirza, H.S. (2001) *Educational Inequality: Mapping race, class and gender*. London: OFSTED.

Greater London Authority (GLA) (2006) *A profile of Londoners by Language.* DMAG Briefing 2006/26.

Hammers, J. and Blanc, M. (1989) *Bilinguality and Bilingualism.* Cambridge: Cambridge University Press.

Hanoman, M. and Mehmedbegović, D. (2004) *Equality in Action: The Pimlico way.* London: City of Westminster LEA.

Hansard Records (2002) House of Lords debate on MFL.

Inner London Education Authority (ILEA) (1982) 'Policy towards bilingualism'. In C. Brumfit, R. Ellis, and J. Levine (1985) *English as a second language in the UK.* Oxford: Pergamon Press.

Institute of Public Policy Research (IPPR) (2005) *Diverse Futures, Equal Opportunity.* Report.

Kenner, C. (2000) *Home Pages: Literacy links for bilingual children.* Stoke-on-Trent: Trentham Books.

— (2004) *Becoming Biliterate: Young children learning different writing systems.* Stoke-on-Trent: Trentham Books.

— Gregory, E. and Ruby, M. (2007) 'Developing bilingual learning strategies in mainstream and community context', *London Digest: Multilingual Learners*, 1. London: London Education Research Unit, Institute of Education (IOE).

London Challenge (2006) *London's Key Issues.*

May, S. (2001) *Language and Minority Rights: Ethnicity, nationalism and the politics of language*. Longman.

Mehmedbegović, D. (2003) 'Researching attitudes and values attached to first language maintenance'. *Language Issues Journal for practitioners*, 15(II).

— (2004) *Bilingualism in Mainstream School: What do headteachers make of it?* London: Institute of Education, unpublished EdD study.

NALDIC (2006) <www.naldic.org.uk/docs/news/archive/news>

— (2006) NALDIC letter to DfES: *DfES Review of school funding arrangements for EMAG from 2008.* <www.naldic.org.uk/docs/news/archive/news>

— (2007) <www.naldic.org.uk/docs/news/archive/news>

Nuffield Foundation (2000) *Languages for All.* Report.

OFSTED (2001) *Managing Support for the Attainment from Minority Ethnic Groups.* London: DfES.

Qualifications and Curriculum Authority (QCA) (2006) *Community Languages in the National Curriculum.* Report and Guidance

Swann, L. (1985) *Education for All.* HMSO.

Tossi, A. and Leung, C. (1999) *Rethinking Language Education: From a monolingual to a multilingual perspective.* London: CILT.

Vygotsky, L. (1962) *Thought and Language.* Cambridge, MA: MIT Press.

Welsh Language Act, 1993.

## *Conferences*

Chartered London Teachers' Conference, 2007, IOE, London.

Westminster EMA Annual Conference, 2004 and 2006, City of Westminster, London.

## *Media*

*Time Out*, May 2006.

# 10 A pan-London approach to 14–19 learning: a figment of the imagination or a potential reality?

Paul Grainger, Ann Hodgson and Ken Spours

## Introduction

In one sense, in terms of education and training, there is nothing real about either 14–19 or London. A 14–19 phase is still an aspiration because it goes against the grain of existing institutional, curricular, and governance arrangements in England (Hayward *et al.* 2005) and London, as a living economic and social entity, does not fit neatly within clearly defined administrative boundaries. There are many differing institutional structures providing 14–19 learning, a very wide range of achievement and complex 'journey to learn' patterns across the capital, some of which relate to institutional and geographical stratification by age, class, and race. The number of agencies operating at the regional, subregional, and local levels makes developing a distinct vision for learners complex. Some aspects of curriculum provision are the result of historical legacies that are no longer necessarily valid or helpful in terms of current needs. A more unified and inclusive curriculum will require much higher degrees of institutional collaboration than is the case at present. In this essay, we will argue that a fully comprehensive concept of 14–19 education and training is necessary from the perspectives of both social inclusion and economic competitiveness, and that this is particularly the case in a city such as London. Similarly, in terms of the organisation and governance of education and training, there are good reasons for seeing London as a city/region that runs across historic or administrative boundaries and comprises a number of smaller-scale dynamic localities.

## 14–19 learning

While we have suggested above that a 14–19 phase of education and training is not currently a lived reality in England, the concept of 14–19 learning is both meaningful and necessary. Young people at this stage in their lives are in transition and start to move between educational institutions and between education and work – the learning landscape becomes significantly bigger. In this context, the concept of a 14–19 phase has been seen as a curricular attempt to overcome the institutional break at 16+, by encouraging learners to remain in some form of education or training, to achieve more highly and to become active and productive citizens (Working Group on 14–19 Reform 2004; DfES 2005a). Furthermore, a focus on 14–19 learning suggests that schools, colleges and work-based learning providers, many of which operate on either side of the 16+ divide, need to collaborate to promote learner progression rather than simply focusing on achievement within their own individual institutions.

Such a concept of an expanded 14–19 education and training system clearly has implications for the content of the curriculum and approaches to learning and assessment. In terms of government policy, it has meant the introduction of more practical and vocational education into the school curriculum with a demand for institutional partnership to promote a broader range of provision and greater learner choice (DfES 2002; 2005a). Others have argued strongly that this is too narrow; that there is a need for a more comprehensive approach to the 14–19 phase and that reform should extend to the whole curriculum and pedagogy, including general education (Hodgson and Spours 2003; Working Group on 14–19 Reform 2004; Hayward *et al.* 2005). This broader view poses a challenge, not only to the dominance of GCSEs and A-levels, but also to the organisation of secondary, further, and higher education as a whole.

This rationale for a 14–19 phase thus represents a somewhat uneasy 'coalition' of motives. The government currently sees 14–19 reform in terms of three distinct functions: providing an alternative vocational route for those disaffected with traditional GCSEs and A-levels; a way of strengthening vocational education and preparation for employment; and as a means of increasing participation and attainment rates to reach international standards. Others in professional, research, and many policy communities view the focus on 14–19 learning as a way of breaking down long-standing academic/vocational and 16+ institutional divides, thereby building a more equitable and comprehensive upper secondary education system for the future. It is recognised, however, that a future system of this type will require more than curricular change and a broader concept of learning and assessment. These reforms will need to be accompanied by new organisational, accountability, and governance arrangements and a more regulated youth labour market (Hodgson and Spours 2004).

### *Learners*

The 2005 census records that there were around 600,000 Londoners aged 14–19, an annual cohort of approximately 120,000. This figure is rising slowly. The London Regional Learning and Skills Council (LSC) estimates that there were 256,211 16- to 18-year-olds in 2006 rising to 256,764 by 2008, and 259,283 by 2021. Half of all 16- to 19-year-olds in London are from black, Asian, and multi-ethnic groups and this is expected to rise to 80 per cent by 2016. Just under a third of pupils in secondary schools have English as a second language and, for roughly half of this group, this causes difficulty with their education. These figures clearly indicate major changes to the population of London schools and colleges, and will undoubtedly have implications for curriculum, pedagogy, and the organisation of learning opportunities (see Essay 8 for a broader discussion of ethnicity and education in London).

## *Providers*

The education of London learners is the responsibility of a complex range of providers. The statutory requirement for provision for 14- to 16-year-olds and the strategic lead on 14–19 arrangements lie with 33 boroughs, through local authorities that vary greatly in size. The smallest, the City of London, had no publicly funded pupils at the end of Key Stage 4 (KS4), and the largest, Croydon, had 4,359 in 2005. Eighteen of the 33 London boroughs number among the 30 per cent of the most deprived boroughs in England. Most local authorities are democratically accountable bodies, but some are run by independent consultancy arrangements: in Hackney, a Learning Trust; in Islington and in Southwark, an education services company.

There are 421 secondary schools in London. Of these, 207 are their own admissions authority (that is, the decision on which pupils to admit is outside local authority control) and around 185 have sixth forms providing for students over the age of 16. Outside local authority control there are publicly funded independent schools: city technology schools and academies. The DfES *Five-Year Strategy* (DfES 2004) commits to providing 60 academies in London by 2010.

Given this range of school status, the ability of the 33 London local authorities to plan provision varies. In Southwark, for example, no school is directly within the local authority; all are academies or voluntary schools. Furthermore, planning is made difficult by substantial movement of pupils across boundaries. In Hackney, 37 per cent of pupils at Key Stage 2 (KS2) had not been in a Hackney school for Key Stage 1 (KS1). In Lambeth 25 per cent of pupils move school each year. Much of this pupil movement appears unplanned. During 2001, 631 pupils in Haringey joined a school at non-standard times, as did 505 in Westminster. The Association of Local Government (2005) called attention to the disruptive impact this was having on schools.

Recently, however, the influence of local authorities has been increased by two national initiatives, and a restructuring of government departments. 'Building Schools for the Future' requires local authorities to formulate strategic capital bids to replace all secondary school buildings, with implications for institutional structures and size. Responsibility for putting into place the new 14 lines of Specialised Diplomas (now known as Diplomas) was also allocated to local authorities. From 2013, 14 lines of Diplomas covering all major vocational sectors will be offered at Levels 1–3 (DfES 2005b), requiring collaboration between institutions at 14–19, co-ordinated by the local authority, and leading to new partnerships and subregional groupings.

Post-16, an age when attendance at school or college is, at present, voluntary, the situation is yet more complex. The LSC has been responsible for funding provision at 16+. However, in July 2007 the Department for Education and Skills (DfES) was split into two new departments – the Department for Children, Schools and Families (DCSF) and the Department for Innovation, Universities and Skills (DIUS). The former will be responsible for 14–19 education and training, working through local authorities with the DIUS having oversight of younger learners following apprenticeships. The future role of the LSC is, for the present, uncertain.

Responsibility for guaranteeing an individual's entitlement to suitable provision for 14–19, as for example with the new Diplomas, lies with local authorities. However, the majority of learners post-16 attend the 54 further education institutions in London, which are not under local authority control. Of these 36 are general further education or tertiary colleges, 12 are sixth form colleges, and six are specialist designated institutions, mainly working with adults. Since 1993, when further education colleges became independent of local authorities, and employment of staff and ownership of assets were invested in the College Board of Corporation, colleges have developed distinct missions and marketing strategies. Some have entered into partnership arrangements at 14–16 and 16–19, but others prefer to remain outside of such shared arrangements.

The range of further education available to students varies according to locality and this adds to the degree of movement of students around the capital. The catchment area of a college rarely coincides with local authority boundaries (over 50 per cent of students post-16 attend a college outside their borough). In nine boroughs, on average more than 60 per cent of further education pupils opt to enrol on a course outside their home borough. Catholic sixth form colleges frequently draw a majority of their students from boroughs other than those in which they are based, while large further education colleges will draw students from wide areas, becoming, in effect, major subregional hubs.

Estimates of numbers of further education students vary and are increased by around 20,000 16- to 19-year-olds who travel into London for their education. The Association of Colleges London website estimates that 600,000 students enrol annually in London's further education institutions, with 120,000 enrolments per annum of students aged 14–19. Only 16 per cent of all-age further education students are full-time, full-year students, but for many colleges, especially sixth form colleges, full-time students aged 16–19 form the majority of their activity. The Mayor's Office records further education numbers in 2004 of 700,000, of whom 123,868 (18 per cent) were aged 16–20 (Mayor of London 2004).

### *Post-16 participation*

Although plans have been announced for making continuing education compulsory up to the age of 18 (DfES 2007), at present the decision to stay on at 16 is voluntary. Most students choose to remain in education or training at 16, but a significant minority leave at this point (between 8,000 and 10,000 unsettled destinations at 16) and there is further attrition during the first year of study in post-compulsory education. Retention in London at 16 in publicly funded education in 2006 was 86 per cent (compared to 77.6 per cent in 2004). The LSC (2007a) records that in 2004, 73 per cent of 16-year-olds in London remained in full-time education: 57 per cent to an FE institution, 16 per cent to school sixth forms. A further nine per cent go into government supported training (there are 136 workplace learning providers in London), and ten per cent took employment. However, by the age of

17, participation drops to 81 per cent, with only 66 per cent in full-time education. Retention in work-based learning, at 55 per cent, is particularly low, as is the retention of those with low GCSE grades (53 per cent at 16, 42 per cent at 17).

In 2007, the LSC funded 101,780 young people in further education colleges, some following more than one course. Of these, 32,630 were undertaking Level 3 study, 24,850 were undertaking Level 2, and 22,380 were taking Level 1 and Entry Level courses, including 5,850 on Entry to Employment courses. Over 2,500 learners were taking Advanced Apprenticeships (Level 3) with 6,180 taking apprenticeships at Level 2. In all, 36,000 learners were undertaking basic skills qualifications, including 7,330 on apprenticeships (LSC 2007a).

### *Attainment*

Attainment at age 16 across London varies significantly. In 2005, 48.2 per cent of all 16-year-olds gained five A*–C grades at GCSE or equivalent but this ranged from 43 per cent to 70 per cent between the lowest and highest performing boroughs (DfES 2005c). Girls outperform boys in every borough except Kensington and Chelsea. Those boroughs which have low GCSE attainment levels also have lower participation in 16–18 learning. Post-16, a further 16.5 per cent of each annual cohort is achieving a full Level 2 award, usually a vocational qualification, which takes London achievement near to the national average (70 per cent) by the age of 19 (LSC 2006).

In 2006, one-quarter of students aged 16–18 left further education during their course, with significant movement and dropout at 17: of those who stayed, 73 per cent achieved their qualification. In June 2006, 9.6 per cent of young people aged 16–18 were recorded as not being in employment or education (NEET) compared to 8.6 per cent for England as a whole. A further 5.6 per cent were unknown, owing to a failure in tracking, and are likely to have disengaged (LSC 2007a). This NEET group is regarded as at risk of becoming permanently economically inactive and more likely to engage in criminal activity (Prince's

Trust 2007). Numbers in this category are falling slowly, and recent figures suggest that the London NEET figure is now less than the national average (LSC 2007a).

Readiness to progress to higher education (HE) at 18 is generally measured by UCAS points gained in A-level General (GCE) and Vocational (VCE) results. The average point score at 18 in England is 277. Only four London boroughs exceed this average score – Barnet (281), Bexley (279), Havering (285) and Sutton (323). However, this figure is achieved by low numbers of students, largely from grammar schools. Relatively few students go on to HE from the East of London. Under 26 per cent of the cohort progress to HE from eight boroughs. The figure grows to more than 35 per cent for 17 boroughs, generally outer boroughs and those to the west. The national average is 33 per cent. Despite the general improvement in Level 3 achievement, in 2006 there was a fall of 17,184 (3.5 per cent) in applications to HE from London (HEFCE 2007).

It is clear that while there is a wide range of provision and significant areas of success in terms of participation, attainment, and progression in some parts of London, the systems within the capital do not yet fully support learners at all levels of 14–19 education and training. There is, therefore, a clear need for both organisational and curriculum change to meet the needs of very diverse learners and the future demands of a global city like London.

## A pan-London approach

Just as the concept of a 14–19 phase is not yet a reality so, as we will see, the idea of a pan-London approach to learning and skills is still in its infancy. In one sense, this is surprising because, as we discuss later, there has been a rich history of educational planning, initiatives, and innovation.

London has a number of distinctive assets and challenges for 14–19 education and training. It has to be able to produce high levels of skill for a metropolitan and internationally competitive labour market, while at the same time meeting the needs of a very diverse and often needy cohort of young people. London has a vibrant labour market with an enhanced demand for skills at Level 4 and above, and a large number of internationally recognised HE institutions. It also has pockets of very high unemployment and deprivation alongside some of the richest areas in the world (Dorling *et al.* 2007). The capital has a uniquely diverse and fast-changing population, which combines the risk of isolation and division with the opportunity for dynamic interrelationships.

The challenge is to develop an approach to economic and educational development that encourages mobility, breaks down barriers between geography, class, race, gender, and communities and which actively builds on the opportunities that diversity brings. In economic terms, labour markets are London-wide and public transport infrastructure has to be considered on a city- or region-wide basis. While post-14 education can be seen as a local access issue for many learners, the search for vocational specialist facilities or appropriate learning or institutional environments encourages others to travel significant distances and to cross borough boundaries. This can be seen as a useful preparation for a journey to work or HE to access wider economic and learning opportunities or to escape local demographic and economic constraints in order to integrate with the wider community in the capital.

Major recent initiatives, such as London Challenge (see Essay 3) and the move to a regional management structure for the LSC in 2004, means that London is seen as one area in terms of the funding and organisation of post-16 learning, rather than being split into five local LSCs. Together with the announcement in 2006 of the new Skills and Employment Board chaired by Ken Livingstone, the Mayor of London, all of these changes make the concept of a pan-London approach more of a reality.

## National 14–19 policy

Here we provide a brief overview of national policy on 14–19 education and training and the way in which London has responded. While we will argue for a role for London as an innovator in 14–19 learning, it is also important to recognise that its actions will be encouraged or constrained by government policy. For this reason, it is necessary to have a clear perspective on national policy, its direction, and contradictions within it. This provides the context for discussion of a future vision of a more cohesive and proactive pan-London 14–19 approach. It is important that such an approach builds on current innovative practices and networks, but also works with a wider range of regional and local stakeholders to develop an inclusive and comprehensive post-14 system in London that goes beyond the current divisive national policy in this area.

Until 2002, debates about a 14–19 phase were conducted almost entirely outside government and were dominated by two interrelated sets of proposals for a more inclusive and unified system that combined the features of baccalaureate-type qualifications (e.g. Finegold *et al.* 1990) and unitised credit frameworks (e.g. FEU 1992). These two approaches influenced the thinking behind the proposals in the Tomlinson Final Report (Working Group on 14–19 Reform 2004) for a unified and inclusive multilevel diploma system (Hodgson *et al.* 2006).

In 2002, the first national policy document on 14–19 education and training – *14–19 Education: extending opportunities, raising standards* – was published by the DfES. It emphasised the importance of choice, flexibility, and the introduction of more vocational courses and experiences for 14- to 16-year-olds. It provided funding for the Increased Flexibility Programme (IFP) and a number of 14–19 Pathfinders to pilot these proposals. This Green Paper was followed by a consultation process that resulted in a more measured government response (DfES 2003). One of the major proposals of this document was to establish a Working Group on 14–19 Reform chaired by Mike Tomlinson, the ex-Head of the Office for Standards in Education (OFSTED). The Working

Group published three reports in which it laid out principles for the phase, and proposals for a multilevel diploma system covering all types of 14–19 learning that would gradually subsume all existing qualifications for this age group. The aim of this unified diploma system was to blur the academic/vocational divide while building strongly on vocational education; to tackle disaffection; to prevent early specialisation; to create space for innovative learning; and to provide an inclusive climbing frame of progression opportunities for all 14- to 19-year-olds (Working Group for 14–19 Reform 2004).

The government rejected the idea of a unified diploma system covering both general and vocational learning and proposed instead a set of Diplomas (at that point referred to as Specialised Diplomas) focused on broad vocational education (DfES 2005a). Alongside these changes to qualifications for 14- to 19-year-olds, the government is also putting into place a statutory 14–19 entitlement based on access to the 14 Diploma lines, A-levels, GCSEs and apprenticeships and on the study of English and maths to at least Level 2 up to the age of 19 (DfES 2005b). It argues that the delivery of this entitlement will require improved levels of collaborative working between schools, colleges, community organisations, and work-based learning providers. Two further drivers for collaboration are the Diploma Gateway and the development of local 14–19 prospectuses that advertise provision on an area basis. In order to offer the first five Diplomas from 2008, local groups of providers across the country, led by the local authority, had to go through the Gateway process, which involved a complex set of procedures designed to select only those areas of the country where collaboration between schools, colleges, and work-based learning providers is at an advanced stage (DfES 2006).

However, many education professionals, including those in London, question the direction of reform. The government's pursuit of a partial set of reforms of vocational education at Levels 1–3 is open to the criticism of premature specialisation, ignores the needs of entry and foundation learners and leaves a selective and narrow academic track intact. Practitioners and researchers argue that an unreformed academic track will compromise the status and uptake of vocational qualifications (Hodgson and Spours 2007). The Nuffield Review of 14–19 Education and Training in England and Wales has also criticised the government's policies on the organisation of 14–19 provision, concluding that policy drivers for institutional collaboration are outweighed by those encouraging institutional competition (Hayward *et al.* 2005; 2006).

Nevertheless, 14–19 innovation continues to take place on the ground in many parts of the country, including London, stimulated by the IFP, which has provided funding for colleges to work with schools to offer vocational programmes to 14- to 16-year-olds, and by the example of 14–19 Pathfinders in 39 areas of the country, whose role was to pilot aspects of the 14–19 reform agenda (Higham and Yeomans 2006; Tirrell *et al.* 2006).

## 14–19 developments in London – the historical legacy

Despite its size and heterogeneity, there has been a tradition of pan-London education developments and initiatives for 14- to 19-year-olds, stretching back over at least 30 years. The main strands are described briefly below.

### *Bridging courses – early London solutions to tackle disaffection*

These courses were focused on 15- to 16-year-olds (now Year 11) and were intended to improve retention and motivation for pupils identified by schools as needing some form of vocational experience or stimulation during the last year of compulsory education. The course involved one or two days a week attendance at college. Typically, a college would have links with five or six schools. The courses were regulated by the Inner London Education Authority (ILEA), but there were no specific formal or external qualifications offered. Selection of pupils was undertaken by schools and, inevitably, there was a concentration of disruptive, underperforming, and alienated young people in these courses. There were genuine attempts by the managers of this provision and their ILEA supervisors to use access to workplace facilities and hands-on activities to improve motivation and reduce truancy, and they met with some success (DES 1982). However, the resources made available, and regarded as motivational, were often underused facilities within the college, areas experiencing declining recruitment, such as motor vehicle engineering, or which were associated with working-class employment. The word 'vocational' thus carried a connotation of a lack of aspiration.

### *London's experience of national policy initiatives in the 1980s and 1990s*

During the 1980s, within further education, there was renewed vigour nationally to resist the so-called academic/vocational divide, to promote a higher level and range of courses at 16+ and to provide greater access to career choice. There was a will to break down stereotypical attitudes, to promote inclusion, and to give greater status to vocational education (FECRDU 1982). Two major initiatives were the introduction of broad vocational or pre-vocational qualifications, such as BTEC awards and the Certificate in Pre-Vocational Education (CPVE), and the Technical and Vocational Education Initiative (TVEI), both of which were intended to raise the status of vocational education and to encourage schools, and later colleges, to review the ways in which they were approaching teaching for the 14–19 phase.

The potential for these initiatives to constitute a comprehensive 14–19 curriculum planning framework, however, was severely undermined by a number of divisive national policies and strategies relating to the two final terms of Conservative rule (1987–96). The break-up of ILEA was followed by the introduction of the National Curriculum in 1988, with its tight prescription of the content to be studied by each year group, reinforced, in the newly designated KS4 (ages 14–16), by an emphasis on the study of the traditional, academic single subjects. Vocational learning was largely squeezed out of compulsory secondary education. Moreover, in the early 1990s, further education colleges were responding to the implications of incorporation and complete autonomy from LEA control. As newly incorporated organisations, colleges' major focus was on recruiting sufficient learners and reducing costs, rather than on collaborating with school partners and broadening the curriculum.

The early years of the New Labour administration did little to reverse this trend. The Curriculum 2000 reforms of advanced level qualifications served to further reinforce divisions between both academic and vocational curricula and between 14–16 and 16–19 learning (Hodgson and Spours 2003). It was not until the beginning of its second parliament that the New Labour governments put in place two major policies which stressed the importance of 14–19 education and a more planned institutional approach to its delivery with the 14–19 Green Paper (DfES 2002) and the establishment of the LSC in 2001.

What this brief history demonstrates is that national policy never encouraged a holistic and sustainable 14–19 approach in London. Moreover, the effects of policy volatility over the past 20 years have left a rich but stratified and fragmented variety of institutions (Fullick 2006). The succession of administrative boundaries has led to highly localised arrangements. In many ways these reflect the phenomenon of the global city, full of spaces and corridors, segmented by wealth, poverty, class, and race (Lefebvre 1991). There are pockets of intense learner alienation and areas where the royal route to higher education is well entrenched. Managers in London have, over this period, experienced partnerships devised to control disaffected adolescents, to extend curriculum access, to develop new approaches to pedagogy, to develop the skills required for a changing curriculum and technology, and to build loose partnerships around professional development. Partnerships have thus had to navigate their way around frequent changes of policy; varying curriculum structures; different and changing funding bodies, and variations in institutional culture. In summary, 14–19 partnership has often had to work against the grain of policy rather than with it.

## Local and regional developments since 2001 – a platform for the future

Since 2001, however, a number of important building blocks have been put in place to begin the construction of a more planned, coherent, and inclusive 14–19 phase in London, based on a new level of partnership working, both locally and London-wide.

### *Local partnership working*

Recent research on partnership working in London (Fullick *et al.* 2007) indicates that the institutional structure for 14–19 partnerships varies appreciably between boroughs, although there are some common features, for example in terms of core membership. Partly this reflects the initial impetus for the partnership (for example, whether it arose as a means of promoting co-operation between 16–19 providers, or as a means of broadening the curriculum pre-16). There is also a plethora of initiatives at the local level, reflecting different circumstances and priorities. Whilst there is evidence of 14–19 partnership working in all London boroughs, the research shows that this has reached very different stages in terms of promoting specific practical collaborative working.

In terms of scope, the evidence indicates that partnership working is significantly more strongly established at borough level for the 14–16 stage than in 16–19 provision. In part, this is a result of IFP funding, but it also reflects the greater direct influence local authorities have on pre-16 learning. By contrast, 16–19 collaboration is currently more common at the consortium level (typically collaboration between a group of relatively small sixth forms, sometimes also involving local colleges).

Most boroughs have some form of strategic partnership body, whose role is to ensure that 14–19 plans are in line with strategic priorities (for example, the Every Child Matters agenda, Building Schools for the Future, and the government's plans for 14–19 education and training). This is normally led by the local authority and feeds in to the borough's reporting infrastructure. In the main, partnerships link to the local authority at official level, although one or two have also made conscious efforts to forge relationships with elected members as a means of extending their influence. Below the strategic level there is a wide variety of arrangements to give effect to partnership plans or decisions, typically involving working groups made up of practitioners (for example, to draw up protocols and develop particular initiatives) or local consortia below borough level.

The 'core' membership of partnerships normally comprises the local authority, the LSC, representatives of secondary schools in the borough, the local college(s), one or more representatives of work-based training providers and the careers service and careers advice providers. However, there are variations both within and beyond this. For example, the involvement of schools other than community schools is far from uniform – foundation and grammar schools are not always engaged, nor are special schools and pupil referral units; academies and independent schools are rarely involved. Most boroughs have found it difficult to enlist direct employer representatives; some regard the local Education Business Partnership (EBP) as a proxy for employer representation, even when it is run by the local authority and its activities confined largely to arranging pre-16 work experience placements. Partnership working on Diploma Gateway applications has highlighted the difficulties in securing effective employer engagement in many boroughs. The involvement of representatives from higher education, youth services, community organisations, and providers from outside the borough also varies, although there appears to be a trend towards broadening the membership of partnerships as the scope of their work expands. This in turn reflects the fact that in most cases the partnerships operate on the basis of consensus. Insofar as they have any powers, these derive from formal or informal agreements entered into voluntarily by the partners.

Table10.1 below indicates the wide range of specific activities and initiatives taking place across London as a result of partnership working.

**Table 10.1** Examples of borough 14–19 collaboration

- KS4 pupils travel to participate in work-related provision with college providers both within and outside the borough [Bexley]
- A successful prototype for the Diploma for 14- to 16-year-olds, an accredited programme involving 12 providers (work-based learning and FE colleges), offering new provision going beyond what schools could provide [Newham]
- A collaborative arrangement between two schools, a college and the EBP, to provide a post-16 transition programme for those not yet ready to move straight to college or into work-based training [Enfield]
- Apprenticeship in Sports Management and Leadership with some 50 places available from September 2007, mainly targeting the NEET group [Camden]
- Harmonised timetabling for one day per week and a single cross-borough offer of an alternative flexible curriculum at KS4, currently involving just over 400 pupils (c. 15 per cent of the cohort) and funded under IFP [Bromley]
- Borough-wide prospectuses for 14–16 and post-16 (with electronic versions from this year), including single prospectus for 14–16, incorporating all 'out of school' provision [Barking and Dagenham]
- A 16–19 course directory distributed directly to Year 11 pupils and their parents (also available on line) and a 14–16 prospectus of vocational opportunities across a range of colleges, schools, and work-based training providers, with a common application/admission process [Bromley]
- Development of a post-16 competition submission to the LSC on behalf of all secondary schools and the local FE college to collaborate in two consortia to deliver a 14–19 programme [Richmond]
- A forum to manage a '14–19 guarantee', in a borough where there are no local authority schools [Southwark]
- Establishment of a Diploma Centre as a school-based company, involving four schools (including an academy) and a local employer [Ealing]
- Harmonised timetabling across 14–16 and 16+ within the borough, to allow movement of students between schools [Barking and Dagenham]
- Development of protocols covering issues such as admissions, health and safety, roles and responsibilities of different partners, funding arrangements for a new additional provision programme; and an

'enabling document' to set the parameters for 14–19 partnership, within which more detailed protocols and procedures can be drawn up [Newham]

- Joint staff development between schools and colleges [Enfield, Bromley]
- Arrangements for data co-ordination and sharing, involving collaboration between different data providers (local authority/schools; colleges; Connexions; LSC) [Barking and Dagenham, Enfield]
- Strong co-ordinated careers information, advice, and guidance [across all boroughs in the South London Partnership]

---

Boroughs have typically appointed a 14–19 co-ordinator to take the lead in managing partnership infrastructure. Hitherto, this post has normally been funded by the LSC although in most cases filled by a local authority officer or consultant, usually with experience of working at senior level in or with schools. The amount of additional staff resource varies greatly (from limited part-time administrative and/or consultancy support to a dedicated team of half-a-dozen or more staff). In one borough (Bromley), the collaboration is intentionally independent of the local authority; this is seen as a strength because it is 'owned' by all the local partners, although it is not the typical model. The extent of the boroughs' direct influence depends very much on the pattern of local providers, both pre- and post-16; where there are few or no providers directly within the local authority's jurisdiction, or where there is a strong tradition of school independence, the local authority has less direct influence.

### *London-wide developments*

Alongside these developments at the local level, the establishment of the LSC in 2001 reintroduced a planning regime across the whole spectrum of post-compulsory education in England, with five local LSCs covering London. In its first years, the LSC instigated area-wide 14–19 inspections and strategic area reviews which focused institutional attention on planning post-14 provision across an area, although these have now given way to reviews linked to the government's broader Every Child Matters agenda, which does not focus primarily on 14–19 provision. The five London LSCs, however, sat uneasily with both borough boundaries and the concept of London-wide planning. It is perhaps not surprising, therefore, that this arrangement for London was short lived, being replaced by a regional structure in 2004 and a number of Local Partnership Teams aligned with local authorities as part of the so-called 're-shaping' of the LSC under Mark Haysom (Hodgson *et al.* 2005). The London region LSC sits alongside other London-wide bodies, such as the Government Office for London, which co-ordinates central government policies at regional level, and the Regional Development Agency, which is responsible for business and regeneration in the capital. While this focus on the role of the region suggests that the regional tier of government has a future, there may well have to be some rationalisation in order to make it workable. The shift in responsibility for 14–19 learning (announced in July 2007) to the new DCSF, working through local authorities, could be seen as weakening this move towards regional planning.

This brings us to a third and very significant related development. From 2007, Ken Livingston, the Mayor of London, has chaired the London Skills and Employment Board, which, for the present, will be serviced by the newly constituted London region LSC. This means that for the first time since the abolition of ILEA, there is a real prospect of London-wide planning of education and skills linked to employment. However, as we have suggested earlier, the move from the DfES to the DCSF and DIUS, with the former taking over responsibility for 14–19 education and channelling funding for it through local authorities rather than partially through the LSC, means that the future role of the LSC is now unclear. Under the Education and Inspection Act 2006, local authorities are seen as lead partners for the development of the 14–19 phase and are now responsible to the new DCSF. While the London regional LSC, working closely with the Mayor's Office and the democratically elected London Regional Assembly, will want to integrate the work of local authorities and their 14–19 partnerships into a broader pan-London approach, the mechanisms by which this may happen have not yet been decided.

The rationale for future collaboration will be the need to respond to the development of London as a dynamic city/region with particular transport, infrastructure, and regeneration demands highlighted, in particular by the coming Olympics and the continued development of the Thames Gateway (see <http://www.thames-gateway.org.uk/> for more details on this development). Recent research, for example, indicates very little co-ordinated curriculum planning for the skills required for a successful Olympic Games (Duckett *et al.* 2007). In terms of a London-wide approach to 14–19 education and training, therefore, the capital is not starting from scratch. It has inherited a disrupted but real legacy of partnership working to which has been added a number of longer-standing and more recent pan-London planning and development structures.

In this final section of the essay, we outline a framework for a more holistic and inclusive 14–19 London-wide vision and strategy that draws on 'policy memory' as a means of harnessing valuable past experience; uses the building blocks that have appeared over the last five years; exploits the new dynamic relationship that is being forged between local, regional and national policy and governance; and adopts a more unified vision of 14–19 learning with the aim of connecting and building on innovative local practice.

## A 14–19 future for London – beyond the government's agenda

### *A distinctive vision*

Given the diverse nature of London both socially and organisationally, a learning system for the capital will require some form of 'glue' that binds the wider actors together in preparing young people for adult life and lifelong learning. One major starting point will be the forging of a shared educational vision with strong underpinning values and clearly articulated purposes for the 14–19 phase. Such a vision would have to be facilitated by the Regional Assembly, promoting a regional coherence that involves a range of stakeholders and experts rather than being led by the DCSF or LSC. This will need to go well beyond the current *Vision for 14–19 in London* (DfES *et al.* 2005), which is largely a restatement of government policy. A vision that would be meaningful for the capital would have to combine themes of inclusion, innovation, challenge, and an appreciation of the unique opportunities offered by London. This inevitably would take it further than the current government agenda.

### *Learning, curriculum, qualifications and assessment – a unified and inclusive approach*

Our view is that at the heart of any London-wide vision for the 14–19 phase lies its approach to learning, curriculum, qualifications, and assessment. We would argue that the unified and comprehensive approach to curriculum, qualifications, and learning, outlined earlier in the essay, is likely to be more inclusive and effective for London 14- to 19-year-olds – because it allows them to keep their options open for longer (and certainly beyond the age of 14), to have access to a broader range of pedagogy, assessment, and learning experiences that go beyond narrow subject boundaries – and, above all, because it privileges progression over selection. A unified approach, based broadly on the Tomlinson Final Report but going beyond it, will mean balancing features of coherence and national frameworks with local determination and personalisation. It also suggests the need for a new type of participative pedagogy and strong support for expansive learning in a variety of challenging contexts, including the workplace (Unwin and Fuller 2003). This is most likely to be facilitated by shifts in approaches to assessment away from the dominance of external examinations and towards the development of more teacher-directed assessment with standards secured through local or regional quality assurance systems involving a range of stakeholders.

London is in a good position to innovate in this way but, as its history demonstrates, it cannot remain outside national policy. Regional development of this type will require further qualifications and assessment reform at the national level. Moreover, the vision for a unified and comprehensive approach to curriculum and learning is based on a realisation that a pan-London approach will only be fully realised when it is supported by strongly collaborative organisational and governance arrangements and a more regulated youth labour market. It is to these dimensions that we now turn.

### *Strongly collaborative local learning systems*

While the overall vision for London may be best set at the regional level, its enactment will be local. Under the new Education and Inspection Act 2006, the provision of learning opportunities for the majority of 14- to 19-year-olds, and certainly for all 14- to 16-year-olds, will be organised by local authorities. It is important, however, that this does not become a return to purely local authority administration but develops into a new form of leadership of strongly collaborative local learning systems, involving employers, voluntary and community organisations, and independent training providers, as well as schools and colleges, to satisfy the complex demands of 14–19 learning.

Strongly collaborative local learning systems will attempt to frame existing provision and qualifications into a comprehensive latticework of progression opportunities from entry level upwards and to ensure that they are understood by learners, parents, educational professionals, employers, and higher education providers. This type of latticework will afford learners the possibility of crossing curricular boundaries between general and vocational learning and access to coherent and expansive learning programmes, linked to local and regional resources, of which London has a rich array. The aim of the approach is not simply to provide the necessary skills and opportunities for progression, but also to develop the learning and problem-solving capacities that London's young people will need for the future.

We have argued elsewhere that the development of strongly collaborative learning systems will involve building on the current 14–19 Partnerships but going beyond them (Hodgson and Spours 2006). Currently, as we have seen, 14–19 Partnerships are, on the whole, narrowly conceived as relationships between schools or schools and colleges. The delivery of expansive learning outlined above will need to involve a much broader range of partners reaching into the workplace and the voluntary and community sectors, driven by a stronger regional coherence. While the majority of relationships will be forged within the locality, some forms of learning, particularly those involving specialist facilities, may require a regional approach.

It may be useful to see the locality as a 'local ecology' in which the actions of one partner affect the health of others (Stanton and Fletcher 2006), implying limits to institutional autonomy. The concept of an interdependent local ecology also highlights the relationship between education and its wider socio-economic context, recognising that in the 14–19 phase, the labour market and the wider community play a strong role in motivating and supporting young people to remain within education and to achieve (Spours *et al.* 2007). It recognises too that 14–19 education and training needs to be seen as a stage in lifelong learning.

The development of strongly collaborative local learning systems will require changes to both accountability frameworks, such as targets, funding, and performance tables, and to governance of the system, because the current arrangements promote competitive rather than collaborative behaviour and disrupt the development of local or regional planning (Hodgson and Spours 2006). Localities and regions need greater control over their actions through devolving certain policy and accountability mechanisms, which are currently situated at the national level, to the local and regional levels. Highly specified national targets, for example, which cascade down the system from the Treasury via DCSF and DIUS and LSC, could be replaced by broader policy narratives indicating the direction of development, but leaving it to the local and regional levels to determine how best to meet the needs of the learners in their localities. This will involve some degree of local and regional autonomy which appears to be the direction of government policy (DCLG 2006). This would mean that the wide range of partners at local level could be bound by more collective targets and forms of mutual accountability, potentially offsetting some of the costs of collaboration – complexity, bureaucracy, and time.

### *Employment, employers and the labour market – a regional approach*

Earlier we have argued that to realise a 14–19 vision for London will involve a more overt focus on the role of employers and employment because the aims of 14–19 education and training include successful transitions to working life. Currently, young people receive mixed signals from the labour market about what is valued in terms of qualifications and skills (see Hayward *et al.* 2005). This creates difficulties for young people in making choices about whether to continue participation in education and training or what type of programme they should follow. A successful 14–19 phase for the capital will, therefore, require the closer integration of 14–19 programmes, work-based learning opportunities, and employment. This is likely to involve stronger patterns of 'licence to practise' vocational training, generated nationally and regionally, which bind together the employer, the provider, and the young person in a common agreement to support the process of initial qualification. The Health and Science Pathway in East London, a collaboration between a local NHS Trust, Tower Hamlets College and a number of 11–18 schools, provides an innovative example of developing coherent skills and progression routes across a range of partners.

It is now widely recognised that the challenges of employment and regeneration have to be addressed at a regional level. While London houses a very large number of small and medium enterprises, some of which operate very locally, there are also many who work and recruit at a metropolitan or wider level. Those responsible for education, skills, and employment in London have clearly identified the need to make more overt links between the education and training system and the needs of London employers and employment. Currently, there are a number of regional organisations and initiatives focusing on 14–19 education and training, either as their sole focus (e.g. London 14–19 Forum and the Pan London Vision) or as part of a broader skills and employability agenda (e.g. the newly formed London Skills and Employment Board chaired by the Mayor of London).

A brief analysis suggests the following three patterns of development:

***Regional initiatives to implement government policy*** – for example, *Vision for 14–19 in London 2005–2008* (DfES *et al.* 2005), which seeks to reduce the present inequality of provision through a London-wide learner entitlement that includes the acquisition of functional skills, an increase in apprenticeship places, and access to the new Diplomas through both physical and virtual learning arrangements.

***Co-ordinating a 14–19 London landscape through regional collaboration*** – several regional agencies are working together in the 14–19 London Forum to develop an e-prospectus of learning opportunities across the capital, to map specialist training providers, including FE colleges and Centres of Vocational Excellence, to maximise employer engagement and to disseminate good practice to support both regional and national needs.

***A democratically determined and distinctive London approach to skills and employment*** – the London Skills and Employment Board, chaired by Ken Livingstone, was announced in July 2006, giving the Mayor responsibility for adult skills in the capital. This statement from a recent speech by Ken Livingstone (2006) indicates that he will prioritise London needs rather than simply follow national government policy:

> I do not have the slightest doubt that we can make a big impact by crafting that skills strategy to London's needs rather than the present situation where we are part of a national strategy. London's economy is so different that we need to have, quite specifically, a skills strategy that answers our needs.
>
> (Annual Public Meeting of the London Development Agency, 12 September 2006)

While this view represents a step change in regional governance in England (because it includes the majority of publicly funded adult education and training) it does not yet extend to 14–19 education.

## Conclusion

In this essay we have argued that a pan-London 14–19 education and training system needs to become more than a figment of the imagination. We have described how current national 14–19 policy, which focuses primarily on a narrow set of reforms designed to raise the profile of vocational education, holds only half the solution and how regional planning, while still in its infancy, could become a powerful force for change in London. If London is able to develop a more holistic and inclusive approach to 14–19 learning to meet the needs of its diverse population and dynamic economy and is able to organise learning and skills in a more cost-effective and democratic way, then the capital could set the example for the country at large as to how the concept of a city/region might become more than a new form of rhetoric. We have concluded by proposing that four dimensions need to be brought together – a distinctive vision linking learning, inclusion, innovation, and future employment; a unified curriculum and qualifications system forged out of current developments; the creation of strongly collaborative local learning systems as dynamic entities within a regional framework; and, finally, a democratically accountable approach to regional employment and employer engagement linked back to the 14–19 education and training system.

**References**

Association of London Government (2005) *Breaking Point: Examining the disruption caused by pupil mobility*. London: ALG.

Department for Communities and Local Government (DCLG) (2006*) Strong and prosperous communities: The Local Government White Paper.* Norwich: HMSO.

Department of Education and Science (DES) (1982) *The ILEA Bridging Course. Report from the English national evaluators.* DES/EEC Transition to Work Programme. London: DES.

Department for Education and Skills (DfES) (2002) *14–19 Education: Extending opportunities, raising standards.* London: DfES.

— (2003) *14–19: Excellence and Opportunity: Government response to the 14–19 Green Paper.* London: DfES.

— (2004) *Five-Year Strategy for Children and Learners.* London: DfES.

— (2005a) *14–19 Education and Skills.* London: DfES.

— (2005b) *14–19 Implementation Plan.* London: DfES.

— (2005c) *GCSE and Equivalent for Young People in England 2004–5: Provisional Statistical First Release* 46/2005. London: DfES.

— (2006) *The Specialised Diploma Gateway*. London: DfES.

— (2007) *Raising Expectations: Staying on in Education and Training Post-16.* London: DfES.

DfES, Government Office for London and LSC (2005) *Vision for 14–19 in London 2005–2008: Pan London Actions.* Nottingham: DfES.

Dorling, D., Rigby, J., Wheeler, B., Ballas, D., Thomas, B., Fahmy, E., Gordon, D. and Lupton, R. (2007) *Poverty, Wealth and Place in Britain, 1968 to 2005.* Bristol: Policy Press.

Duckett, I., Grainger P., Smith D. (2007) *Skills for the Olympics.* London: LSN.

Finegold, D., Keep, E., Miliband, D., Raffe, D., Spours, K. and Young, M. (1990) *A British Baccalaureate: Overcoming divisions between education and training.* London: IPPR.

Fullick, L. (2006) '14–19 in London: current achievements and future challenges'. Speech at the Institute of Education, University of London, 11 July.

— Grainger, P., Hodgson, A., Spours, K., Truelove, J. and Waring, M., (2007) '14–19 Partnership Working in London: Towards effective and Inclusive local and regional collaborative learning systems'. Paper prepared for the London Learning and Skills Council.

Further Education Curriculum Review and Development Unit (1982) *A Basis for Choice: Report of a study group on post 16 pre-employment courses.* London: FECRDU.

Further Education Unit (FEU) (1992) *A Basis for Credit?* London: FEU.

Hayward, G., Hodgson, A., Johnson, J., Oancea, A., Pring, R., Spours, K., Wright, S. and Wilde, S. (2005) *Annual Report of the Nuffield 14–19 Review 2004–5.* OUDES Oxford: University of Oxford.

— Hodgson, A., Johnson, J., Keep, E., Oancea, A., Pring, R., Spours, K., Wright, S. and Wilde, S. (2006) *Annual Report of the Nuffield 14–19 Review 2005–6.* OUDES Oxford: University of Oxford.

Higham, J. and Yeomans, D. (2006) *Emerging Provision and Practice in 14–19 Education and Training. A report on the evaluation of the third year of the 14–19 Pathfinder initiative*. DfES Research Report RR737. Nottingham: DfES.

Higher Education Funding Council for England (HEFCE) <www.hefce.ac.uk/polar> (accessed April 2007).

Hodgson, A. and Spours, K. (2003) *Beyond A Levels: Curriculum 2000 and the reform of 14–19 qualifications.* London: Kogan Page.

— (2004) 'Reforming 14–19 learning: towards a new comprehensive phase of education'. *New Economy*, 11 (4): 217–23.

— (2006) 'The organisation of 14–19 education and training in England: Beyond weakly collaborative arrangements'. *Journal of Education and Work,* 19(4): 325–42.

— (2007) 'Specialised Diplomas: transforming the 14–19 landscape in England?'. *Journal of Education Policy,* 22 (6): 695-711.

Hodgson, A., Spours, K. and Wilson, P. (2006) *Tomlinson and the Framework for Achievement: A unified answer to a divided system.* Leicester: NIACE.

Hodgson, A., Spours, K., Steer, R., Coffield, F., Finlay, I., Edward, S. and Gregson, M. (2005) *A New Learning and Skills Landscape? The LSC within the learning and skills sector.* ESRC TLRP Project 'Impact of Policy on Learning and Inclusion' Research Report 1. London: Institute of Education, University of London.

Lefebvre, H. (1991) *The Production of Space.* Oxford: Blackwell.

Learning and Skills Council (2006) *Targeting Worklessness in London – Socio economic analysis.* London: LDA.

— (2007a) *The London Region Strategic Analysis 2007–8.* London: LSC.

— (2007b) *The London Learning and Skills Plan; Regional Commissioning Plan for London 2007–08*. London: LSC.

Livingstone, K. (2006) 'Vision for London'. Speech to the APM, 12 September, <www.lda.gov.uk/server/show/ConWebDoc.1621> (accessed February 2007).

Mayor of London (2004) *Higher and Further Education in London. A Review.* London: GLA.

Prince's Trust (2007) *The Cost of Exclusion, Counting the cost of youth disillusion in the UK*. London: the Prince's Trust.

Spours, K., Coffield, F. and Gregson, M. (2007) 'Mediation, translation and local ecologies: understanding the impact of policy levers on FE colleges'. *Journal of Vocational Education and Training,* 59(2): 193–211.

Stanton, G. and Fletcher, M. (2006) *14–19 Institutional Arrangements in England – A research perspective on collaboration, competition and patterns of post-16 provision.* Paper prepared for Nuffield Review of 14–19 Education and Training Seminar, 12 July.

Tirrell, J., Winter, A.M. and Hawthorne, S. (2006) *Challenges Facing Partnerships: current developments towards implementation of 14–19 in local authorities.* Sheffield: LEACAN 14+.

Unwin, L. and Fuller, A. (2003) *Expanding Learning in the Workplace*. NIACE Policy Discussion Paper. Leicester: NIACE.

Working Group on 14–19 Reform (2004) *14–19 Curriculum and Qualifications Reform: final report of the Working Group.* London: DfES.

# 11 Adult learners in a global city

Leisha Fullick

## Introduction

London is a dynamic city that currently is enjoying the status of one of the exemplar global cities of the early twenty-first century. It also clearly manifests what Castells describes as the 'sharp divide between valuable and non valuable people and locales,' where highly educated prosperous elites derive benefits from the city that are denied to increasingly marginalised and insecure social groups (Castells 1998). Thus, in common with other advanced, prosperous global cities, achieving social justice and combating inequality present considerable challenges. Improvements in schooling in London have, as described elsewhere in this book, enjoyed much attention as a key means for achieving greater social inclusion in the city. But the importance of adult learning to the economic and social health of London, which has been a constant theme in the capital since the end of the nineteenth century, is now also enjoying the highest profile it has ever had. New Labour governments since 1997 have taken the education of adults more seriously than any other political administrations in the UK in the twentieth century and have given substantial policy attention and funding to the promotion of adult learning in England (Taylor 2005). This has led to an expansion of learning opportunities for adults in London in the last ten years, and to massive reforms in the structures and mechanisms for delivery.

This essay reviews and analyses the nature and impact of this expansion in the context of the proposition that the public provision of effective education opportunities for adults is fundamental to the success of diverse global cities such as London. It examines the characteristics of current and potential adult learners in London in the socio-economic context of the city and reviews the supply of adult learning in a complex policy environment that encompasses a national framework, a powerful Mayor, a fragmented education system, and an employer structure that includes many major global corporations (including one-third of all Fortune 500 companies), very large public employers such as the NHS, and thousands of small- and medium-size enterprises.

This essay will seek to offer a wider definition of the goals and objectives for adult learning in London than the one that has developed since New Labour came to power in 1997. The commitment to improving education opportunities for adults, which has been a feature of the last ten years, has become increasingly narrowly focused. The term 'adult education' itself has all but disappeared from contemporary discourse, and the concept of lifelong learning (which enjoyed some vogue in the early years of the New Labour government) has not really been developed in current policy. Instead, we have a policy that is primarily about skills formation in order to promote economic competitiveness and growth. While economic and employment growth are rightly seen as fundamental to combating social exclusion and promoting social justice, they have become increasingly seen as the only way to do this, and there is now an absence of a conceptual framework for learning throughout the lifespan which embraces richer notions of social and human capital development. While unemployment and worklessness are prime drivers of poverty, and cities with more jobs tend to have less poverty and social exclusion, to achieve the levels of participation in learning that a more inclusive city would require there needs to be a broader approach with a better balance between adult learning as an investment good, a social good, and consumption good.

London of course has a long and proud history in the education of adults. The political leadership of London, stretching back to the first

London School Boards of the 1870s, always recognised its role in promoting vocational opportunities for adults linked to London's industry, and the importance of education for personal and creative development in a socially and culturally diverse city (Maclure 1990). This led, in Inner London, from the 1950s onwards, to a comprehensive system of adult learning opportunities, increasingly focused on giving access and opportunity to disadvantaged groups. While this essay will not cover in detail the history of those developments, which have been well documented elsewhere (Cushman 1996), the importance of this tradition to the capital should not be underestimated. It was a powerful lever for promoting social cohesion and it successfully nurtured vocational excellence in many areas of importance to London's economy. It is a tradition that lives on within many London providers in the further education, higher education, and the voluntary and community sectors. It deserves recognition and respect for what it might teach us for the present and the future education and training of adults in London.

## London's adults

As Lupton and Sullivan detail in Essay 1, there are high levels of income and education polarisation in London and huge differences in economic and social opportunity between different ethnic groups, between men and women, and between younger and older people. This polarisation provides the backdrop to understanding need and demand for adult learning in London and gives some indication of the size of the challenge presented to policy makers, employers, and providers concerned with adult learning in the city.

The challenge in many ways is one of success. London is a prosperous city characterised by strong growth in population, employment, and earnings. London is literally rejuvenating itself, as a consistently large flow of well-qualified young adults from overseas and elsewhere in the UK enters the capital to take up the new employment opportunities: 42.8 per cent of the population is aged 20–44 while only 14.4 per cent of the population is over 60 (LDA 2005a). The workforce is generally well qualified – currently around 30 per cent of the workforce is qualified to level 4 (equivalent to first degree level) – the highest overall level of any English region (LDA 2005a).[1]

However, the growth in opportunity has been highly uneven and has left large numbers of people behind. London's employment growth has been fuelled by increases in managerial, professional, and technical jobs, while skilled manual work in trade and manufacturing as well as lower grade administrative jobs have been in terminal decline over the last 20 years. Many more Londoners face an increasingly unfriendly labour market (GLA 2002). The new jobs in London require skilled labour and it is predicted that 47 per cent of all jobs will require higher level skills and qualifications by 2014 (LSC 2007). Those in unskilled jobs have not benefited from the marked growth in real earnings arising from London's economic prosperity. Lower paid workers, particularly women and part-time workers, have seen much lower growth in earnings (GLA 2002).

London has the lowest percentage of its working-age population actually in employment (70 per cent overall) of any region in England, and Inner London has the highest levels of unemployment in England (LDA 2005a). Most economically inactive people have never had a job at all or have been out of work for more than two years. Attempts to explain the high rate of non-employment among working age Londoners point to strong competition for lower skilled jobs, and the comparatively high numbers of women and young people in this category, many of them from minority ethnic groups (Gordon 2006).

Employment levels are closely linked to education levels, and this polarisation in earnings and employment opportunities is reflected in the education qualifications of London's residents. The proportion of London *residents* with higher level qualifications is lower than that of the London workforce as a whole and residents represent a disproportionate number of the low qualified in work, indicating that commuters from elsewhere occupy many of the higher skilled jobs.

Overall it is estimated that 23 per cent of London's white population and 28 per cent of black residents are only qualified to level 1 or not at all (LDA 2005a). Nineteen per cent of unemployed people and 28 per cent of the economically inactive (workless) have no qualifications at all (LDA 2005a). The education background and skills of refugees and asylum seekers is above average in comparison with the host population (GLA 2001). However, there are many obstacles to marrying labour market demands with the skills and motivation of refugees and asylum seekers, and Refugee Council research shows that there are disproportionately high levels of unemployment among refugees and asylum seekers (Penrose2002).

Recent research suggests that there are 900,000 people of working age with literacy problems in London and a staggering 2.3 million with very poor numeracy skills (LDA 2006). These problems are compounded by underachievement of many young people in London's schools. While there have been huge improvements in the numbers of young people in recent years gaining a level 2 qualification (equivalent in standard and breadth to five good passes at General Certificate of Secondary Education (GCSE) level, in 2005–6 10,000 young people in London failed to gain GCSE passes in English and maths and 2.5 per cent achieved no passes at GCSE (DfES 2006). In addition it is estimated there are 600,000 people who may have need of ESOL (English as a second or other language) provision (LDA 2006).

While London has the image of being a city of young people, the over 60s represent 1.2 million people, of whom a quarter of a million are over 80. The number of older people is projected to increase by nine per cent by 2021 (GLA 2006). Even though employment rates for those over 50 have risen in recent years, only 68 per cent of those between 50 and pensionable age are in work, compared to 76 per cent in work between the ages of 25 and 49. Worklessness among older minority ethnic groups and women is higher than that of men. Qualification levels among older workers are much lower and older workers are less likely to be given training opportunities in the workplace (GLA 2006). There is considerable evidence nationally of the exclusion of people aged 55 to 65 from the labour market and from volunteering (Tuckett and McAuley 2005). Evidence of participation in adult learning consistently shows people over the age of 55 being the least likely to participate in any form of adult learning, and that participation correlates strongly with levels of qualification and socio-economic status (Tuckett and McAuley 2005). This is a serious issue for the London labour market. The skills needs of the London workforce cannot be met solely by young labour market entrants. As the twenty-first century progresses, there will not be enough young people in the cohort to fill all the jobs the economy requires. By 2020 25 per cent of the UK population will be over 60, with only about half the population under 45 (Leitch 2006). While in London the high levels of inward migration of working age young people and adults look to continue, there will also be the need to train and retrain mature people to enable them to enter and to remain longer in the workforce.

All in all these statistics point to the fact that there are a considerable proportion of London residents who are not able to take advantage of the opportunities this prosperous global city has to offer. Low skills are increasingly a significant barrier to participation in the labour market in a way they were not in the past. Particular groups are disproportionately affected – older people, people from minority ethnic and linguistic backgrounds, disabled people, and migrants. Supporting these marginalised groups into education and employment is a social justice as well as a labour market imperative. Unless more adults in London gain the skills they need to participate in employment and civil society then the high levels of poverty and social exclusion will continue. Unfortunately, the organisation and nature of the provision for adult learners in London, and the policy approaches that underpin that provision have many features that militate against London rising to that challenge. These are discussed in more detail in the rest of this essay.

## Adult learning in London: the move from local to national leadership

Developments in the last 15 years have meant that the adult learning strategy in London has become increasingly determined by national policy imperatives. This was not always the case. The development of publicly supported adult learning provision in London was firmly rooted in local government. While there was never a coherent London-wide approach to adult learning, the Inner London Education Authority (ILEA) (which was until 1990 responsible for education in the 13 Inner London boroughs) had a vigorous and comprehensive strategy for adult education and ran what was regarded as the finest such provision for adults in any city in the world. Most of the Outer London boroughs (who were individually responsible for their education services) also maintained a strong tradition of supporting a system of vocational and non-vocational opportunities for adults, where adult learning needs were seen as important to the economic and social fabric of the community and were catered for at every level. This leadership and funding through local government encompassed further education (FE) colleges, some higher education (HE) institutions, adult education institutes and centres, and grants to the Workers Education Association (WEA) and other voluntary bodies (McClure 1990). It was the type of education that had been seen as particularly important to London for well over 100 years, meeting social, economic, and community needs in highly responsive and innovative ways. It was a popular, low cost, largely voluntary activity, much of it non-accredited, with a broad curriculum determined by student demand, professional passion, and social and political commitment (Cushman 1997).

This system came to an end in 1992 when the Further and Higher Education Act removed further education colleges from local authority control and funding for FE and most adult education passed to a new quango – the Further Education Funding Council (FEFC). Colleges were no longer within a local authority planning framework, and were expected to operate competitively and independently of each other. In

London, as elsewhere, local authorities ceased to be the main providers of adult learning from that date. However, the vast majority of London boroughs did seek to continue to play a role in adult education – as indeed they had the powers and the legal duty to do – either through their own structures or through contractual arrangements with local FE colleges. This role was not easy to sustain, as the 1990s was a period of considerable structural and financial turbulence in local government, and by the end of the decade there had been a significant decline in the local authority adult education provision in London, with consequent loss of expertise in, and funding for, the kinds of programmes described above. However, through the 1990s many FE colleges expanded their provision for adults, mostly through the large growth in funding for accredited courses. While this growth in adult access to accredited programmes did to some extent offset the decline in adult provision overall, in London in the 1990s it has been estimated that non-vocational non-accredited provision in London had declined to 25 per cent of pre-1992 levels by 1997 (Cushman 1997).

The trend for national as opposed to local leadership of adult learning instituted by the establishment of FEFC has accelerated since 1997 with the shape and scope of the supply of adult learning in London increasingly determined by national funding regimes and structures. The New Labour government since 1997 have devoted a huge amount of policy attention to adult learning and have produced a number of major reports focused on improving adult skills in England. Over time the focus on economic 'human capital' imperatives has become stronger and the concept of lifelong learning has changed to a concept that is primarily about acquiring or improving employability skills. The first ever comprehensive National Skills Strategy was published in 2005. The main thrust of the Skills Strategy is to ensure employers have the right skills to support business success and individuals have the skills to be employable and personally fulfilled. The main mechanisms proposed to achieve this are to vastly improve qualification levels of the English workforce (using these as a proxy for skills levels), to raise the number of working age adults qualified to at least level two (considered by the government to be the basic measure of employability) and to make the provision of learning opportunities more demand led (DfES *et al.* 2005).

The main motivation for this approach has been concern about the competitive pressures on the economy arising from globalisation, and the recognition that the UK will struggle in the future to maintain its strong economic position in the face of growing economies such as those of China and India. Improving the skills levels of the UK population is seen as the main means to counter this threat. The Skills Strategy was given added impetus in 2006 when the Treasury commissioned a further major review of skills – the Leitch review. The Leitch Report, which has now been accepted by government as the platform for the next phase of reform, recommended acceleration in this process and for the UK to become a world leader in 'economically valuable' skills by 2020.This will mean doubling the 2005 levels of attainment by that date. In order for this to be achieved, the Leitch Report has called for a revolution in attitudes to learning in England, leading to a massive increase in learning undertaken by individuals and provided by employers. The strategy for achieving this revolution in attitude is the creation of a new 'demand led' system for adult learning with funding placed in the hands of individuals and employers to enable them to purchase employment-related skills training (Leitch 2006).

## Adult learning in London: the regional landscape

This strong national focus on increasing adult attainment levels has led to almost continuous restructuring and the proliferation of government agencies and strategies charged with fulfilling a growing number of targets and plans in the lifelong learning area through an equally large number of initiatives and funding streams. There has also been an increasing focus on the involvement of employers in the new structures and in the planning and provision of publicly funded adult learning opportunities. This has led to the presence in London of a number of regional bodies working alongside local government, education and training institutions, and private sector companies to widen participation in adult learning. While the regional focus, employer involvement, and the emphasis on partnership working have all been welcome developments, they have led, in London, as elsewhere, to a system of considerable complexity that has lacked a holistic approach to the planning of responsive and effective provision (Coffield 2006).

## The Learning and Skills Council

The biggest regional player for adult learning in London since 2001 has been the Learning and Skills Council (LSC). The creation of the LSC in 2001 was the most important structural initiative of New Labour in its drive to revolutionise adult learning and skills in England. It was the first national public body to be given the remit to promote adult learning and increase the participation of adults (Fullick 2004). On its establishment, the LSC took over the funding of further education from the FEFC and brought together funding and policy for the vast bulk of education and training post-16 (excluding higher education). Training and Enterprise Councils (TECs), established in 1989 to provide and promote employer-based training and workforce development, were also incorporated into the LSC. Huge importance was attached to the role of the LSC in widening participation, driving forward improvements and bringing greater coherence and responsiveness to the whole of the post-16 education and training system. The national grant to the Learning and Skills Council more than doubled from 2001–2 to 2006 while investment in FE colleges has increased by 48 per cent since 1997 (Coffield 2006).

In London the LSC became the biggest public funder of adult learning opportunities (£560m in 2006–7); initially through five local LSCs and latterly through a unified regional structure, it became the lead body for the funding and planning of the bulk of post-16 education and work-based learning in the capital, presiding over a massive wave of expansion and reform in the education of adults, focused on meeting national skills improvement targets, delivered largely through nationally devised programmes and initiatives. The top priority has been to improve basic skills and intermediate (level two) and technical skills levels (level three). Growth in participation and qualification levels in these areas has been achieved through fee remission strategies, better advice, guidance, and marketing and, most notably, through the 'Train to Gain' initiative, a brokerage service which subsidises employers who release staff to achieve first full level 2 qualifications (equivalent to five GCSE grades A*–C) and basic skills qualifications. Reflecting the level of need in London, provision for 'basic skills' (deemed to be literacy, numeracy, English as a second or other language (ESOL) and IT skills) have been the biggest growth area for adults in recent years. In 2005–6 there were 71,695 enrolments by adults on literacy, numeracy, and other key skills courses in London and 155,787 enrolments on ESOL courses, the ESOL provision accounting for half of all such provision in England.[2]

## Tackling poverty, unemployment, and social exclusion

Over the same period as the expansion of LSC activity, other new regional developments arising from government strategies have shaped the range and nature of adult learning opportunities in London. Much of this has taken place through the growth in national strategies to tackle social exclusion, poverty, and unemployment in urban areas. Another regional agency – Government Office for London – has the role of supporting a 'coherent regional approach' to sustainable development, regeneration, and social inclusion and it does this through its own raft of government programmes, such as the National Strategy for Neighbourhood Renewal, New Deal for Communities and the oversight of the Every Child Matters strategy. Programmes delivered through these strategies by schools, local authorities, health agencies, employment services such as Job Centre Plus, prisons, the voluntary sector, disability organisations, and others often have a significant adult education component that recognises the role it plays in the well-being of deprived urban communities. Largely because of the fragmentation and complexity of much of this activity, the impact of these programmes on the scale of lifelong learning in London is under-researched and difficult to gauge but it is clear that it has made a substantial contribution to sustaining lifelong learning in London. The Neighbourhood Renewal (NR) strategy in particular has seen innovative approaches to raising education and skills levels of adults in deprived urban areas as being essential to achieving social cohesion and regeneration , with London receiving considerable NR funding (£129m in 2005–6) covering nineteen boroughs across the capital (see <www.neighbourhood.gov.uk>).

Nationally initiated regional economic and governance policies have also had a major impact on adult learning in London. Nine Regional Development Agencies (RDAs) were established across England in 1998. A unique regional governance structure for London was established in 2000 with a directly elected Mayor and regional assembly (the Greater London Authority). The London RDA – the London Development Agency – was made accountable to the Mayor. RDAs were given the task of developing Regional Frameworks for Employment and Skills Action (FRESA) designed to 'enhance the development and application of skills relevant to its area' (Fullick 2004). The Mayor early on established the London Skills Commission to develop a London skills action plan and to create cohesive and complementary approaches to skills development in London alongside the Mayor's economic development strategy. As well as promoting skills development, the LDA funds a range of projects under its own Skills and Employment Programme devoted to increasing employability skills for disadvantaged adults. In addition, the LDA in 2005–7 contracted out £9.8 million European Social Fund monies to support further education, training, and employment for disadvantaged adults in London. The LSC's ESF programme for adult skills was £152.5m for the same period.[3]

The importance of these adult learning developments, many of which were designed to tackle social exclusion, unemployment, and poverty, was highlighted in research undertaken by London Metropolitan University in 2006. This research presents a very rich picture of public, private, and voluntary sector activity in London, supporting the learning of disadvantaged groups including ex-offenders, refugees and asylum seekers, homeless people, and disabled people, in order for them to gain access to the labour market. However, the report also presents a picture of rigid and target driven funding arrangements, lack of co-ordination between funders and agencies, and fragmented and short-term funding with attendant lack of continuity and difficulty in being able to take a holistic view of client needs and to tailor provision to individual needs (Beutal and Paraskevopoulou 2006).

## Universities and colleges

At the same time the historic major providers of adult learning in London, the further education colleges and higher education institutions have been a significant part of the regional infrastructure. London has one of the greatest concentrations of universities in the world, which supports much of London's highly skilled workforce. London's 44 HE institutions have 350,000 students and over half of them are adults aged over 25. Over one-third of students are part time (GLA 2004). There are a further 20,000 London based adults studying in the Open University. There are 36 further education and tertiary colleges, as well as five specialist adult colleges (the Specially Designated Institutions) catering for adult students. Recent developments, such as two year Foundation Degrees and lifelong learning networks, which promote links and progression between FE and HE in key sectoral vocational areas, emphasise the importance of university and college-based adult learning to the London economy and labour market. The decline of university 'extra mural' liberal adult education, which accompanied the mainstreaming of adults into accredited university courses and degrees in the 1980s and 1990s, has perhaps been less marked in London than elsewhere, with colleges such as Birkbeck and Goldsmiths maintaining solid non-vocational as well as vocational programmes for adults. London also has a long history of part-time vocationally oriented HE for adults, much of it delivered through former polytechnics such as the University of Westminster and London South Bank University, and these as well as many other HE institutions have a wide offer of continuing education and professional development that provides training and skills development for adults working in London's economic sectors and public services.

The Leitch Report has proposed that 40 per cent of all adults in the workforce should have degree level (level four) qualifications by 2020 (Leitch 2006). To achieve this figure, even in London, where the number of level four qualifications is relatively high, the effective contribution of HE and FE is fundamentally important. However, the potential has yet to be fully realised, particularly as far as FE is concerned.

The House of Commons Education and Skills Select Committee in its report on Further Education (House of Commons 2006) criticised the 'complex and unwieldy morass of planning funding and stakeholder bodies that overlay further education'. Many of London's colleges were, and are, large, confident, well-led institutions providing their student body and wider community with an education offer appropriate to its diverse cultural and social profile. Their contribution to the London adult learning system has been immense over more than 100 years. In London the new management system post-2001 with its five Learning and Skills Councils was an unhappy combination of national central command and inappropriate local delivery structures, which found it difficult to take account of the reality of London as a unified travel-to-work and travel-to-learn area with colleges that have a large regional reach. The five local LSCs struggled and failed to achieve a London-wide perspective on learning and skills strategy and further education's role within it. Despite attempting a series of major strategic area reviews in the early years of the twenty-first century a London-wide strategic vision for a coherent and confident further education and post-school system across London was never achieved. Further education, still a key to the delivery of an effective adult learning strategy for London, now faces a further set of uncertainties. The Leitch Report has recommended that by 2010 all public funding for adult vocational skills, apart from community learning, should be routed through employers and learners. And the new post-Leitch policy that only courses approved by Sector Skills Councils should receive state funding in the future means that there could be a prospect of the 'turning off' of funding for a range of provision and qualifications currently on offer in London colleges that does not fit government and employer priorities.

## Participation in adult learning

While this legacy of a proliferation of agencies, initiatives, and funding regimes, and policies that are often incoherent or contradictory still remains, there is no doubt that London does have a richness of provision which has been effective in widening opportunity and participation for adult learners in recent years.

While there is no one easily accessible source of information about participation in adult learning in London there are a number of indicators which point to relatively buoyant levels of demand and participation in recent years. In 2005–6, the LSC reported that there were around 442,000 adult learners in LSC-funded further education (FE) and University for Industry (UFI) provision in London and 5,920 adults in work-based learning provision ranging from advanced apprenticeships to Entry for Employment programmes. An estimated 130,990 students participated in LSC-funded community education programmes (the LSC's new Personal and Community Development Learning and other programmes) largely delivered through local authorities, London's five adult colleges (known as the Specially Designated Institutions) and the voluntary sector (all figures provided to author personally by LSC London Region). All London boroughs, with the exception of the City, provide adult education for their residents – some going well beyond LSC-funded courses in the scope and level of their provision. 'Floodlight', a well-established listing service for part-time day and evening courses in all London boroughs, listed over 40,000 courses, including HE courses and courses offered by private colleges in 2007 (Floodlight 2007). Further numbers participate in adult learning programmes through voluntary activity, the University of the Third Age, and London's 250-plus museums and galleries. It would perhaps be reasonable to assume that the total adult participation figure is at least double the numbers funded by the LSC. This could mean that perhaps at least 1 million adults out of an adult population of approximately 5 million are participating in learning delivered through London public and voluntary sector education.

Learning provided by employers (other than LSC-funded work-placed learning) is likely to be equally significant but even more difficult to estimate. The National Institute for Adult and Continuing Education (NIACE) conducts a national annual survey of adult participation in learning, which showed that in 2005, 44 per cent of adult Londoners reported recent or current participation in learning (McGivney 2006). The NIACE and other surveys also show that you are much more likely to be engaging in learning if you are at work (OECD 2004). The National Local Area Labour Force Survey, which specifically surveys people in the workplace, shows 50 per cent reporting on participation in taught learning in the London region 2004–5. The London participation figures are the highest after the South east and the South west regions (Mcgivney 2006). The National Employers Skills Survey, undertaken by the LSC, states that employers in London spend £5.8 billion on training employees (LSC 2006b). Training by employers is five times more likely to go on highly skilled workers than on low-skilled workers and there is no evidence to suggest London is any different in this respect.

While this high level of reported participation gives some indication of the strength of the contribution of London's employers to learning in the capital, a large task remains to be done to understand the nature and impact of the employer contribution to the London adult learning landscape. In addition, the lack of a complete overview of adult learning participation and the fact that there is no overall policy drive to raise participation as such (all the focus is on funding particular qualification outputs) are yet further ways in which a coherent approach to lifelong learning in London is undermined. The new employer-led Employment and Skills Board, discussed later in this essay, will hopefully be able to develop this overview and to enable an integrated understanding of how the whole private and public sector provision adds up for the benefit of Londoners.

## The risks to adult learning in London

Whatever the positive aspect to these participation figures, it is not the whole picture and there are no grounds for complacency. The NIACE 2005 participation survey shows 55 per cent of London respondents saying they are unlikely to be taking up learning opportunities in the future (Aldrich and Tuckett 2005). Nationally, such intentions are strongly linked to age, class, and current participation and, given the social and demographic profile of London adults described above, this would suggest that many less well qualified, poorer, and older Londoners are showing little sign of a willingness to participate in learning.

And, for all the good intentions of current policies, it is possible that their effect is making things worse, not better, for some Londoners. Nationally we know that the number of adult learners has not grown significantly in the last ten years (Aldrich and Tuckett 2005) and is now declining. In 2005–6 the number of adults on LSC-funded programmes decreased by nearly 700,000. At the same time, adult and community-based learning numbers fell by nearly ten per cent and the numbers in first level and entry level programmes fell by 19.9 per cent. Participation by older learners has declined markedly with a loss of around 22 per cent of 50- to 60-year-olds and a loss between 2004 and 2006 of around one-third of students over 60 years of age (Flint 2007). A NIACE survey in May 2007 indicated that a half a million adults have been lost to learning in 2006–7 (Aldrich and Tuckett 2007). This trend is likely to continue. The LSC has planned that in 2007–8, 45 per cent of its college funded provision in London will be for young people; 15 per cent will go on ' Skills for Life'; 16 per cent will go on level two; and 13 per cent will go on level 3. It has planned a 3.7 per cent cut to the adult further education budget; 'other' adult education will only amount to about three per cent of funded provision overall.[4]

This drop in the number of adults learning has been a direct consequence of a national policy priority to focus on funding increasing participation and improved education outcomes for the 16–19 age group and to put the bulk of national funding for adults into the 'economically valuable' parts of adult learning – the obtaining of qualifications either at basic skills level or at level two. While it should be recognised that the investment in basic skills and level two qualifications for adults has delivered to large numbers of people the important fundamentals of learning, and has focused real resources on some of the poorest and least qualified adults, the consequences of the policy have also been to threaten London's rich learning market for adults and the diversity and the responsiveness of its provision.

From 2005–6 there have been big fee increases for adult classes in London and the closure of a wide range of courses that did not fit into priority categories. Much of the decline in provision has occurred because students were not able or willing to pay sudden and high fee rises, but entry level courses for the most disadvantaged and learning support have also disappeared as funding has been redirected to increasing the number of qualifications at level two. The disappearance of mainstream provision because people are resistant to paying higher fees affects everyone and leads to the loss of that provision for low-income people attending such courses on reduced fees. This, together with any threat to the volume of entry level courses and community-based courses that do not fit the priorities, could result in a decline in the overall demand for learning and make it even more difficult to move disadvantaged Londoners into the qualifications based learning they desperately need. This is serious in London where approximately one-third of Londoners are not educated to level two and where high levels of social and economic need demonstrate that many people are very far from aspiring to this level.

This wider adult education curriculum is also essential to social connectedness, culture, creativity, and citizenship. Research shows that the adult learning of any kind has individual and wider societal benefits such as health, civic participation, and racial tolerance (Schuller *et al.* 2004). Such issues are of enormous importance to London. As well as being social goods in their own right, they also ultimately have an economic value. While London currently may be able to import more than its fair share of highly qualified young workers, if the city's own social and cultural capital is not strong then it will struggle to continue to attract the human and financial investment it needs. In the context of globalisation, with the constant risk that finance and business will go elsewhere, London also needs a social and civic base that will maintain its attractiveness and world city status; and a wide diversity of learning opportunities makes an important contribution to such a status.

While a tightly focused national adult learning strategy based upon a demand-led, employer-led system offering a basket of accredited skills to individuals will work well for some Londoners, it is not the solution to the complex and diverse societal structure of London. We need provision that is sensitive to the full range of determinants for adult learning for men and for women and for people from different cultures. Research on adult learning shows that education programmes that are responsive to a very broad range of personal motivation are often most effective and aid progression (Mcgivney 2001). As well as listening to adults themselves we also need to listen to London providers who probably know better than most about how and why adults in the capital learn and the range of factors influencing people's willingness to engage in learning. The current national strategy may aspire to achieve a cultural step change in attitudes to learning but its narrow approach to economically valuable skills and to demand-led provision is in danger of actually reducing choice in the London context and destroying a whole raft of activity proven to be successful in engaging people in learning and moving them on to employability.

## New developments and challenges

To be fair, more recent policy statements are according more importance to ensuring that learning for social as well as direct employment benefits will be available at affordable prices (LSC 2006a) and there is also more interest in a more holistic approach to the delivery of adult learning. There are signs of a renewal of focus on the importance of adult learning through local government. Local Area Agreements (LAAs) have been initiated to pool various funding streams from central government, including health, community safety, and regeneration, to give local authorities and their partners the flexibility to devise local solutions to local problems. It is intended that Personal and Community Development Learning (PCDL) commissioned through the LSC will be brought together in the Local Area Agreements to support community development, health, and community cohesion through the provision of leisure, community related, and family learning in a wide variety of contexts. In London the hope must be that the LAA mechanism will enable local authorities and others to continue to develop and deliver a socially responsive, coherent, and co-ordinated adult education provision in their local areas.

At the same time the Lyons Inquiry into the role of local government has recognised the importance of the links that need to be made between planning for local learning and skills needs and local government's role in economic regeneration and employment. Lyons' call for local government to play a stronger 'place shaping' and economic development role would seem to imply that local authorities may engage more with skills issues in the future, working with employers on local Employment and Skills Boards (as proposed by the Leitch Report) to influence the development of skills training at local level (Lyons Inquiry 2007).

## The London Skills and Employment Board

Most importantly, for London there is now the prospect of better co-ordination at regional level. New legislation in 2006 gave the Mayor of London a new role in relation to adult skills, and powers to establish and chair a new London Skills and Employment Board with the remit to help to equip Londoners with the skills that best meet employer needs. The Board, established in December 2006, is employer-based and has responsibility for the strategy for adult skills in London. While it is supposed to work within the framework of the national skills strategy and to meet national skills targets it also has a remit to address London-specific needs. It will create its own strategy, which will drive the spending decisions of the LSC in London. There is no doubt that giving the Mayor overarching responsibility for economic development and adult skills strategy in London could give the impetus for a more effective and responsive approach to increasing the number and range of adult learners in the capital.

However, the big danger is that the change to current arrangements for the strategy and planning for adult learning and skills in London will simply result in another layer to be negotiated, leading to even more lack of responsiveness. The picture remains a very complex and uncertain one. The long phase of reform of the national framework, structure and institutions of adult learning, begun in 1992 and still continuing, has left a system in London that it is in danger of collapsing under the weight of its own contradictions. London still has its three 'heavy hitter' regional bodies (the Mayor, GOL and the LSC) with an interest in adult learning. To this may now be added the structures associated with the London 2012 Olympics and Para Olympics, both of which have been given targets to effect a permanent reduction in worklessness in London, particularly in the five 'host' East London boroughs. There is an urgent need for a less cluttered and confusing landscape and a better focus on meeting London's specific and economic priorities.

In this context it will be interesting to see how the LSC and further education, both essentially driven by national policy imperatives and funding priorities, will be able to become part of a new Mayor-led system aspiring to be responsive to the real needs of London residents and employers, and how this will integrate with social and economic programmes led through GOL. In particular the contradiction between a national policy based on unswerving commitment to a 'demand led system' which only funds specific nationally determined programmes and qualifications and the realities of the demands and needs of real people in London is likely to come into sharp relief as the new more regionally focused policies develop. Under the new arrangements the LSC retains its role as the biggest single funder for public sector adult learning in the capital and is now charged with implementing a new skills strategy for London led by the Mayor. However, following the recommendations of the Leitch Report, its planning role will be curtailed and its main task from 2010 will be to ensure there is a functioning marketplace for most adult learning in the capital driven by employer and consumer demand. Its attention will be on stimulating competition and developing capacity for new providers in an ever more diverse marketplace. Given this context the Board faces a considerable challenge in creating a balance of influence across the LSC, the LDA, GOL, the local authorities, and the plethora of other agencies, and in moving the focus from national policy imperatives to what London really needs in relation to lifelong learning.

## The future

The big challenge confronting the Skills and Employment Board is to get more London residents able to meet the level of skills that the London economy requires. Not only does the Board face the challenge of persuading many more individuals in work to invest in their own learning and many more London employers, particularly small employers, to invest in the skills levels of their workforce, it also means facing the equally big challenge of engaging large groups of Londoners in learning who are either out of work or at the margins of the labour market. While many employers do not have the incentive to do this because they can access good quality recruits from elsewhere, this challenge has to become more widely accepted as an economic and social imperative for London.

The attitude of such workers to engaging in further education and training and acquiring qualifications is very different from younger workers. Working with employers to meet this particular challenge will require a lifelong learning approach to skills acquisition and will require developing a braver and harder edged policy framework for lifelong learning in London. London needs to maintain and expand a diversity of approaches that engage with a wider framework which includes the work of the local authorities, extended schools, health, and the voluntary sector. Adult learning must be recognised as a crosscutting theme that is relevant to most main social and economic policy agendas and that this is the essential underpinning to an effective London skills strategy.

There is now an opportunity to be seized at Mayoral level to promote in London for the first time a cohesive adult learning system. The range and diversity of London agencies tackling education disadvantage is calling out for such a framework. The London skills strategy would then be part of an approach that not only recognises access for all to employability as the key to the future wellbeing of all Londoners but also recognises the role of learning in sustaining and enriching cultural value and social cohesion in London, and as highly relevant to the prosperity of London in its widest sense.

But this will only happen if it is recognised that the imperative to raise the skills levels of the workforce to meet the needs of the London economy is indivisible from the imperative of maintaining a high volume, broad, and flexible curriculum offer for adults in London. Such a curriculum offer is the foundation for a lifelong learning culture in London and a key to the future wellbeing of the city.

Many of the structural changes of the last 15 years were designed to ensure local delivery of national policy and to override the importance of local initiative in the adult learning field. This has been successful in establishing a priority for a learning society and expanding opportunity in some very important areas. However, there are real signs that the national system has led to a lack of responsiveness to local conditions and a diminution of opportunity for many adults who want to learn. Now London, by virtue of its history and social and economic dynamism, has the opportunity to become the national and international site of the first real ' big city strategy' for adult learners.

**References**

Aldrich, F. and Tuckett, A. (2005) *Better News This Time? The NIACE survey on adult participation in learning.* Leicester: NIACE.

Aldrich, F. and Tuckett, A. (2007) *The Road to Nowhere? The NIACE survey on adult participation in learning.* Leicester: NIACE.

Beutel, M. and Paraskevopoulou, A. (2006) *Tackling Disadvantage, Disengagement and Discrimination in London's Labour Market.* London: London Metropolitan University.

Castells, M. (1998) *End of Millennium, Volume 111.* Oxford: Blackwell.

Coffield, F. (2006) *Running Ever Faster Down the Wrong Road: An alternative future for education and skills.* London: Institute of Education.

Cushman, M. (1997) *The Great Jewel Robbery: Adult education in inner London since the break up of the Inner London Education Authority.* London: National Association of Teachers in Further and Higher Education.

Department for Education and Skills (DfES) (2006) *Secondary Schools (GCSE and Equivalent) Achievement and Attainment Tables.* London: DfES.

DfES, DTI, HM Treasury and DWP (2005) *Skills: Getting on in Business, Getting on at Work.* London: The Stationery Office.

Flint, C. (2007) 'Where now for Adult Learning?'. *Adults Learning*, 18(6): x, January 2007.

Floodlight (2007) *London's Original Course Guide*. London: Hotcourses.

Fullick, L. (2004) *Adult Learners in a Brave New World: Lifelong learning policy and structural change since 1997.* Leicester: NIACE.

Greater London Authority (GLA) (2001) *Refugees and Asylum Seekers in London: a GLA perspective.* London: Greater London Authority.

— (2002*) London Divided: Income inequality and poverty in the capital.* London: Greater London Authority.

GLA Economics (2004) *World City, World Knowledge: The economic contribution of London's higher education sector*. London: Greater London Authority.

— (2005) *Our London. Our Future. Planning for London's Growth 11: Summary Report.* London: Greater London Authority.

— (2006) *Annual Report.* London: Greater London Authority.

Gordon, I. (2006) 'London's economy and employment'. In Kochan, B. (ed.) *London Bigger and Better?* London: LSE.

House of Commons Education and Skills Select Committee (2006) *Fourth Report on Further Education.* London: The Stationery Office.

Learning and Skills Council (2006a*) Delivering World Class Skills in a Demand Led System.* Coventry: Learning and Skills Council.

— (2006b) *National Employers Skills Survey; Main Report*. Coventry: Learning and Skills Council

— (2007) *London Strategic Analysis*. London: Learning and Skills Council.

Leitch, S. (2006) *Leitch Review of Skills: Prosperity for all in the global economy – world class skills.* London: The Stationery Office.

London Development Agency (2005a) *Economic Development Strategy.* London: Greater London Authority.

— (2005b) *World Class Skills for the Global City: The London Skills Commission 2005/6 regional skills action plan.* London: Greater London Authority.

— (2006) *The London Skills for Life Strategy*. London: LDA.

Lyons Inquiry into Local Government (2007) *Place Shaping: A shared ambition for the future of local government.* London: The Stationery Office.

Maclure, S. (1990) *A History of Education in London 1870–1990.* London: Allen Lane.

McGivney, V. (2001) *Fixing or Changing the Pattern: Reflections on Widening Adult Participation in Learning.* Leicester: NIACE

McGivney, V. (2006) *Adult Learning at a Glance 2006.* Leicester: NIACE.

Mayor of London (2006) *Valuing Older People: The Mayor of London's older people strategy.* London: Greater London Authority.

Organisation for Economic Cooperation and Development (OECD) (2004) *Thematic Review on Adult Learning, United Kingdom (England).* Paris: OECD.

Penrose, J. (2002) *Poverty and Asylum in the UK.* London: Oxfam and the Refugee Council.

Schuller,T., Hammond, C., Bassett-Grundy, A. and Preston, J. (2004) *The Benefits of Learning: The impact of education on health, family life and social capital.* London: Routledge.

Taylor, R. (2005) *'Lifelong learning and the Labour governments 1997–2004'. Oxford Review of Education* 31(1): 101–18.

HM Treasury (2007) *Employment Opportunity for All: Tackling worklessness in London.* Norwich: The Stationery Office.

Tuckett, A. and McAuley, A. (2005) *Demography and Older Learners: Approaches to a new policy challenge.* Leicester: NIACE.

**Notes**

1 This essay refers to four of the levels in the National Qualifications Framework: level 1 Foundation level equivalent to GCSE D–G , Foundation GNVQ and NVQ level; level 2 equivalent to GCSE A*–C, Intermediate GNVQ and NVQ2; level 3 equivalent to AS/A-level, vocational A-level and NVQ3; level 4 equivalent to undergraduate degree and NVQ4.
2 Data provided to author by London LSC.
3 Data provided to author by LDA and London LSC.
4 Information provided to the author by London LSC 2007.

# 12 London: present lessons – future possibilities

Tim Brighouse, Leisha Fullick, Ruth Lupton and Anne Sofer

## Introduction

There are many ways in which London has been a major success story in the last 25 years. Its economy has flourished, its population has grown, and it is a major city for arts and culture. It presents a dynamic and optimistic image as one of the leading 'global' cities of the world. It is a highly diverse city and has many characteristics that it make it unique, not only in the UK but among other global cities. Essay 1 shows how London's size and population growth, its age structure, its economic structure, wages and housing market, and its high levels of inequality and child poverty all mark it out among British cities. So too does its ethnic diversity, especially among young people. Just 34 per cent of Inner London's Key Stage 4 (KS4) students (aged 15) in 2004 were from the white British ethnic category, and 51 per cent in Outer London, compared with 84 per cent in England as a whole, 86 per cent in Leeds and 93 per cent in Liverpool. Only Birmingham, England's second largest city, has anything approaching London's diversity, with figures similar to those of Outer London. Essay 2 shows that in terms of the ethnic diversity present in many groups, the school population of London is more mixed than that of New York or Chicago.

London education also has a number of differentiating features.

Nowhere in the UK is the governance of education more fragmented. There is no unifying structure for education in the city and the funding and governance of education is managed through a bewildering variety of agencies and local and national government mechanisms. The capital's school system is unusually diverse, with relatively high proportions of private schools, single sex schools, faith schools, and academies, as well as many community and supplementary schools. London education services have had many years of struggle, with political instability, staffing difficulties and shortages, poor buildings, and insufficiently strong leadership. Services have often had a very poor image, particularly in the schools sector. But, like London itself, education in the capital is now changing rapidly. One of the most interesting aspects of much current education policy and practice in London, which is reflected in this book, is its sense of optimism.

Traditionally, urban education analysis and policy has been surrounded by notions of crisis, and the problems of educational underachievement in urban areas have been explained away by a focus on the political, economic, and cultural disadvantage suffered by many in urban areas. It is heartening to witness the huge cultural change that has taken place in many education institutions across the capital, which is based upon the belief in success for everyone. Schools are undoubtedly improving and ensuring the success of many more of London's young people. As essays in this book describe, there is more understanding of, and confidence about, the leadership of schools and the processes of teaching and learning in urban contexts. There is also more collaborative working across the capital – collaborations between schools, between different agencies, professionals and institutions, and across boroughs to solve the challenges that many pupils and students in London face. Many of these changes are now becoming embedded in the fabric of life in the capital. Significant new approaches and strategies have been developed, such as extended schools, new approaches to the curriculum and its delivery for 14–19 year olds, and new types of education provision linked to wider urban regeneration and community strategies.

But there are further economic and social changes on the horizon, which mean that education cannot stand still. If – and it is a big if – we can assume that the international economic and political stability on which London is entirely dependent will last , it appears that London is set to continue to grow. Our book shows how this has many social costs attached, in housing, prices, congestion, and social complexity. These impact most on its poorer citizens, presenting major challenges to planners both in retaining middle income populations and in ensuring equitable access and outcomes for the city's varied populations. London's ethnic, religious, and linguistic diversity is also likely to continue to grow, and technology is transforming modes of learning and communication, as well as young people's social and emotional lives. These issues will shape the future of education in London and mean that further strategies will need to be developed to challenge the huge inequalities in education that characterise the city as much as any promise of opportunity. We refer to some of these inequities below, particularly as they relate to the combined adverse impact of school autonomy and separate admission criteria for the acceptance of pupils.

A significant achievement gap remains in London, therefore, and the ambition to break the link between poverty and underachievement in education, which has become a very welcome part of the political discourse, still remains. While this is a very exciting time for education in London, it has a somewhat fragile feel to it, and many intractable issues must be overcome if the gains made in London are to be sustained and improved for the future. This final essay therefore highlights two big themes from this book that require much more focus, discussion, and debate for the future.

## Social justice and social cohesion

Our first big theme is social justice and social cohesion. Our argument is that there should be a much more ambitious strategy to tackle inequalities in the next phase of London's education history.

Essay 1 clearly demonstrates that educational disadvantage based upon race, class, and concentrations of poverty is the most fundamental feature of education in London. There are significant differences in attainment between rich and poor boroughs, and to an even greater extent at school level. Students in receipt of free school meals (FSM) lag behind others at every stage of the school curriculum, in some boroughs by as much as 30 per cent. Attainment for the most successful ethnic groups is twice as high as for the least. Essay 4 graphically describes the extent of stratification in London's school system, and how that is in danger of increasing, with the possibility of even more social sorting according to race and class determining access to the many different types of schooling in London

London has had a long tradition of recognising that education outcomes are as much a matter of what is happening 'beyond the school gate' as in the classroom. The ILEA from the 1960s to 1990 placed great importance on developing an integrated approach to meeting the needs of children and families in London's diverse and rapidly changing communities (McClure 1990). However, this tradition was all but obliterated with the reforms of the 1990s so it is particularly welcome that in recent years London has once again become a key site for innovation in urban education. First, it has become accepted that disparities between neighbourhoods should not be allowed to 'explain away' differences in education outcomes, but that due recognition should be given to schools which, because of concentrations of social disadvantage, face a 'heightened challenge' requiring the best support, the best leadership, and the best teachers. This has been a defining principle of the changes in the last few years, as our essays on the London Challenge, the school workforce, and leadership in London show. Second, the emphasis on a holistic long-term approach driven by changes to mainstream services has also been a significant feature of many developments. Whatever the weaknesses of current lifelong learning strategies, as described in Essay 11, the notion that a range of social policy and economic initiatives in the capital such as Neighbourhood Renewal, Sure Start and Excellence in Cities are integral to education achievement for young people and adults has become a constant theme. It is also, most importantly, reflected in the development of integrated services for deprived children and young people through the Every Child Matters (ECM) strategy.

However, while there is no doubt that there is now a strong consensus that a range of strategies are required to combat inequality and to achieve greater social justice in the city, it is clear that the approaches described in this book need to become more effective if they are going to make a real impact on some of the most intractable problems. Many of the essays in the book provide strong evidence that education is still struggling to catch up with the growing problems around the social, religious, and ethnic isolation of certain groups and the extreme economic disadvantage suffered by particular communities.

Every Child Matters is a hugely ambitious national programme, which in theory embraces a very radical agenda. But, as Essay 5 shows, the challenge of tackling the issues of violence, child poverty, child mental health, and the social exclusion of particular groups in London has yet to be met. Extended schools, which deliver a cluster of services and engage with the wider community, are key to tackling many of these 'wicked issues' and should be part of the lifeblood of education in London. However, there is a real danger that financial constraints and test performance will continue to be stronger imperatives for many schools in London than embracing a community leadership role. What is needed for the future is more secure and sustainable funding (such as London weighting for secondary school pupils according to prior attainment at age 11, regardless of borough of origin) combined with a much more radical and integrated vision for what education in general, and schools in particular, can really do for deprivation in London. The potential of schools to embrace community engagement and the development of shared values and trust between different groups of people is essential to the future of social cohesion in London. This should be linked to the new discourse on lifelong learning that is argued for in Essay 11.

Provision for the 14–19 age group is also very important to the social justice theme. As Essays 1 and 11 show, people with no educational qualifications now face great difficulty in obtaining work. There is massive income inequality between those in low-skilled jobs and the rest. Essay 10 gives evidence of the 'long tail of underachievement' at 16, which means that the economic and personal future of a significant section of young people continues to look bleak. The stratification and competition that is a feature of London's education market impacts particularly on young people as they move into adulthood and it is unlikely, as Essays 4 and 10 argue, to be sufficiently counteracted by the collaborative arrangements that are now being encouraged between London's schools and colleges. Massive improvements to the education opportunities, curriculum, and qualifications available to all young people across the board need to feature much more significantly in the next phase of education reform in London.

London in the twenty-first century has been defined to date by its constant flow of new populations, and that trend looks set to continue. While everyone agrees that the single most distinguishing characteristic of schools and colleges in London is their diversity, in our view the issue is still not getting the policy attention it requires. The challenge of diversity, particularly when linked to social class and language, still remains a huge one for the education service in London. This challenge encompasses a range of issues such as the pace of change, high levels of pupil mobility, racism both personal and institutional, the social and religious segregation and isolation of particular groups, and attitudes to multilingualism. While several of our essays show that some groups are making significant strides in attainment, shocking disparities still remain. In 2004, the London Development Agency described as 'catastrophic' the situation facing black Caribbean boys in the education system in London (LDA 2004). Further developments in London in capacity building, both at school and across communities, involving minority ethnic parents, pupils, and staff to improve both access and achievement for a number of ethnic groups is an urgent necessity for the future.

While there have been many excellent responses at policy level to the issues that we have highlighted, and there is no doubt responses are also getting stronger at practitioner level as knowledge increases about what approaches and investments work, it seems to us we have by no means exhausted the means to achieve our ambitions in these areas. There is no room for complacency. Our call now is for the launch of a new London-wide debate about inequality in education in the city, with a focus on holistic, practical, long-term solutions that everyone can and should sign up to.

The generation of such a city-wide approach highlights our second main theme arising from consideration of the essays in the book. Concerns about fragmentation, coherence, and sustainability have arisen frequently and for this reason we also think there should be a debate about governance.

## Governance

Reference has already been made to the unusual nature of educational governance in London, in the context of other global cities. It is exceptional within England for being the only English city without its own single authority responsible for education. The vacuum this leaves for strategic planning is considered below. Nevertheless, no one is seriously advocating a reversion to the pre-1990 arrangements. For one thing, there is no longer (if there ever was) a logic in the distinction between the Inner London and Outer London boroughs.

Moreover, the role of local authorities has now changed significantly and in ways few people anticipated 20 years ago. Contrary to the prediction that they would disappear, they have, as the former BBC education correspondent Mike Baker has put it 'been bumped off and come back to life in a new guise' (Parker *et al.* 2007: Foreword). That new role is as children's services authorities, champions of parents and children rather than direct managers of schools. Their responsibility for integrating services for children in order to deliver the five outcomes of the Every Child Matters agenda is undoubtedly wider than in the past. But it could also be argued that it is more appropriately exercised over a recognisably local rather than regional area.

This new arrangement can genuinely be described in two much overused words: innovative and radical. It has been matched at national level by the creation in 2007 of the Department of Children, Schools and Families (DCSF). Like most radical innovations it may be promising more than it can deliver and it will, in any case, take time to bed down. But given the rising concern about the wellbeing of children in today's Britain, highlighted by the recent UNICEF report (UNICEF 2007), and the issues of equality highlighted in the earlier part of this essay, it is an experiment that deserves a fair wind. In our view this amounts to an argument for leaving borough boundaries and powers largely as they are for the time being.

But the issue of the complexity of governance arrangements in London remains and other recent legislation has done little to reduce it. On the contrary, the Education and Inspections Act 2006 adds, in the name of diversity, yet more complexity. The categorisation of the ever-increasing number of types of school, and the different regulations governing each category – how and by whom the status of each is to be proposed and determined, who is to be consulted, and how – has now become a subject so abstruse that it is doubtful that many teachers and administrators, let alone parents and governors, understand it. (A useful summary can be found in the NFER publication *Education and Inspections Act 2006* (Parker *et al.* 2007).)

This is of course national legislation, but in London the diversity of schools as described in Essay 4, the large number of admission authorities and the high level of cross-boundary traffic, especially of secondary and further education students, adds to the potential for chaos. The knock-on effects of decisions relating to any one school or borough are hard to calculate, but currently nobody has overall responsibility for making this assessment.

One interesting feature of this legislation is the increased power it gives to the School Adjudicator, an appointed rather than elected post and an innovation of the first 1997 Labour government. This office not only adjudicates on admissions disputes – likely to become more frequent and contentious during the early stages of the implementation of the new *Admissions Code* – but also on disputes that arise in relation to competitions for the establishment of new schools. It will act as judge of these competitions even where the local authority is itself a contestant.

Will this come to be seen as a 'Bank of England' decision – that is, analogous to the government's handing over to an independent agency control of the bank rate in 1997, hitherto notoriously and damagingly subject to political manipulation? This may indeed happen, and the new arrangement may result in a greater degree of equity.

There are, however, two possible objections. The first is the obvious democratic deficit in such important decisions being made by an unelected body. The second is that an adjudicating body, however wise, can only react to what is brought before it. Again, our argument for paying increased attention to social justice issues in London would call for a more proactive approach.

To compound these issues the Office of the Schools Commissioner, also created by the 2006 legislation, is charged with promoting yet more choice and diversity in schooling. Although this is balanced by the School Admissions Code, which charges the local authority with the task of ensuring that the outcome of these processes in practice adds up to a 'fair' and equitable system, it is hard to see how any individual borough, given the huge interborough movement of pupils at the start of secondary school, can exercise that role effectively. In short, there is no guarantee that the sum of the 'diverse' parts will add up to an 'equitable' whole. Where is the proactive agency to plan a rational disposition of schools of different sorts across London as a whole, to ensure that opportunities are fairly spread, that geographical 'bare patches' do not appear where choice of school becomes effectively limited?

Two other issues are particularly relevant to this governance debate. The first of these is about the necessity of having a proper London overview of education. As we have argued, the success of education in London is going to be increasingly dependent on a holistic approach to the complexities of what is going on in the capital and how this interrelates with London education institutions. The development of the use of data is fundamental to this.

Of course at the level of the school, as Essay 3 on the London Challenge has illustrated, data are used both to optimise 'choice' and 'diversity' for parents (for example, through the publication of exam and test results) and to enable schools not only to learn from each other (for example, through the use of the 'Families of Schools' data) but also to help individual children to succeed better through its use in formative assessment. But at the level of the city as a whole these better educational data need to be harnessed with those for health, housing, employment, and social wellbeing in order that those responsible for making strategic decisions are better informed. Essay 11 graphically illustrates how, despite the collection by many agencies, no one body yet has an overview of the number or nature of adult learners in London. This is a common problem. At the moment, data sets are not synthesised and are diversely collected by a plethora of agencies and bodies. The Greater London Authority (GLA), the Mayor and his individual agencies, Government Office for London, the Learning and Skills Council, 32 London boroughs, various government departments, all the health service agencies, the police, the universities – all create data sets, some of which replicate each other with subtly different definitions over slightly different time frames.

Decisions affecting the provision of services could be so much better if this issue were addressed. But it is also the case that decisions on strategic issues of concern to the future of education are not being addressed because no one body has the remit to take this overview.

The final issue we want to highlight where a better London-wide strategic approach would help is staffing. High-quality staff will remain essential to London's future success and Essay 6 describes the extent of the staffing issues in London's schools and some of the measures taken to alleviate them.

In the private sector, particularly the City of London, high salaries are necessary and forthcoming to attract the very best candidates to jobs on which profitability and pre-eminence depend. In public services, however, it is not so easy to do likewise, partly as a result of restraints on expenditure but also because national pay structures have meant that, outside the university sector where there is some flexibility, there are limits on how much can be paid.

At the start of the London Challenge, when the secondary schools were thought to be in a staffing crisis, the position was immediately relieved in part by a salary hike and a dispensation, backed by specific funding, for schools to use 'retention allowances' to increase the salaries of staff they wished to appoint or retain. Other measures, as described in Essay 6, have been the 'Teach First' scheme, whereby the very best graduates from leading universities contract to teach in the most challenged schools in London for a specified period, a scheme to subsidise housing mortgage costs, and the Chartered London Teacher (CLT) which has sought to create a pan-London identity for the work and professional development of London teachers. Despite these measures, an acute dependence on overseas trained teachers and considerable fragility in staffing, particular in relation to senior and middle managers, remains.

There is a further staffing factor that affects not just the supply and retention of high-quality school staff but also the quality of the necessary support services to schools and pupils. The governance arrangements that mean that the 32 small London boroughs (and the Corporation of the City of London) act as self-contained education authorities, rather than the single strategic agency, have resulted in the rapid turnover and the variable quality and effectiveness of education officers, advisers, inspectors, and other specialist support staff. Of course, it can be argued that after the 1988 Education Act, the shift of management and other powers away from the local authority to schools or the national government has meant that high-quality local authority staff is less important than it was earlier. Moreover, for whatever reason, successive governments have continually changed and diminished the role of the 'middle tier', i.e. local government. The outcome has been that staffing at local government level, especially in education, has become a real issue. Nor has any greater clarity emerged with additional powers and responsibilities being given to local authorities through the Every Child Matters agenda, other than that large numbers of small boroughs continue to compete with each other for a relatively limited supply of skilled staff.

It is hard to escape the conclusion that a pan-London approach to staffing and professional development is necessary for a sustainable future to be assured for many of the initiatives in education described in this book.

Regional governance within the English structures of governance has become something of an uncomfortable subject. The prospects of anything like genuine regional government seemed to die with the failure of the North-east referendum in 2004. While its lack of popularity with the electorate in the north of England did not seem to be the case in London when the office of Mayor and the Greater London Authority were created in 2000, government rhetoric about the 'restoration' of self-government to London did not disguise the fact that in the event, the powers ceded to the Mayor and Assembly have proved strictly limited.

Yet we believe there is a an argument, as these essays reveal, for a 'voice for London' on issues of common concern to all the London local authorities; for instance, teacher supply, their professional development, school improvement services, and issues that impact on the wider context of education, including planning for greater equity and access across the capital. This includes school and college planning, data, and charging policies. It is to the credit of the Labour government that it has created an effective and successful *ad hoc* solution – the London Challenge – to deal with most of these issues. It is, however, *ad hoc* even though its life has been extended to 2011. At the end of that period a debate needs to have been concluded about what the long-term overall pan-London governance arrangements for these functions should be.

Placing these powers with the Mayor and Assembly (the only available London-wide elected authority) would not involve significant additional expense and seems the logical solution. Alternatively, a non-elected body could be established but it would still need to work closely with the GLA, the Mayor and pan-London agencies for other services.

While, as we argued above, we are not calling for wholesale local government reorganisation, it is clear from many of the themes emerging from this book that more imaginative solutions are called for, for some of the big pan-strategic and structural issues. The next phase of reform should start with that debate. Certainly if London's education system is to avoid dangers of fragmentation and in doing so, putting the most vulnerable of its pupils and students at risk, something of this order is needed.

## Conclusion

This book has focused on London. The issues it considers, however, are relevant beyond London. There is a tendency among those of us who have spent a lifetime involved in London's education to dwell on and take for granted its alleged uniqueness. Sometimes this can lead, as it has in one or two of the essays, to claims that the challenges are greater and more formidable than are found in other urban and rural contexts. This must be especially irritating to those working in similar places, especially when the claims are backed by the use of statistics comparing London with national averages when what would be a truer comparison would be to choose some reasonably comparable contexts. Much of what we have addressed, for example many of the remarks about governance, is unique to London, but much else is relevant to educators in many large cities and urban contexts, both in the UK and elsewhere.

We hope therefore that the assembled essays in this volume will stimulate thinking among urban educators in the UK and internationally. We use the word 'international' because globalism/internationalism is an increasingly important issue. And it is our cities which are the focus for the movement of finance, industrial infrastructure, people, and ideas which accompany this internationalism. It is our cities also which have the task of resolving some of the kaleidoscopic social challenges that accompany such rapid change. Major players in creating such solutions are those who work in and around the education systems. They are our audience and while we have focused on London we hope that educators elsewhere will see the debate to which we are contributing as relevant to them.

**References**

London Development Agency (2004) *The Education Experience and Achievements of Black Boys in London Schools 2000–2003*. London: GLA.

McClure, S.A.(1990) *History of Education in London 1870–1990*. London: Allen Lane, Penguin.

Parker, A., Duncan, A., and Fowler, J. (2007) *Education and Inspections Act 2006: The essential guide.* Slough: NFER.

UNICEF (2007) *Child Poverty in Perspective: An overview of child well-being in rich countries.* Florence: UNICEF Innocenti Research Centre.

# Notes on the authors

**Professor Tim Brighouse** was until recently Commissioner and Chief Adviser for London Schools, formerly Chief Education Officer of Birmingham, Professor of Education at Keele University, Chief Education Officer of Oxfordshire and currently Visiting Professor at the Institute of Education.

**Sara Bubb** is an experienced London teacher who helps to develop staff in schools through taking the lead in professional development, assessing, researching, and writing. She is a senior lecturer and was lead director, working with Peter Earley, on the CfBT Education Trust funded project, 'From School Self-evaluation to School Improvement: the role of effective professional development'. She is the London Gifted and Talented Early Years network leader and the new teacher expert at the *Times Educational Supplement*: as well as writing articles she has a weekly advice column and answers questions on its website. Sara is also the consultant for Chartered London Teacher status – a scheme involving over 38,800 teachers. She has published widely and her most recent books include: *Successful Induction for New Teachers: A guide for NQTs and induction tutors, coordinators and mentors* (2007) PCP/Sage; *Leading and Managing Continuing Professional Development: Developing people, developing schools* (2nd edn) (2007) (with Peter Earley) PCP/Sage; *Helping Teachers Develop* (2005) PCP/Sage; *Managing Teacher Workload: work-life balance and wellbeing* (2004) (with Peter Earley) PCP/Sage.

**Professor Peter Earley** is Head of Education Leadership and Management Programmes at the London Centre for Leadership in Learning at the Institute of Education, where he is also Director of Research. He started his teaching career in London working in an inner-city school and an FE college before entering higher education. He was the course leader for the Institute's Educational Leadership and Management MA and co-ordinates the EdD specialist module on 'Leadership and Learning in Educational Organisations'. From 2000 to 2005 he was an accredited external adviser to governing bodies of London schools on headteacher performance management. He has published widely and his recent books include: *Leadership and Management in Education: Cultures, change and context* (2005) (with Marianne Coleman) Oxford University Press; *Understanding School Leadership* (2004) (with Dick Weindling) PCP/Sage; *Improving Schools and Inspection: The self-inspecting school* (2000) (with Neil Ferguson) PCP/Sage; *Improving Schools and Governing Bodies* (1999) (with Michael Creese) Routledge.

**Dr Hilary Emery** is Executive Director of the Development directorate, at the Training and Development Agency for schools (TDA). Prior to joining the TDA, Hilary was Director of the London Centre for Leadership in Learning at the Institute of Education. Alongside her work on leadership development, she fostered cross-Institute teaching and research on the Every Child Matters initiative. Before that, she led the DfES children's services' advisers. She has worked as a teacher, deputy head, researcher, local authority adviser, and teacher educator, becoming Dean of Education and Psychology at the now University of Worcester. Her research interests include self- and peer-assessment, as well as initial and continuing teacher education, including international comparisons.

**Leisha Fullick** is Pro Director for London at the Institute of Education, University of London. She started her professional life in the London boroughs of Hackney and Islington, working on community based learning programmes for adults. She was an Inspector for Further and Higher Education with the former Inner London Education Authority (ILEA). She was Director of Education for the London Borough of Lewisham from 1989 to 1996 and Chief Executive of Islington Council from 1996 to 2002. She has also served as an elected member in London, and on the governing bodies of several schools and colleges and of two universities. She was a founding member of the Learning and Skills Council.

**Paul Grainger** is developing a Post-14 Centre for Research and Innovation at the Institute of Education. Paul has spent 30 years in teaching and FE management, most recently as a College Principal. He chaired the RIBA/LSC Forum which produced *Colleges for the Future* and *World Class Buildings.* He was a member of the Education Experts panel of the Design Council, looking at issues around the Building Schools for the Future programme, and is a core member of the Nuffield Review of 14–19 Education and Training.

**Dr Ann Hodgson** has worked as a teacher, lecturer, LEA adviser, editor, and civil servant, joining the Institute of Education, University of London, in 1993, where she is now a Reader in Education and Faculty Director for Research, Consultancy and Knowledge Transfer. She is currently co-director of the *Nuffield Review of 14–19 Education in England and Wales*, as well as a range of local authority and Learning and Skills Council research and development projects related to institutional organisation, governance, and curriculum and qualifications reform. Ann has published widely on topics related to post-14 policy, lifelong learning, and curriculum and qualifications reform.

**Dr Sandra Leaton Gray** began her career as a London teacher, and is now Lecturer in Education at the University of East Anglia. She was Researcher to Geoff Whitty at the Institute of Education, University of London, from 2006 to 2007. Before that she was an Educational Researcher at the University of Cambridge, and Director of Studies in Sociology of Education at Homerton College. She is a Senior Member of Wolfson College. Her research interests include teacher professionalism, the relationship between education and work, higher education and society, educational technology, continuing professional development (CPD), education evaluation, and professional education in medicine and dentistry. She has written various articles and reports about teachers and the sociology of education. Sandra Leaton Gray is the author of *Teachers Under Siege* (2006) Trentham Books.

**Dr Ruth Lupton** is Director of the London Education Research Unit at the Institute of Education, where she has worked since leaving the London School of Economics in 2004. Ruth's research centres on relationships between poverty, place, and education and she has written extensively on urban and neighbourhood change and its implications for education in disadvantaged urban areas. Recent relevant publications include *Poverty Street: The dynamics of neighbourhood decline and renewal* (2003) Policy Press; *How does Place Affect Education?* (2006) IPPR; and 'Schools in disadvantaged areas: low attainment and a contextualised policy response' (in Lauder *et al.* (2006) Oxford University Press).

**Dr Jan McKenley** has been a teacher, youth worker, counsellor, and HMI. She is now the Director of McKenley-Simpson Limited, a development and research consultancy. She was born in Brixton in 1955 to newly arrived Jamaican immigrants and has been a black Londoner ever since. Her doctoral research was conducted at the Institute of Education under the supervision of Professor David Gillborn and published in 2005.

**Dina Mehmedbegović** recently joined the London Education Research Unit at the Institute of Education. Her research interests are: bilingualism, minority ethnic pupils and minority languages. In her previous job as an Ethnic Minority Achievement Adviser in City of Westminster, LA she led on promoting student voice through student consultations, student conferences, and publications. Previously she worked in Camden as a teacher.

**Janet Mokades** was born in London and educated at University of Bristol, the Sorbonne and University of London. She has lived and worked abroad and in London pursuing a variety of careers in the arts and education. She was involved in some of the first community education projects in London and in many equalities initiatives. She has spent 15 years as an HMI working across the whole range of education. More recently she has worked in the Cabinet Office and in the DfES as a senior education adviser. She is currently an independent education and policy consultant.

**Professor Kathryn Riley** from the Institute of Education's Centre for Leadership in Learning is an international scholar. She began her work in education and public policy in Eritrea and then taught in inner-city schools in London before holding senior academic positions. She was an elected member of the ILEA and has also been a Chief Officer in local government. Her international work includes two years with the World Bank, heading its Effective Schools and Teachers Group and a range of projects for the OECD and UNICEF. Current work focuses on public sector leadership, urban and community leadership, and re-engaging disaffected students in learning. Her extensive publications include: *Whose School is it Anyway?* (1998) Falmer Press; *Leadership for Change and School Reform: International perspectives* (2000) (with K. Seashore Louis) Routledge Falmer; *Working with Disaffected Children: Why students lose interest in school and what can be done about it* (2002) (with E. Rustique-Forrester) Paul Chapman; *Surviving and Thriving as an Urban Leader* ( 2007) Esmée Fairburn Foundation; 'Improving City Schools: Who and what makes the difference?' in C. Sugrue (ed.) *New Directions for Educational Change: International perspectives* (2007) Routledge.

**Anne Sofer** was the Director of Education in Tower Hamlets from 1989 to 1997. Before that she was involved in education variously as a teacher, parent, governor, member of ILEA, and chair of its schools subcommittee and writer. She was a founder member of the Channel Four Television Company, and a member of the Kennedy Committee on widening participation in further education. Since retiring from Tower

Hamlets she has undertaken a number of assignments associated with education and inner cities, including consultancy work for the Department for Education and membership of the Islington Children's Commission. She was Chair of the National Childrens' Bureau from 2000 until 2006.

**Dr Ken Spours** is a Reader of Education and Head of Department in the Faculty of Policy and Society at the University of London's Institute of Education. He is also Director of the Institute's Post-14 Centre for Research and Innovation. Ken has researched and published in the area of the 14–19 curriculum for nearly two decades. His most recent books include *Beyond A Levels: Curriculum 2000 and the reform of 14–19 qualifications* (2003) (with Ann Hodgson) Kogan Page, and *Policy-making and Policy Learning in 14–19 Education* (2007) (with David Raffe) Institute of Education. Ken was a member of the Tomlinson Working Group on 14–19 Reform and is a director of the *Nuffield Review of 14–19 Education*.

**Dr Alice Sullivan** is a Research and Teaching Fellow at the Institute of Education, University of London. Her research interests focus on social class, gender, and ethnic inequalities in education. Recent publications include: 'Class, gender and ethnicity effects on educational attainment in England: an overview' (2007) (with Geoff Whitty) in R. Teese *et al.* (eds) *Education and Equity: International perspectives on policy and practice* (Springer/Verlag); and 'Students as Rational Decision-Makers: the question of beliefs and attitudes', *London Review of Education*, 2006, 4(3).

**Professor Geoff Whitty** has been Director of the Institute of Education, University of London, since September 2000. He taught in primary and secondary schools before lecturing in education at Bath University and King's College London. He then held chairs and senior management posts at Bristol Polytechnic and Goldsmiths College before joining the Institute as the Karl Mannheim Professor of Sociology of Education in

1992. His main areas of teaching and research are the sociology of education, education policy, and teacher education. He has led evaluations of major educational reforms and has assisted schools and local authorities in building capacity for improvement. His recent publications include *Making Sense of Education Policy* (2002) Sage Publications; and *Education and the Middle Class* (2003) (with Sally Power, Tony Edwards and Valerie Wigfall) Open University Press, which won the Society for Educational Studies 2004 education book prize. Geoff Whitty is President of the College of Teachers, former president of the British Educational Research Association, and a member of the General Teaching Council for England. He is also a specialist adviser to the House of Commons Education and Skills Committee.